FLORIDA STATE
UNIVERSITY LIBRARIES

JUN 22 2001

TALLAHASSEE, FLORIDA

LOCAL RESPONSES TO GLOBAL INTEGRATION

Local Responses to Global Integration

Edited by
CHARALAMBOS KASIMIS
Department of Economics
University of Patras
Patras, Greece;
Institute of Urban and Rural Sociology
National Centre for Social Research
Athens, Greece

APOSTOLOS G. PAPADOPOULOS
Institute of Urban and Rural Sociology
National Centre for Social Research
Athens, Greece

Ashgate
Aldershot • Brookfield USA • Singapore • Sydney

© European Society for Rural Sociology 1999

All rights reserved. No part of this publication may be reproduced, stored in a retrieval system, or transmitted in any form or by any means, electronic, mechanical, photocopying, recording or otherwise without the prior permission of the publisher.

Published by
Ashgate Publishing Ltd
Gower House
Croft Road
Aldershot
Hants GU11 3HR
England

Ashgate Publishing Company
Old Post Road
Brookfield
Vermont 05036
USA

Ashgate website: http://www.ashgate.com

British Library Cataloguing in Publication Data
Local responses to global integration
  1. International economic integration
  I. Kasimis, Charalambos II. Papadopoulos, Apostolos G.
  337

Library of Congress Catalog Card Number: 99-73346

ISBN 1 84014 844 6

Printed in Great Britain by
Antony Rowe Ltd, Chippenham, Wiltshire

Contents

List of figures and tables	vii
List of contributors	viii
Preface	ix

1 Introduction: Local Boundaries or Embeddedness in the Global?
   Charalambos Kasimis and Apostolos G. Papadopoulos 1

Part I Globalization, Diversity and Rural Space

2 Modernity, Globalization and the Rural World
   Göran Therborn 21

3 Towards a Theoretical Understanding of the Generation of Diversity in Rural Areas
   Gaston Remmers 41

4 Changing Spaces: The Effects of Macro-Social Forces on Regional Australia
   Geoffrey Lawrence, Ian Gray and Daniela Stehlik 63

Part II Farmers and Farming Women

5 Grounding Globalization Theory: Local Responses to Global Processes in the Light of the Global-Local Links Debate in Rural Sociology
   Luis Llambí, Eliézer Arias and Germán Freire 91

6 Between Global and Local: State Mediation of Gender Relations in Farming
   Sally Shortall 109

v

Part III Communities and Households

7   Social Identification with Local Communities and the
    Globalization Process in Rural Areas of Eastern Europe
    Pawel Starosta and Mariana Draganova   133

8   Global Changes and Individual Responses in Rural Areas:
    The Dynamics of Low Income and Household Economic
    Status
    Esperanza Vera-Toscano and Pollyanna Chapman   153

Part IV Local and Regional Development

9   Globalization and Rural Development: Demographic
    Revitalization, Entrepreneurs and Small Business
    Formation in the West of Ireland
    Perpetua McDonagh and Patrick Commins   179

10 Seeking Local Citizenship: Towards a New Sense
    of the Local?
    Nicholas Mack   203

11 Rural Development Policy in Finland in the 1990s:
    Towards Flexible Specialization or Spatial Taylorism?
    Petri Ruuskanen   223

12 Revisiting the Rural: A Southern Response to European
    Integration and Globalization
    Apostolos G. Papadopoulos   245

List of figures and tables

Figure 3.1	Interaction between plan and performance, and the (re)production of diversity, associated to concepts from Giddens' structuration theory	46
Figure 3.2	The generation of diversity as overlapping cards	49
Figure 3.3	The network: chains of plans (p), contexts (c) and performances (a) in interaction, establishing joint performances	55
Figure 4.1	Australian agricultural policies since the second world war	66
Table 7.1	Strength of social identification by country and community	140
Table 7.2	Regression models of social identification in selected Eastern European countries	141
Table 7.3	Characteristics of types of identification with local communities in Bulgaria, Poland and Russia	145
Table 8.1	Person type, household type and household economic status breakdowns: always rural, always non-rural and movers sub-samples	160
Table 8.2	Person type, household type and household economic status breakdowns according to migration patterns	162
Table 8.3	Reasons for moving	163
Table 8.4	Household economic status and rural/non-rural location: transition matrix	165
Table 8.5	Proportion of time in low income	167
Table 8.6	Probit model estimated marginal effects for conditional probability of low and high income in t given low and high income in t-1	170
Table 9.1	Changes in different categories of population, by birthplace	184
Table 9.2	Origins of business responsibles	188
Table 9.3	Selected characteristics of business responsibles	189
Table 9.4	Size distribution of businesses	192
Figure 11.1	The ideal model of flexible manufacturing network	237

List of contributors

Eliézer Arias, Venezuelan Institute of Scientific Research, Caracas, Venezuela.
Pollyanna Chapman, University of Aberdeen, Aberdeen, Scotland, UK.
Patrick Commins, Rural Policy Research at Teagasc, The Agricultural and Food Development Authority, Dublin, Ireland.
Mariana Draganova, Institute of Sociology, Bulgarian Academy of Sciences, Sofia, Bulgaria.
Germán Freire, Venezuelan Institute of Scientific Research, Caracas, Venezuela.
Ian Gray, Charles Sturt University, Wagga Wagga, New South Wales, Australia.
Charalambos Kasimis, Department of Economics, University of Patras, Patras, Greece; Institute of Urban and Rural Sociology, National Centre for Social Research, Athens, Greece.
Geoffrey Lawrence, Central Queensland University, Rockhampton, Queensland, Australia.
Luis Llambí, Venezuelan Institute of Scientific Research, Caracas, Venezuela.
Nicholas Mack, Action Research Unit, Rural Development Council for Northern Ireland, Cookstown, Northern Ireland, UK.
Perpetua McDonagh, Rural Economy Research Centre at Teagasc, The Agricultural and Food Development Authority, Dublin, Ireland.
Apostolos G. Papadopoulos, Institute of Urban and Rural Sociology, National Centre for Social Research, Athens, Greece.
Gaston Remmers, Department of Sociology, Wageningen Agricultural University, Wageningen, The Netherlands.
Petri Ruuskanen, Chydenius-Institute, University of Jyväskylä, Jyväskylä, Finland.
Sally Shortall, Department of Sociology and Social Policy, Queen's University Belfast, Belfast, Northern Ireland, UK.
Pawel Starosta, Institute of Sociology, University of Lodz, Lodz, Poland.
Daniela Stehlik, Central Queensland University, Rockhampton, Queensland, Australia.
Göran Therborn, Swedish Collegium for Advanced Study in the Social Sciences, Uppsala, Sweden; University of Göteborg, Göteborg, Sweden.
Esperanza Vera-Toscano, Arkleton Centre for Rural Development Research, University of Aberdeen, Aberdeen, Scotland, UK.

Preface

The European Society for Rural Sociology held its 17th Congress entitled 'Local responses to global integration: Towards a new era of rural restructuring' in Crete in August 1997. The Congress theme set the context in which it was discussed whether globalization, as an economic and social process, has taken a more pervasive form, leading to an increasing similarity of production and consumption patterns and a world wide movement of products, people, services and cultures. However, it was indicated that such a development has not necessarily led to an all-embracing homogenization process.

Rural areas have undoubtedly experienced the impact of such a process adopting new functions as both producers and consumers. Their roles today are not characterized by uniformity; integration or resistance being rather a reflection of their accumulated history. In other words, the crisis of the regulatory framework has led to a reconsideration of globality as expressed so far. In the Congress it was revealed that new forms of production and consumption have developed and localities, as specific social spaces, have put forward their own diversities, seeking their own 'autonomy of being'.

This book publishes a selection of papers presented at the Congress which best reflects the Congress theme and the issues raised above. One of the main criteria for our final selection was the diversity of theoretical and methodological approaches used. As a result, authors from Australia, Bulgaria, Finland, Greece, Ireland, the Netherlands, Poland, Sweden, the United Kingdom and Venezuela are represented with their research work touching upon an even wider spectrum of countries.

We gratefully acknowledge the support of the National Centre for Social Research (EKKE) in Greece for this publication of this volume. Special thanks go to Vaggelis Zouridis for his work connected with the technical preparation of the book and to Voula Galinou for her language and other editorial help. Finally, we would like to thank all the contributors to this edition who patiently worked with us over the past year.

C. Kasimis
A.G. Papadopoulos

1 Introduction: Local Boundaries or Embeddedness in the Global?

CHARALAMBOS KASIMIS AND APOSTOLOS G. PAPADOPOULOS

Globalization: the concept and the arguments

Reference to the global aspect of economic, social, political and cultural processes has been very popular in the majority of analyses of the 1990s. The concept of globalization conditions the whole discussion concerning the social and economic restructuring of different localities and/or regions in any part of the globe. Moreover, in many treatments the 'globalization process' is used as a shorthand for describing the character of rapid changes occurring across the globe, referring to the increasing inter-connections among different localities, practices and systems as well as illustrating the impact of particular incidents or processes which have occurred in specific areas upon the rest of the world. Often the globalization process is considered as an exogenous factor to particular localities, thus stressing the significance of macro-structures and macro-processes for explaining micro-instances and/or concrete cases. Moreover, it is based upon an implicit assumption of an increased concentration of power (e.g. economic, political, cultural), which tends essentially to push towards the intensification of integration processes within wider social and economic contexts. In respect with the impact of globalization upon specific localities it is normally considered that the latter are based upon wider processes and interdependencies for their existence and that the world space is the arena for local action (indicative is the expression, 'think globally act locally' Holton, 1998, p. 18). The primacy of the global space over the local is stressed by the inter-connectivity and networking of localities and the domination of trajectories leading to a formation of a global economic and social system.

Rural space, as any other space, constitutes an arena of the globalization process. The alleged specificity of 'rural' local responses only reinserts the common theme of different forms of local reflexivity towards globalization.

Despite the discussion concerning the particularity of agriculture for the capitalist integration or, in modern terms, of global integration, we do not consider the agricultural sector as a special case presenting problems for the integration of concrete localities in the global economy. Agricultural production relations constitute just one set of relations along with other sectors within concrete localities in geographical space. In this respect, the utility of the socioeconomic restructuring thesis for examining localized processes of social change appears to be increasing (Marsden et al., 1990). The tendency to treat agriculture as an example of the wider process of globalization, increased economic integration and subordination of family farming to large agro-industrial capital, has gained significant weight and merits particular attention especially when studying the spatial implications of internationalized commodity production and circulation chains (Friedland, 1991).

One of the basic arguments regarding globalization, refers to the novelty of this process (Weiss, 1997). In fact, globalization signifies changes which have started long ago during the 16th century. However, it refers today to a transformation of the elementary time-space relationship, it initiates a reflexive process of change, designates the decline of universalism and particularism; and combines an ambiguous mixture of risk and trust (Waters, 1995, pp. 62-64). The 'sociology of globalization' intricately links such trajectories closely to the all-encompassing concept of 'modernity'. Apart from a specification of modernity, Giddens describes globalization as a 'stretching process' between local and distant social forms and events, 'in so far as the modes of connection between different social contexts or regions become networked across the earth's surface as a whole' (1990, p. 64). This 'stretching' process has triggered off contradictory tendencies at the local level. Local transformation is increasingly caught between the lateral extension of social relations over time and across space and the reiterated need for local autonomy, regional identity and cultural specificity. For Giddens, such a process of uneven development signifies the 'incompleteness' of modernity as a 'Western project' (1990, p. 175).

In this context, globalization is considered either as a 'late modern' or a 'post-modern' project referring to 'Western' societies. Giddens' view that 'modernity is inherently globalizing' implies a particular variant of modernity (i.e. 'reflexive'). Two reservations on Giddens' version of globalization have been raised. The *first* is Mouzelis' (1997) consideration of modernity drawing from the distinction between 'formal and substantive differentiation' as a basis for defining 'variants of modernity', leading to a 'multi-polar' conception of global economy and society. The *second* is Therborn's (1995) analysis of 'routes to/through modernity' allowing for open possibilities and institutional differentiation against a dynamically developing and multiply defined modernity. Therborn treats globalization as a spatial concept, thus stressing the decentralized character of modern development processes (see Therborn, Chapter 2). Both critics reject the 'hyper-globalization' thesis which connects globalization with the deconstruction of the nation-state and the fragmentation of the wider economy and society into its basic elements. Instead, they acknowledge the significance of new phenomena, such as the prevalence of the logic or values of one institutional subsystem and their 'colonization' of other institutional spheres (Mouzelis, 1997, p. 39), or that a notion of 'global village' which 'stands a chance as another global modernity, thriving from local responses, rather than from central fantasies of power' (Therborn, Chapter 2, p. 38).

Apart from being a socioeconomic process globalization is part and parcel of a sociopolitical discourse and cannot be conceived in terms of any kind of inevitability, as is often the case in the neo-liberalist or neo-conservative literature (Koc, 1994). Nevertheless, globalization does not constitute an era although it significantly marks a 'post-developmentalist' period in world economy. For McMichael (1996), globalization labels the project which succeeded the so-called 'development project' that predominated in the post-war period until the early 1970s. McMichael examines globalization retrospectively and seeks its 'legitimization' as a 'project' in a world-view perspective. Globalization in itself signifies both the process and the end-state of global integration dynamics. The periodization of world economy implies some sort of evolutionism and externality of social change. In McMichael's conception of globalization economistic arguments are implicit under the view that 'the globalization project represents an institutional form for stabilizing capitalism' (1996, p. 39). Although such a *political economy* approach conceives a significant part of globalization in both its political and institutional implications, it reproduces the preconception that it is essentially another variant for the spatial reflection of capital and labour (Friedland, 1994). However, one cannot deduce from this that the global-local relationship can be conceived wholly in these terms. Neo-liberalism has not yet completely dominated world economy and the local should not be reified in terms of local voluntaristic responsiveness. In reality, the particular character of the 'local' can only be conceived in view of the global-local interconnections. Moreover, far from merely constituting an alternative sociopolitical regime, globalization only creates the space for reconsidering the locality dynamics and, in fact, allowing for local diversity. In the more recent sociological literature globalization cannot be dissociated from localization processes. In this connection, one should not neglect to examine the ways and types of local or regional specificities of rural/local production processes which deserve in-depth analysis not only for dealing with regional development issues but also, and more importantly, for responding to external and 'top down' policy design or implementation (see Papadopoulos, Chapter 12).

Globalization cannot be defined as the inverse of localization, but rather as a concept which incorporates a dual identity of 'the global in the local' and 'the local in the global'. This dual identity of globalization is better described in the use of *'glocalization'* as a more precise term dealing with the time-space and homogeneity-heterogeneity axes of the restructuring process (Robertson, 1995, p. 40). It should not be forgotten that such an analysis concerns processes referring to the nation-state, the cultural interactions and the localities. For example, 'glocalization' has been considered useful for international relations and political analyses (Holton, 1998) while it provides the basis for dealing with concrete cases in terms of interlocking global and local processes. It suffices here to say that the analysis of the global-local relationship faces, in spatial terms, a seemingly unbridgeable dilemma. Within a rapidly changing socioeconomic terrain, the 'locale' or the region may be of two variants: a locality or a region which 'wins' and a locality or a region which 'loses' (Lipietz, 1992). This structuralist analysis of a virtually 'closed' socioeconomic setting does not leave space for an 'intermediate' position for localities or regions.

On the part of the specific locality or the region, choices are not self-evident since they require an evaluation of a number of factors, such as entrepreneurship, networking, availability of (skilled) labour force, availability of resources, subsidiarity of state actions at a macro-economic level etc., in order to obtain a 'winning' case status and clearly initiate an endogenous development process (Barquero, 1991; Verschoor, 1997). In this respect, it has been argued that localities apart from being defined as localized social structures, they may also undertake the role of an agent. Stressing the agency part of localized social structures (taking into account class analysis), Cox and Mair (1991) aim at producing a radical redefinition of localities as virtual or potential agents. In this discussion, we may distinguish two programmatic options concerning local development: *one* which stresses the reconstitution of the local essentially in view of a 'bottom up' approach (see Mack, Chapter 10); and a *second* which takes account of the larger state (regional and/or rural) policy orientation to redefine the context of local development opportunities and its character in view of the restructuring dynamics (see Ruuskanen, Chapter 11).

Moreover, a modern analysis of local integrity or local identity, may also involve an evolutionist consideration, within a rapidly changing postmodern and - consequently - fragmented socioeconomic reality, and may well argue that the local is still significant to study for its particularities (see Starosta and Draganova, Chapter 7). Local integrity and identity are often considered in cultural terms, while the importance of the social fabric and social bonds is underlined for the maintenance of local or cultural specificity which is considered to downplay the impact of the globalization process (see Vera-Toscano and Chapman, Chapter 8). The persistent stress on social bonding, which in fact constitutes the gist of the 'community spirit', identifying itself with a cultural variety of social capital (Putnam, 1993), has been criticized for being conservative and disorientating from the actual (i.e. the contradictory) question of social cohesion and social integration at the local level (Portes, 1998).

This discussion brings us to the issue of global-local relations which is, in real life, a tug-of-war between macro- and micro-social dynamics conditioned by economic restructuring, political and cultural processes. In order to differentiate among various types of global-local relations, we may refer to basic trajectories of the social construction processes. Analytically, there are two different modes of social construction or structuration: one is through *conflict* and the second through *consensus*. In this respect, and considering these two modes of social construction as elementary ideal types upon which 'civil society'[1] may be based, we classify local responses to global integration along two basic (not necessarily contradicting) variants: *'the local as a boundary'* which formulates the local in contradistinction to the global and where the local postulates its recognition or its reinstatement; and the *'local embeddedness' in the global* which describes a coexistence of local opportunities and global needs and where external calls are transferred to internal mechanisms reflexively. In this way, the 'local as a boundary' may well imply conflictual conditions for local responsiveness to global integration, whereas the 'local embeddedness' may be based upon collective agreements, social pacts or consensual actions and/or practices.

Local responses to global integration

The dynamics of the local, according to the restructuring thesis, can only be conceived with respect to the global situation, the socioeconomic integration trajectories and the growing internationalization of industrial and financial capital. In such a world, the local is defined in terms of local social structures which, however, are increasingly linked to wider issues of class formation and civil society (Marsden et al., 1990). On the other hand, the conceptualization of the local on the basis of the restructuring thesis does not leave much space for local 'reactions' to wider processes. This is the reason why, often more action-oriented schemes were employed to illustrate the new character and dynamics of the local. Mixtures of structural explanatory schemes and situational socio-cultural analyses have been proposed to examine the local occurrence of social transformation. More particularly, rural local resistance to global processes may be treated as the inter-penetration between intended and unintended effects of purposive, and socio-historical actions signifying the existence of countervailing forces (see Llambí et al., Chapter 5).

The discussion so far has raised some challenging questions about the globalization process. In this respect, one may argue that any local boundaries posed to globalization are neither circumstantial or implicit. Rather they can be systematic and visible only when local and/or national concrete socioeconomic conditions are examined and/or appraised. Thus, the diversity and the specificity of the local signifies not only the *modus operandi* of the globalization process but also, and more importantly, the limits to this process (Papadopoulos, 1999). The strength that local resistance is expressed with depends upon a number of factors linked to the socio-political, economic and cultural sphere. For Scott, there are three axes along which limits to globalization are raised: a) the contestation and resistance to this process; b) the complexity of culture and agency; and c) the resilience of the nation state (Scott, 1997, pp. 18-20). All these three axes provide the coordinates for studying local responsiveness.

The role of the state remains a central issue of debate in the discussion of globalization. Often, the simultaneous trajectories of market integration (e.g. EU, NAFTA, WTO) and state disintegration (e.g. USSR, Czechoslovakia, Yugoslavia) appear to contradict each other forming a new situation (post-Cold War period), which allegedly points to the existence of a multi-polar globe (Roumeliotis, 1996). For example, even official documents of the European Union acknowledge the need for adapting to the emergence of a multi-polar world (EC, 1997). However, on the part of the individual nation-states there is great diversity in their domestic capacity, that is in the ability to exploit opportunities of international economic change and adapt to trajectories of international integration. This situation presents a more unpredictable future for nation-states than the one put forward by the globalization orthodoxy (Weiss, 1997).

In this respect, the role of the state may prove negative either for undoing local resistance or for perpetuating local incapacity to gain momentum under external pressure for social change. In the first case, the state itself, by succumbing to neo-liberalism and withdrawing from basic spheres of social welfare and cohesion, cedes vital space to capital functions and to the erosion of the local social capacity for resistance (see Lawrence et al., Chapter 4; Ruuskanen, Chapter 11). In the second case, the state may continue to play a significant role in maintaining, through its power, the historical, cultural, social and economic referents and fabric for local cohesion or resistance to externally induced changes (see Shortall, Chapter 6).

The impact of larger processes on small spatial units is mediated by capital and state strategies and conditioned by a number of factors (i.e. institutional forms, networks, norms, culture) effecting local cohesion (Cloke and Goodwin, 1992). There are cases where local responses may be posed as a structural characteristic of global integration. This is either because globalization is self-induced or because there is a consensual agreement (both theoretical and institutionalist) that local diversity constitutes a *sine qua non* term for social (re)construction. The intensification of the globalization process does not lead to increasing homogenization, but it is rather related to 'heterogenization at the local level' (Amin and Thrift, 1994, p. 7).[2] In such a process, the local is part and parcel of the global and regionalism or localism are not just forms of resistance to globalism, but they signal the success of globalization. In these cases, the local does not clearly compete against the global but fights to override (or else out-compete) other localities.

It is particularly significant here to stress the view expressed by Granovetter, who argued that 'economic action is embedded in structures of social relations, in modern industrial societies' (1985, p. 481). Although, all economies are 'embedded' in social relations (Barber, 1995), the notion of *embeddedness* has more concrete outcomes when it refers to 'developed market economies' (Granovetter, 1985, pp. 482-483).

It is no surprise that the more economically successful cases of regions or localities tend either to be located in developed countries or in dynamic areas in other countries with strong traditions of networking, entrepreneurship, local resources etc. In the current period of globalization the *local embeddedness* of labour processes is crucial for identifying responsive regions or localities to external market calls or social challenges (Marsden et al., 1992).

In this respect, in cases when agricultural production in rural areas truly interacts (not without mediators of course) with the market, one may analyze the micro-macro linkages in agriculture as a locally embedded socioeconomic process (Hebinck and van der Ploeg, 1995). Moreover, the *'relocalization'* of agricultural activity constitutes a major outcome of the globalization process (van der Ploeg, 1992, p. 37), which increasingly becomes reflexively intentional for concrete localities or regions. The relocalization of agricultural activity is part of a purposive programme which values and appraises resources, action and outcomes. Thus, relocalization induces a 'rational choice' logic which is internal to the impact of globalization in concrete localities or regions. This is counterdistinguished from the 'local-as-a-boundary', which considers globalization as an externally induced process. Furthermore, the notion of heterogeneity can be attributed to globalization as a (re)structuring process linked to localization, while the notion of diversity refers to types that the local is responsively engulfed or integrated through the globalization process.

The local embeddedness concept thus signifies the ability of the local to react by continuously reformulating its 'plan and performance' and maintaining its entity by diversifying itself. This local structuration process, which is particularly interesting for rural areas, keeps pace with the exogenous impact and adapts global elements by localizing and sustaining development (see Remmers, Chapter 3). The relocalization of economic activity fits well with the opportunities and means provided for by the operation of the globalization process. In this respect, rural industrialization in certain localities may well be linked to the cross-fertilization of different local factors depending upon the 'local capacities' and local capabilities of endogenous resources (see McDonagh and Commins, Chapter 9).

The two underlying analytic stances (local 'boundaries' and 'embeddedness') described in the previous paragraphs provide two diverse modes of appraising globalization and, consequently, local responsiveness and/or resistance. Resistance as an action is mainly attributed to radical or marginal reactions to global integration. In this connection, the notion of local boundaries has a potentially negative connotation for the action or impact of the globalization process, while local embeddedness contains a positive meaning with respect to the globalization process.

However, there is significant discussion on the degree of flexibility and permeability of the boundaries or embeddedness (Scott, 1997, p. 17). The analysis of the spatial peripheral societies and of the processes, which marginalize people and places in the course of development (Lobao, 1996, p. 92), provides a central issue within modern discussions of rural restructuring. The highlighting of the impact of larger processes upon 'spatial periphery', be it in bounding or embedding, provides a major means for policy planning that is more relevant to rural populations (Singelman, 1996).

We tend, therefore, to consider the global more as a *condition* and less so as an explanatory category. Although, in many writings, the global appears to have explanatory power, it also encompasses both local responses and wider processes to these responses. The global cannot simply be an 'exogenous' factor which provides the context and poses rules for the local. We argue that it also conditions the 'endogenous' potential of the local. In this way, the local due to its relationship with the 'hyper-local' cannot be conceptualized as an autonomous or marginal unit of analysis. The marginality or embeddedness of local existence or actions is thus considered in view of a 'top down' conceptualization of the globalization process. Rather the concept of the local itself underlines its ties with the hyper-local. As Massey puts it, the local is in constant negotiation and reformulation since, as time goes by, new relations are initiated, new links with the hyper-local are integrated into its frame (1993, pp. 148-149). In this respect, Kilminster's argument on the conception of globalization seems relevant:

> Globalization both fosters forms of cosmopolitan consciousness *and* stimulates feelings and expressions of ethnicity. It is not surprising, therefore, that the dominant contemporary sociological conception of globalization is of a Janus-faced process of global incorporation and local resistance. The younger generation of social scientists who emphasize the Janus-faced character of globalization themselves work within those dominant nations which are structurally affected by globalization in ways that are conductive to their psychological ambivalence. This may account for the strong evaluative weighting that has become attached to the latter component of the conception of the Janus-faced tension, i.e. 'resistance', as well as to the ideal of cultural pluralism (Kilminster, 1997, p. 280).

Kilminster's reply to those who see globalization as a 'post-modern project' by stressing the 'ideologization' of the inconsistency of the global integration process is of utmost importance here. This critique, in fact, elucidates the 'social construction' character of 'local resistance' as an active project either by linking local responsiveness to a particular component, within the locality, or by assuming voluntaristic schemes of social (re)action.

Overview of the book

This edited volume includes theoretical and empirical research which represents and reflects a diversity of national, comparative, sociological and economic traditions and research backgrounds. Our target here has been to provide a contextual discourse for locating each particular chapter, reflecting not only our own theoretical concerns, but also underlining the authors' arguments and positions. Each chapter maintains its own specificity which cannot be surpassed by our Introduction. The authors' styles of writing have been preserved, while joint effort was made to reveal the particular significance of local responsiveness for each particular case.

The book is divided into four parts comprised of particular concerns which the chapters reflect. Part I, 'Globalization, Diversity and Rural Space' includes 3 chapters. In Chapter 2, Therborn, drawing extensively from historical sociology, discusses globalization and globality as spatial concepts and thus highlight the contribution of rural studies to the analysis of spatial formations and spatial relations. The author acknowledges that the rural world of today is characterized by an increasing divergence between the agrarian and the rural, the diminishing agricultural distinctions in the occupational and income structure of the population and finally the decreasing importance of the family as a unit of production. He argues that there is an interaction between what he calls a post-agrarian political economy and the spatial nature of rural landscape which needs to be seriously studied. In Therborn's view, as a spatial concept, globalization is in need for further analytical clarification and specification. Spatial relations between global and local, regional and local, regional and national and centre and local are complex and multidimensional relations, while the 'social capacity' of the 'local', determined by knowledge and skills provided by the advancement of modernity well beyond the 'centre' or the urban, is increasing.

Remmers, in Chapter 3, constructs a theoretical model drawing from Giddens's structuration theory and Richards's 'plan and performance' notions in order to mark out diversity and localization as 'an ongoing process at the heart of the generation of diversity', against the homogenization forces of globalization. Diversity, largely evident in empirical observations of agricultural modernization, is the result of a continuous 'struggle' for one's identity and survival often managed within the 'room for manoeuvre' that exists between the state or its institutions and farmers. This 'peasant resistance' is expressed in the creation of new situations and localities. Remmers presents empirical examples from his research in marginal areas of Southern Spain to highlight the creative process of common people often ignored by the administration and policy makers since there is no constructive interaction with the farmers. In his opinion this creativity intervenes in the production of diversity by unravelling possible alternative development paths and policy options. In other words, local actors can transform and adapt global elements and thus localize development.

Chapter 4, written by Lawrence, Gray and Stehlik critically, presents the changes occurring in rural Australia as a result of both the expansion of the globalization process and the increasing adoption and implementation of neo-liberalist policies by the Australian Government. After a short presentation of what constitutes the 'farm problem', the new, post-modern features of Australian rural society, are presented. Emphasis is placed on the negative effects of recent developments: the decline of rural population and the weakening of social capital in rural areas; the detraditionalization of rural society and the undermining of the family, social cohesion and cooperation; the growing adoption of a self-help approach for local communities almost in place of state accountability; and the growth of a racial and ethnic blame for the economic and social problems of the country. The 'withdrawal' of the state and the increasing role of the TNCs leading to the 'de-industrialization' of Australian rural regions produce negative outcomes for rural areas. In the authors' view, the latter seriously hinder the very capacity of rural areas to respond to macro-changes under the pretext of supporting a model of integrated rural/regional development. For Lawrence et al., there are positive results as well, connected with the expansion of new technologies, however of a lesser importance as they bring rural regions closer to metropolitan districts and they relatively transform rural areas into consumption spaces where other economic activities can develop to assist rural-based populations.

Part II entitled 'Farmers and Farming Women' includes 2 chapters. Chapter 5 by Llambí, Arias and Freire introduces the discussion on the relationship between globalization and local rural restructuring. This discussion is built upon what they consider complementary rather than contradictory perspectives. The first is the *neo-Marxian political economy* perspective represented by Phillip McMichael which grounds theory in history and sees globalization as a 'political project' designed and implemented by a global elite. The second, drawing from Norman Long's work, is the *post-modernist ethnographic approach* which sees rural transformation as the outcome of the 'complex dynamics between the processes of globalization and localization'. A critical synthesis of the two perspectives is attempted in the analysis of the application of structural adjustment programmes (SAPs) in two neighbouring horticultural communities of Venezuela and Colombia in the Andes. They view globalization as a combination of intertwined multiple historical trajectories, the unintended effects of both purposive actions and countervailing trends. Their argument is that SAPs, a reflection of current globalization processes, not only influence local agriculture and rural livelihoods, but they also generate local responses of either an adaptive or a non-adaptive nature, which are historically and culturally specific.

In Chapter 6, Shortall attempts a comparative analysis of the farm women's situation in three different national contexts. She argues that the way farming is practiced depends on the different social, economic, cultural and historical contexts in which it is embedded and on the actors involved. More specifically, drawing her empirical evidence from Norway, Canada and Northern Ireland, she confirms that the way local responses to a global unacceptability of gender inequalities are shaped is a matter of distinct national political ideology and culture. In Norway, a good example of institutionalized and legitimated gender equality, there is a new law of succession which gives the right on the farm to the eldest child, irrespective of gender. In Canada, a pluralist state and multicultural society with strong farm women's groups, the Canadian Farm Women's Network has taken up and managed to get support for issues connected with equality in land ownership, representation in farming organizations, the farmers' media and the recognition of work roles. Finally, in Northern Ireland, where the 'breadwinner model' predominates, gender equality is not as important as religious and nationalist identities. Shortall's main argument is the reinstatement of the role of the state as a mediator between global gender equality values and forms of local responses.

Part III, 'Communities and Households' includes 2 chapters. In Chapter 7, Starosta and Draganova examine the question, whether and to what extent globalization produces the same consequences for local identities in countries of different cultural backgrounds as well as for local responses to such processes. They draw their evidence from a comparative study of local communities in Bulgaria, Russia and Poland. They assume that if local identification in countries of different historical and cultural background is attaining the same characteristics, then one may conclude that 'global political, economic and cultural processes are producing similar effects'. Their findings indicate that in Bulgaria, there is low emotional bonding and high level of interest for the locality and its affairs. In Poland the situation is rather the opposite, that is high emotional bonding and low interest in local issues. Finally, in Russia both are high expressing a more cohesive type of local identification. As a result, the authors do not dispute the impact of globalization on localities. However, they emphasize the importance of local factors in contemporary social and political life.

Vera-Toscano and Chapman, in Chapter 8, examine the patterns of population movement between urban and rural areas and explore the reasons for such moves in the consequences of the restructuring rural areas are experiencing due to the globalization process. Drawing their evidence from the British Household Panel Survey (BHPS) they come to a number of interrelated conclusions: migration is in both directions between rural and urban areas and it is employment-led; single, non-elderly households show higher mobility; the main reasons for counter-urbanization are employment, family and housing conditions rather than the 'way of life' or the 'scenery'; low income households in rural areas are more extensively present; the more members of a household in employment, the less likely the possibility for persistently low income categorization; and the probability to move above the poverty line increases with the increase in the number of people employed. Indicating that in fact local responses to global integration are not as straightforward as many people imagine, the authors stress that there needs to be further research into these questions taking into consideration issues like the costs of living, gender and quality of employment.

Part IV, 'Local and Regional Development', contains 4 highly diverse chapters. Chapter 9, written by McDonagh and Commins, discusses 'relocalization' of economic activity as a counter and seemingly contradictory trend to globalization. The authors argue that despite the importance of the influence of globalization upon local economies and their development capabilities, attention needs to be paid to the role of 'local agency' in the shaping of a 'new rural economy'. Drawing from empirical research on rural restructuring as manifested in the establishment of SMEs in three, mainly rural, counties of Ireland, the authors found that there is a strong correlation between in-migration and firm formation. As a conclusion, they state that their research illustrates elements of both integration and resistance strategies to globalization. The first concern the attraction of external capital, the development of export markets, the linkage to modern communication technologies and the industrial production systems. The second are connected to the development of local resources and capacity, local entrepreneurship and the establishment of niche-markets by non-movers who show a higher sense of local identity.

In Chapter 10, Mack focuses his attention on the distinction between those local responses sharing a global culture and goals and those of independent, genuine local identity. As far as the first are concerned, the emphasis is on the use of local resources for a global integration whereas for the second, the emphasis is placed on 'a sense of the local and its integrity in a global setting'. Mack draws on evidence from Northern Ireland to claim that the development organization and the policy and planning processes are rather concerned with the first form of responses. In order to 'improve on the capacity for social inclusion and sustainable development', the building of local citizenship is instead put forward as a suggestion. What should be sought for is the enhancement of the local 'as a component of the global to integrate localities, not replace them for a seamless, referenceless whole'. Furthermore, the author suggests that local consciousness and focus for action should be encouraged since being local is of important value to people in rural areas. What is needed, therefore, is a refocus on 'the local' and it is rather 'this consciousness, its inclusiveness, intensity and content, which forms the basis for a development of a new local, and of local citizenship'.

Ruuskanen, in Chapter 11, discusses the rhetoric and the new content of rural policy in Finland as it is set out in the Rural Development Programme of the country in the 1990s. Giving an historical account of rural policy in Finland, the author presents the shift from a strong, paternalistic government planning of the economy, based on a vocabulary of welfare state rhetoric, to a market-led policy rhetoric. More particularly, instead of a state-supported agriculture and a welfare system for the rural population, 'entrepreneurship and new sources of livelihood' become central elements of rural policy. He states that there is a clear move from an objective of a self-sustaining agriculture to a 'relatively self-sufficient social structure'. Further, in the new rural policy, agriculture becomes centralized experiencing the results of globalization. Jobs lost will be replaced by the creation of 'new sources of livelihood and services'. This shift presupposes a change of attitude, which has been traditionally connected with a resistance to change and a prevailing climate of opinion that poses obstacles to this development. Ruuskanen sees the strategy of flexible specialization and industrial networking facilitated by an emphasis on entrepreneurial training, as it is clearly stated in the Finnish rural policy, as 'a new application of Taylorism'. Ruuskanen disputes the possible positive outcome of the new rural policy in Finland and claims that this policy 'may well undermine the long-term possibilities of local initiative of rural areas and will certainly exacerbate the social inequality between them'.

Finally, Chapter 12 written by Papadopoulos attempts to model Southern European rurality within a discussion of agrarian and naturalist traditions in Europe as expressed in the distinction between the production and consumption conceptions of rural areas. The author believes that no 'grave distinctions' exist between urban and rural areas in Southern Europe. He discusses its rurality along three themes which help him account for the 'difference or convergence with the rest of Europe': a) the differentiation of farming in Southern Europe; b) the peripheral construction of the rural; and c) the crosscutting conception of the rural. Having posed his most basic assumption that the South European countries are treated as a heterogeneous whole, the author comes to the conclusion that the strong

Introduction: Local Boundaries or Embeddedness 15

bonds between urban and rural areas create a distinctive 'social fiber', characterized by different types of family farming, employment patterns and survival strategies which can provide the basis for a sustainable endogenous development option. For Papadopoulos, rural restructuring in Southern Europe needs a 'modernization project' which will support the maintenance of social networks, local empowerment, socio-spatial heterogeneity and cultural diversity.

Notes

1. The notion of 'civil society' is used here as an exegetical concept which allows for a characterization of the social bonding or cohesion as it is historically treated in the study of modern nation-states that are placed at different levels and degrees of socioeconomic development. For a recent anthropological-historical analysis of civil society which aims at criticizing socio-political and cultural homogeneity, see Gellner, 1994.
2. A significant example illustrating the seemingly contradictory nature of globalization is featured in the case of EU integration process. As long as the European market unification process intensifies, the regional policies and scenarios undergo significant renaissance. According to Keating the 'new context for regionalism is provided by globalization' (1997, p. 23). Although one may define different forms of regionalism (e.g. defensive, integrating, autonomist) regions/localities, however, provide the main mediator of economic and social development in a European context (McAleavy and De Rynck, 1997). Moreover, it should be stressed here that both forms or traditions of regionalism and the definition of regions/localities are state-led concepts conditioned by administrative-political traditions and, consequently, enabled to operate in the European context by their national structures (Benz and Eberlein, 1998).

References

Amin, A. and Thrift, N. (1994), 'Living in the Global', in Amin, A. and Thrift, N. (eds) *Globalization, Institutions and Regional Development in Europe,* Oxford University Press: Oxford.

Barber, B. (1995), 'All Economies are 'Embedded': The Career of a Concept, and Beyond', *Social Research*, Vol. 62, No 2, pp. 387-413.

Barquero, A.V. (1991), *Local Development: A Strategy for the Creation of Employment,* Papazisis: Athens (in Greek).

Benz, A and Eberlein, B. (1998), 'Regions in European Governance: The Logic of Multi-Level Interaction', *Working Paper RSC No 98/31,* European University Institute, September.

Cloke, P. and Goodwin, M. (1992), 'Conceptualizing Countryside Change: From Post-Fordism to Rural Structured Coherence', *Transactions of the Institute of British Geographers*, NS, Vol. 17, pp. 321-336.
Cox, K.R. and Mair, A. (1991), 'From Localized Social Structures to Localities as Agents', *Environment and Planning A*, Vol. 23, pp. 197-213.
European Commission (1997), *Agenda 2000. For a Stronger and Wider Union*, Office for Official Publications of the European Communities: Luxembourg.
Friedland, W.H. (1991), 'Introduction: Shaping the New Political Economy of Advanced Capitalist Agriculture', in Friedland, W.H., Busch, L., Buttel, F.H. and Rudy, A.P. (eds), *Towards a New Political Economy of Agriculture*, Westview Press: Boulder.
Friedland, W.H. (1994), 'Globalization, the State and the Labour Process', *International Journal of Sociology of Agriculture and Food*, Vol. 4, pp. 30-46.
Gellner, E. (1994), *Conditions of Liberty. Civil Society and its Rivals*, Hamish Hamilton Ltd.: London.
Giddens, A. (1990), *The Consequences of Modernity*, Polity Press: Cambridge.
Granovetter, M.S. (1985), 'Economic Action and Social Structure: The Problem of Embeddedness', *American Journal of Sociology*, Vol. 91, No 3, pp. 481-510.
Hebinck, P. and van der Ploeg, J.D. (1997), 'Dynamics of Agricultural Production. An Analysis of Micro-Macro Linkages', in de Haan, H. and Long, N. (eds), *Images and Realities of Rural Life*, Van Gorcum: The Netherlands.
Holton, R.J. (1998), 'Introduction', in *Globalization and the Nation-State*, Macmillan Press Ltd.: Basingstoke and London.
Keating, M. (1997), 'The Political Economy of Regionalism', in Keating, M and Loughlin, J. (eds), *The Political Economy of Regionalism*, Frank Cass and Co Ltd: London.
Kilminster, R. (1997), 'Globalization as an Emergent Concept', in Scott, A. (ed), *The Limits to Globalization*, Routledge: London and New York.
Koc, M. (1994), 'Globalization as a Discourse', in Bonanno, A., Busch, L., Friedland, W., Gouveia, L. and Minzione, E. (eds), *From Columbus to ConAgra: The Globalization of Agriculture and Food*, University Press of Kansas: Lawrence.
Lipietz, A. (1993), 'The Local and the Global: Regional Individuality or Interregionalism?', *Transactions of the Institute of British Geographers*, NS, Vol. 18, pp. 8-18.
Lobao, L. (1996), 'A Sociology of the Periphery versus Peripheral Sociology: Rural Sociology and the Dimension of Space', *Rural Sociology*, Vol. 61, No 1, pp. 77-102.
McAleavy, P. and De Rynck, S. (1997), 'Regional or Local? The EU's Future Partners in Cohesion Policy', *Working Paper RSC 55*, European University Institute, October.
Marsden, T., Lowe, P. and Whatmore, S. (1990), 'Introduction: Questions of Rurality', in Marsden, T., Lowe, P. and Whatmore, S. (eds), *Rural Restructuring: Global Processes and their Responses*, David Fulton Publishers: London.

Marsden, T., Lowe, P. and Whatmore, S. (1992), 'Labour and Locality: Emerging Research Issues', in Marsden, T., Lowe, P. and Whatmore, S. (eds), *Labour and Locality: Uneven Development and the Rural Labour Process*, David Fulton Publishers: London.

Massey, D. (1993), 'Questions of Locality', *Geography*, Vol. 78, No 339, pp. 142-149.

McMichael, P. (1996), 'Globalization: Myths and Realities', *Rural Sociology*, Vol. 61, No 1, pp. 25-55.

Mouzelis, N. (1997), 'Modernity: A Non-European Conceptualization', in Keyder, C. (ed), *Tradition in Modernity: Southern Europe in Question*, ISA Regional Conferences.

Papadopoulos, A.G. (1999), 'The Indefinable Boundaries of Globalization: Reconsidering the Relationship between Globalization, Local Development and Family Farming', *EKKE Working Paper 5*, National Centre for Social Research, Institute of Urban and Rural Sociology (in Greek).

Portes, A. (1998), 'Social Capital: Its Origins and Applications in Modern Sociology', *Annual Review of Sociology*, Vol. 24, pp. 1-24.

Putnam, R.D. (1993), 'The Prosperous Community: Social Capital and Public Life', *The American Prospect*, No 13, pp. 35-42.

Robertson, R. (1995), 'Glocalization: Time-Space and Homogeneity-Heterogeneity', in Featherstone, M., Lash, S. and Robertson, R. (eds), *Global Modernities*, Sage Publications: London.

Roumeliotis, P (1997), *The Route to Globalization: The European Strategy for the 21st Century*, Nea Synora: Athens (in Greek).

Scott, A. (1997), 'Introduction. Globalization: Social Process or Political Rhetoric?', in Scott, A. (ed), *The Limits to Globalization*, Routledge: London and New York.

Singelmann, J. (1996), 'Will Rural Areas still matter in the 21st Century? (or) Can Rural Sociology Remain Relevant?', *Rural Sociology*, Vol. 61, No 1, pp. 143-158.

Therborn, G. (1995), 'Routes to/through Modernity', in Featherstone, M., Lash, S. and Robertson, R. (eds), *Global Modernities*, Sage Publications: London.

Van der Ploeg, J.D., (1992), 'The Reconstitution of Locality: Technology and Labour in Modern Agriculture', in Marsden, T., Lowe, P. and Whatmore, S. (eds), *Labour and Locality: Uneven Development and the Rural Labour Process*, David Fulton Publishers: London.

Verschoor, G. (1997), 'Entrepreneurship, Projects and Actor-Networks. Reconceptualizing Small Firms', in de Haan, H. and Long, N. (eds), *Images and Realities of Rural Life*, Van Gorcum: The Netherlands.

Waters, M. (1995), *Globalization*, Routledge: London and New York.

Weiss, L. (1997), 'Globalization and the Myth of the Powerless State', *New Left Review*, No 225, pp. 3-27.

Part I

Globalization, Diversity and Rural Space

2 Modernity, Globalization and the Rural World

GÖRAN THERBORN

One of the first things noticeable when reflecting upon the world and upon social science from the angle of the countryside, is the persistent size and importance of the rural world. While farmers have become rare, outside the Balkans, Poland, the lands of the former USSR, and the Third World, 40 to 50 per cent of the population in many of the rich OECD countries are still rural. That is the case of Scandinavia, except Norway where almost 60 per cent of the population was rural in 1990, in USA, Canada, and Ireland, but no longer in Greece, Portugal, France, or Spain, which are about a third rural. Most urbanized are the peoples of the Low Countries, less than ten per cent rural (OECD, 1996a, p. 36).

Now what is 'rural' is probably not uncontroversial among rural sociologists, and the OECD definition as communities with less than 150 inhabitants per square kilometer, is one among many. But it was not made for reasons of special pleading, and it indicates the size of the tasks of ambitious rural sociologists.

Rural perspectives on social science

Social science in general and sociology, as the most wide-ranging of the social science disciplines, in particular, have, in fact, much to learn from using a rural lookout, from listening to country people, and from reading rural sociology. This is not primarily in the self-evident sense of learning about rural life, but in the sense of learning and developing the trade of social analysis. Two rural themes of central significance to general sociology are selected here, the theme of space, and the theme of change.

Space is the most obvious one. Rurality, the defining criterion of the object of rural sociology, is, of course, a spatial concept. The rural/urban contrast refers to different forms of spatial organization and utilization. True, it has mostly been taken for obvious, and space is one of the most underdeveloped key concepts of social science, often relegated to the walled-off compound of geography, alternatively re-interpreted as an attribute of cities only, manifested only in urban space.

Globalization and globality are spatial concepts, and we should expect rural angles to provide us with new insights about the globe. They do, but I shall come back to that later in this chapter.

The relationships, historically usually exploitative and domineering, occasionally protective as well, between *the local and the exterior* are classic components of peasant experience. Henri Mendras (1995, p. 14) made them into defining characteristics of a peasant society. Something similar was taken over by Immanuel Wallerstein (1974) and his disciples in making centre-periphery relations a key to the analyses of the 'modern world system'.

However, some familiarity with rural localities, with local cunning, with the frequent gaps between central presumptions and local realities, should inspire inquiries into more complex spatial relationships. Local responses to global integration indicate a transcendence of the earlier centre-periphery conceptualization. The well-known inter-relationship of supranationality and regionality in the EU is another pointer into a new spatial direction.

Spatial orders and relationships are extremely important to social organization. A rural sociology perspective offers us an excellent vantage point for looking at spatial arrangements.

Social *change* is another phenomenon that can never be properly understood without including a rural perspective. Rusticity has always occupied a special place in literary and in everyday conceptions of change, a position of contrast or polarity, of quiet, equilibrium, sometimes interpreted as harmony, of slowness, in brief as the opposite of the noise, the pace, the tensions, the volatility, the feverish change of urbanity. This should lead us to suspect that the study of rural societies has something important to tell us about social change. Hitherto, there has been little of this, although some of the first scientific studies of the diffusion of innovations were made in the countryside, by pre-WWII American rural sociologists.

What could be rural sociology contributions to the grasping of social change? One frequent weakness of general conceptions of social change is their lack of attention to the enormous role of physical displacement, in causing changes in the places of destination, in those of departure, and in the culture of the people displaced, be it through long- or short-distance migration, uprooting through wars and destruction, or simply through temporary military service more or less far away. From a rural perspective it is impossible to overlook physical movements under preoccupations with social revolutions, technology, and learning.

It seems that another elementary lesson from rural studies is the intricate and widely variable imbrication of change and conservation. The urban stereotype of the peasant has been effectively challenged by John Berger, the British art critic, writer, and close participant observer of peasant life (in Haute Savoie). 'Each day a peasant experiences more change more closely than any other class', Berger (1979, p. 206) points out, referring to changes of the season, the weather, of domestic and of wild animals, of plants, etc. Modernity and change are not synonymous, and change and tradition are not incompatibles.

Modernity

Modernity is a central concept to at least two very different social approaches. One defines 'modernity' as a set of particular institutions and/or patterns of institutional outcomes, such as urbanization, literacy, usually those of the author's society or ideal society. That is the mainstream of self-consciously 'western' sociology, from Max Weber, via Talcott Parsons to Anthony Giddens and Ulrich Beck. In a more popular, missionary form this conception was also known as 'modernization theory', which may be encountered on the Balkans in rather low-keyed form in the collection on *Diverse Paths to Modernity in Southeastern Europe*, put together some years ago by Gersamios Augustinos.

The other main definition of modernity developed out of historiography, out of the history of art, culture, and concepts. Its main contemporary proponent is the German conceptual historian Reinhart Kosellek, but one finds it also among historically oriented sociologists, like Niklas Luhmann, Alain Touraine, and Göran Therborn.

Modernity, in this second sense, is defined as an epoch or culture dominated by a certain temporal mentality, a certain orientation to time. The rise of modernity, in this view, means a discovery of the future as an open, unknown, but reachable horizon, and a conception of the present as under an obligation to break with the past and to prepare for a new future. Modern - and pre- and post-modern - orientations may best be studied in specific institutional areas, in those of learning and knowledge production, in art, in the economy, in politics. They refer then to conceptions of knowledge, in terms of growth, development, the positive value of change and novelty. In certain periods, these orientations take a high profile, in commitments to the avant-garde, to progress, to liberation and emancipation, to continuous reform or permanent revolution. In others, they are more low-keyed, or challenged by backward-looking, cyclical, or directionless occasionalist conceptions.

From an institutionalist conception of modernity, rurality and peasantry are a priori without intrinsic interest, as pre-modern by definition. From a temporal viewpoint, peasant experiences offer new food for thought.

The temporality of modernity is not simple that of a pervasiveness of change, as a reading of urban sociology from Georg Simmel onwards might lead us to assume. But it is in the countryside that the break between the cyclical time predominant of pre-modernity and the future-directed linear time of modernity is most tangible. Modernity arrives, when there is something new and unforeseen glimpseable beyond the regularity of the seasons and the recurrent contingencies of good harvests, bad harvests, and disasters. New modes of cultivation, new crops, new employment or pursuits.

A major advantage of a temporal conception of modernity is its inadequacy to ethnocentric bias and its amenability to spatial comparisons. From a global study of the history of the right to vote, I learnt, that the myriad of modern historical experiences may be summarized into four major routes to and through modernity (Therborn 1992; 1995). These routes, it seems to me, also make sense of the sociopolitical history of global agriculture.

Agrarian modernity, defined in terms of temporality, refers to agriculture and agriculturists, oriented towards exploiting the opportunities of a new future. Concretely, this means an agriculture oriented towards expectations of new future yields and sales - expectations nourished by new technical knowledge and by anticipations of consumer demands -, rather than to given needs of subsistence or given outlets for sale and delivery, to conjectures about the future rather than to the wisdom of the past and the urgencies of the present. How agrarian modernity in this sense developed, and to what extent and why it became a permanent feature of agriculture or remained an occasional moment succeeded by a new tradition, are fascinating questions to a history of modernity, a project which largely remains to be written.

A Swedish village vignette

A completely unrepresentative illustration may be how this modernization reached the village in Southeastern Sweden, where I grew up, a fairly prosperous, although somewhat off-the road, kulak-dominated plain of Northern European mixed farming. The village, or hamlet rather, was what geographers call a chain-village, a row of nine farms and some non-farm houses, including one smith and machine repairman, one shoemaker, two seamstresses, and a score of workers' cottages, spread-out along a road. There was a village council for some common affairs but no spatial intimacy.

Modernity came and settled in two waves, one was productivity-driven, the second was driven by its attention to market outlets. The first succeeded with my father's generation, he was born in 1905. When it started I cannot tell, but it was not triumphant and secure before World War II. It was only after the war that the tractors came, then the harvester combines, the milking machine systems, and soon an endless stream of bigger and better machines. Farms were merged upon the retirement of the older generation, and the farm hands, not more than a few per farm, began to disappear. Auto-consumption of the farm produce ceased.

Only in the second wave did the product mix really change, although it had of course occasionally altered in the past. The traditional distinction between farmers and other entrepreneurs disappeared. Now, to be modern meant to find out what might be profitable products, and to specialize in them, as long as they were more profitable than other alternatives: it could be an industrial production of pigs or chicken, the raising of beef cows, the cultivation of strawberries and vegetables, variably supplemented with cereals and/or root crops.

In my village, this second wave of modernization was brought about by relatives and neighbours of my generation, establishing themselves in the 1970s-early 1980s. Theirs is no longer a special farming culture - not to speak of a Balkan or Savoyard peasant culture - but a rural middle-class lifestyle, with riding-horses for the girls, regular exercise at the town gym, and biannual skiing holidays. The peripheral crofter cottages, on the edge of the forest, which were de-populated in the first wave, are inhabited again, by working class and lower middle class families commuting to the town or to other distant non-farm workplaces.

Modern rurality tends to become pure space, and no longer a specific mentality.

Ruralities and the four global routes to/through modernity

From this little local story, let us leap to the global. I am not competent to outline a comparative history of agrarian modernity. But let us see, if my general perspective on the four major roads to and through modernity in the world, originally an empirical generalization from a study of the right to vote, has anything to say about global agrarian modernity.

What relates the sociopolitical and cultural-political analysis of modernity to peasants and farmers, is the 'englobing society' of the latter, in the sense of Henri Mendras.

Global modernity arrived along four main routes, each of them of course allowing for a considerable amount of individual driving. The European, that of the New Worlds, the Colonial, and fourthly, the road of Externally Induced Modernization, first and most successfully taken by Japan. The four routes, discovered by empirical induction (Therborn, 1992), differ structurally by the different location, internal or external, of the forces for and against modernity.

In Europe both forces were indigenous. Indigenous were the path-breaking door-openers to a new future, in British science from the early 17th century, asserting the cumulativeness of knowledge, in French art and aesthetics from late 17th, arguing that contemporary art could equal and even surpass the Ancient models, in the Scottish Enlightenment portraying human history as one of successive stages of economic development, in rationalist German philosophy and French proto-sociology reflecting upon the meaning of the French Revolution. And equally indigenous were the forces of anti-modernity, the Churches, Catholic, Protestant, and Orthodox, the backward-looking admirers of Antiquity, and all the guardians of ancient customs and privileges, the Romantics and the reactionaries in the wake of the Revolution. The oceanic voyages and the colonial conquests of Europe from about 1500 widened the horizons of Europeans, but did not per se and directly open Europe to modernity. They started as extensions of medieval seafaring, trade, and war. The Iberian conquest of the Americas was a continuation of the 'Reconquista' of the Iberian Peninsula from Muslim rule.

In the rest of the world, the rise of, and the battles for and against modernity always involved a crucial relation between the external and the internal. In the New Worlds, the forces of modernity were internal, like in Europe, sectors of the European settlers, but a major force of tradition was the European Empire, Britain in the case of North America, Spain and Portugal in Latin America. To the Colonial Zone, modernity arrived literally out of the barrel of guns, from the colonial conquerors, providing novel role models to a growing part of the colonized, who then challenged colonial rule in the name of absorbed nationalism. Finally, there was a group of countries in which modernity was externally induced, by external threats and challenges to traditional ways of ruling, but actually undertaken from above, by a part of the indigenous elite, selectively importing new techniques, institutions, and ways of thinking from threatening external forces of modernity.

The four main roads to modernity may each be sub-divided into lanes. The division closest at hand is one of dichotomization. Each route had, for various reasons, a fast lane and a slow one. In this way, it is often useful to distinguish Northwestern Europe from the rest of Europe, North America with Australia and New Zealand from Latin America, Colonial Asia from Colonial Africa, and Japan from slower drives of Externally Induced Modernization.

While referring to actual historical trajectories, the four routes may also be used as ideal types, capturing the process of modernity in a particular country as a combination of two or more roads. Russia, for instance is part of European history, but it also has features of imported modernization, by Peter I and by Lenin and Stalin, which resemble the modernization of Japan. Nineteenth century Greece, under its imported German dynasty, would be another example. Or take China, once a semi-colonial society having crucial experiences in common both with India and with Japan or Turkey.

The British Industrial and the French Revolution were the crucial events in the coming of European modernity, the Wars of American Independence to the New Worlds, the conquest of Bengal and the independece of India, the 'scramble' for Africa and African independence, to the Colonial Zone, and the Meiji Restoration in Japan or the Kemalist revolution in Turkey to Externally Induced Modernization.

Only in Europe did rural and agrarian issues and forces play a specific and significant role in the key events of modernity, in the agricultural transformation laying the basis for the industrial take-off and in the anti-aristocratic insurrection in France. Agrarian settlement was also a defining feature of the New Worlds, but agrarian issues and conflicts were not central to the Wars of Independence. The modern dialectic of the Colonial Zone was typically urban, and so was the center of the externally inspired revolutions from above. But in East Asia we may distinguish a second phase of a modern breakthrough, in which a rural transformation was essential.

Europe

Europe was the pioneer of modernity, but the meaning of this forerunner position is seldom realized. Modernity in Europe was the fulcrum of endogenous conflict, with the forces for and against both well anchored within European society. The European route to modernity was, above all else, the route of *civil war*, between the forces of tradition and of modernity, both endogenous to European society. Because of this, but also because of the pre-modern social organization of estates and because

Europe became the only continent having societies dominated by industrial employment, class, class consciousness, class organization, class conflict became uniquely important in the European journey to and through modernity.

Peasants and farmers of Europe also organized themselves as a class to unique extent, beginning in mid-19th century Scandinavia and then spreading in the course of the first third of the 20th century all along the East-Central strip of Europe, from Finland to Bulgaria. In Western and Southern Europe, farmers' parties did not grow, but economic and cultural class organizations did.

The rural classes of Europe could be mobilized as shock troops of anti-modernity, but the rural class struggle was often a crucial contribution to urban modernism, from 1789 to 1917. Agrarian modernity in Europe rose in the welter of internal social conflict and competition, however the agents of modernity differed from one country or epoch to another, be they landowners, big individual farmers, cooperative movements, or urban planners. The civil war modernity of Europe pitted peasants against landowners, peasants against urbanites, landless labourers against landowners and/or big peasants, and crofters against big peasants. The French revolutionary Scare of 1789, and the reforms from above in Denmark and Sweden at the same time inaugurated the new era. The '18th Brumaire' of Louis Napoleon Bonaparte in 1849 and 1851 manifested the electoral predominance of rurality. The Romanian peasant uprising of 1907 and the red revolution of the Finnish crofters in 1917-18 constitute, with the Russian peasant rebellions of 1917, the major bids for a peasant power.

In their revolutionary forms, the peasant assertions were all defeated. However, European modern peasants were rarely fully defeated. On the contrary, farmers became everywhere in capitalist Europe a benefiting part of 20th century *class compromises*. And in most of the new late 19th century-post-WWI nations, the class of farmers became a crucial and self-conscious part of the ruling blocs. Elsewhere in Europe, peasants/farmers have remained a major, non-hegemonic social group till this day. Within the European Union, the policy of agrarian support is the major economic game being played (claiming a good half of the total EU budget).

The New Worlds

In the New Worlds, of early European settlement, modernity also emerged internally, but the main forces of anti-modernity were external, those of the originally settling, Old World, and, less powerful but more culturally persistent, the natives, who were also regarded as external to settler society.

Settlement meant new agriculture, of plantations or farms, although modernism often did not remain a constant orientation. Nevertheless, in the agrarian history of the world, the New Worlds and their settled lands conquered from native nomads constituted a spearhead of productivity and of intercontinental exports. How modernist the slave-run plantations, of sugar, tobacco, cotton etc., were, we do not know, but they fed significantly into new global consumption patterns. And the European countryside and European food consumption were revolutionized in late 19th century by the arrival of North American and Argentine grain, of meat from the US, from Argentine and Uruguay, of meat and dairy products across two oceans from Australia and New Zealand.

Rural conflict in the New Worlds took on an ethnic in addition to a class character. Settlers, land robbers, planters, agrarian capitalists versus natives be they native peasants or native nomads and/or versus alien slaves constituted the agrarian frontlines, from Canada to Argentina, from Australia to New Zealand. In the plantation region, from Southern United States to Northern Brazil, via the West Indies, slavery, racism and the denial of humanity were the basic issues.

More generally, the European cleavage of the people versus the privileged upper class was superseded by the divide of us the people and the rest, the non-people. In the New Worlds, at the south as well as at the north of the Rio Grande, people had rights. But who belonged to the people and who defended the rights of the people? Were the natives part of the people? Were the slaves and the ex-slaves? The recent immigrants?

Not even the decadal epic and the final success of the Mexican Revolution undid this settler-native divide, as the recent rebellion of the Chiapas natives has shown.

The (Ex-)colonial zone

To the Colonial Zone modernity arrived from overseas, by violent conquest and destruction. The cultural arsenal of the conquerors was gradually mastered by new generations of local élites, embarking upon paths other than their forefathers and mothers, and then turning against the foreign masters the culture of nationalism and that of people's and individuals' rights.

The colonial countryside was often subject to enforced cash-crop cultivation and generally to some form of monetarizing taxation. By and large, however, the colonial countryside remained outside that inter-elite cultural exchange and conflict. On the contrary, the distant colonial power usually bolstered up the traditional rural elites and their local rule, such as that of the Tutsis over the Hutus.

The new anti-colonial counter-elites, which colonialism fostered through its own contradictions, were typically urban, whether professional gentlemen like Nehru or Jinnah or school teachers, clerks, or non-commissioned officers, like the 'verandah boys' of Ghana and of other African nationalisms.

Colonized peasants could sometimes be successfully mobilized by modernist social revolutionaries, pitting the peasants against the powers of alien urbanity and modernity, as well as against local settlers and landowners, and providing a focused national political goal to the unleashed energies of pent-up peasant frustration.

However, the gap, the mutual exteriority of the metropolitan state and countryside, has continued into the gap of urban modernity and rural tradition. It has been reproduced by the ex-colonial states, in spite of some scattered regional exceptions, from the Ivory Coast to the Punjab and Java.

The enormous peasant mobilizations, from semi-colonial China to colonial Algeria, succeeded as anti-colonial revolutions, but not as peasant assertions. Urban superordination, parried with traditional rural evasiveness, rather than an autonomous class deal or settler pride seems to have characterized the ex-colonial rural world. Modernizing impulses have continued to come into the countryside mainly from outside.

Externally induced modernization

Finally, we have the passage to modernity through external threat but short of conquest, the pass of Externally Induced Modernization. Here, modernity descended from the pinnacles of re-constituted power onto a sullen agrarian population. Japan of the Meiji Restoration opened the route, and was followed, in part, by China, by Siam turned into Thailand, by the Ottoman Empire transformed into Turkey, by Iran, and a few other countries.

Here, the peasantry was not mobilized by the modernist faction of its traditional, indigenous rulers. Traditional patterns of cultivation were not overthrown. Nor could any endogenous peasant autonomy develop, like in Europe. However, landlord-peasant relations got subordinated to the modernizing drive of the ruling elite.

The peasantry was kept, and re-organized, as a basis for conservative culture and politics, while being gradually transformed into a force contributing to modern national development, putting its savings at the disposal of industrial investment and its sons and daughters for pliable industrial labour.

In East Asia, a new pattern emerged with the Sino-Japanese War and with World War II. Now agrarian transformation became central. In China and North Korea, it was part of the Communist extrapolation of the struggle for national liberation, as occurred somewhat later also in Vietnam. In Japan and in South Korea, later setting examples to Taiwan and other countries, agrarian reform became a central feature of a US attempt at capitalist modernization. Japan had become an original modern country before agrarian reform and before Hiroshima, but there seems to be general agreement that agrarian reform and transformation have been crucial contributions to the later East Asian 'economic miracle'.

The rural world of today

Shifting gear, from the history of modernity to recent agrarian change, there are four aspects to be signaled.

One is the widening divergence between the agrarian and the rural. While agrarian employment in Western Europe tends to vary between 2 and 5 per cent of the labour force, with a couple of outliers like Portugal and Greece, between a third and half of the Western European population lives in rural conditions. While the agricultural trend is steadily downwards, we have had tendencies towards counter-urbanization or re-ruralization since the 1960s in Britain and West Germany, since the 1970s in France, in the Low Countries, and in Denmark and Sweden (Jordan, 1996, pp. 313-14). Re-ruralization has not been a consistent trend, but all OECD countries, save Finland, Greece, and New Zealand, increased their rural employment in the 1980s. In Belgium, Germany, and the UK, rural employment grew more than urban (OECD, 1996a, p. 52).

In the Scandinavian welfare states a major part of this new rural employment are in public social services. But, like in Ireland and elsewhere, there is also an economically significant increase in rural telecommunications- and computer-based services, of booking, selling, and billing. In those post-industrial services you have a good 'local response to global integration'.

Secondly, the distinctiveness of agriculture as an occupation is diminishing rapidly. One part of this, is the declining, but also cross-nationally very variable share of farming income among farm owners. In Western Europe, the share of farm income among the total household income of farmers ranges from a fifth in Denmark, not quite a third in Italy, and less than half in Spain and Germany, to about two thirds in France,

Greece, Ireland, and Portugal, three fourths in the Netherlands, and to 87 per cent in Switzerland. US and Japanese farmers derive only 15-16 per cent of their current income from their farms. Wages make up the bulk of other income, except in France, Italy, and Spain, where welfare state benefits are most important, in Italy slightly more important than the farm (OECD, 1995, p. 190 and national tables).

A manifestation of this lack of distinctiveness is also that farmers' incomes tend to resemble those of the rest of the population, although again with some significant cross-national variation. Total farmers' incomes in the OECD generally lie in the range of 90 to 110 per cent of the national average, in Sweden slightly lower. In three countries, farm-owners have much higher income than the national population, in the Netherlands (80 per cent more), Norway (50 per cent), and Japan (33 per cent). The early modern pattern in Europe, on the other hand, was more like the current Mexican share, of less than half the average national income (46 per cent of it) (OECD, 1995, national tables).

Thirdly, the increasing complexity of farm incomes indicates, among other things, the lesser importance of the family as one common economic unit of family farming. While familism is still a distinctive feature of probably most farm households, it is important also to underline the enormous importance of the state. European agriculture successfully resisted capitalist wage-labour enterprise by the family farm. So far, it has also successfully resisted neo-liberal privatization.

Public subsidies net constitute half of the value of EU agricultural production in the mid-1990s. It is less in the US, one fifth, but higher in two countries with small welfare states, four fifths in Switzerland, and three fourths in Japan (OECD, 1996b, p. 119).

Fourthly and finally, in agriculture, the general failure of post-Communist Europe to realize liberal promises and recipes seems to have taken two different directions.

One is a tendency to de-modernization, back into small-scale, low technology subsistence agriculture. A process to be found in large parts of Russia and of other former Soviet republics, and in the Balkans. On the enormous fields of Romania, for instance, you can suddenly spot groups of people, mainly but not exclusively women, bent over manual labour, weeding or collecting, with no piece of machinery in sight.

The other is an enduring survival of collectivist agriculture in new legal forms, as corporations, new style cooperatives, in complex systems of leasing and tenancy. This pattern is most striking in the most developed parts of the ex-Communist world, in Hungary, Czechia and Slovakia, and in eastern Germany. In Germany this means, that the income of agricultural households in the former GDR, after the exodus of a large number of workers, is higher than in the old Federal Republic, particularly higher than farmers' income in southern Germany (OECD, 1995, p. 16; Lhomel, 1997).

Spatial formations

The rural and the urban are spatial concepts, referring to a still largely under-theorized and underdeveloped aspect of social analysis. From a sociological point of view, space has at least four crucial dimensions, *expanse* or area, *connectivity*, i.e., linkages of transport and communication, thirdly, *density*, of population, of social activities, and finally sociophysical significance, *landmarks*. Rurality contrasts against urbanity by having lower density and lower connectivity, which usually goes back to having a larger expanse. Rurality also means that the landmarks, the spatial expressions of familiarity, respect, and admiration, the most significant points of orientation, are natural, features of a landscape, rather than constructed buildings.

What we call societies, often without much reflection, are always spatial formations, among other things. What have they meant to social relations? For instance, what are the implications of size differences in rural settlements ranging from the agricultural towns of up to 20-30,000 inhabitants, in southern Italy, southern Spain, and eastern Hungary, to the typical Germanic village of a few hundred people (Jordan, 1996, p. 273)? What does it mean, to social relations, to cultural symbols, to social consciousness, the fact that, for example, Denmark still has a significant, 42 per cent according to the OECD, rural population, and the Netherlands is overwhelmingly urban? The only true answer is that we do not know.

The countryside is being changed from an agricultural space into something else. One change is, of course, the tourist and leisure area. Mass tourism started in the mid-1950s, roughly simultaneous to the decisive de-peasantization of Europe. The urban family country house began to become a mass phenomenon a decade or two later. Part of the rural world has become a commuter park, a landscaped environment to old or new homes of households commuting to urban work.

The Mediterranean coastline, to a considerable extent, is becoming a string of old people's homes, migrating across national borders or within, distributed according to land values and wealth. The countryside has turned from the source of capital accumulation to a vast receptacle of public funds, for public service employment - catering for the aging ex-agrarian population - for agricultural subsidy, and for social entitlements, of pensions of various sorts. The interaction of this new, post-agrarian political economy and the spatiality of the rural landscape is so far largely unexplored.

A few spatial notions have got established, the US 'frontier', the 'immenseness' of Russia, the proximity of the sea and the threat of the tides in the Low Countries, the consciousness of being an island in Britain, or in Crete. Others have got ideologically discredited, like Lebensraum (living space), or geopolitics, still others are socio-spatial proper names, the Far North in Scandinavia, the Deep South, the Mid-West, and the Far West in the US, the Far East in Russia, the Deep North in Australia, the West (Mahgreb) and the East (Machrek) in the Arab world.

Rural sociology and anthropology, and most recently biological history, have provided us naive urban social scientists with a breathtakingly broad spatial delimitation. The agricultural sociology of Ester Boserup, the family anthropology of Jack Goody, and the biological history of Jared Diamond have demonstrated to us the different flora and fauna, the different agriculture, and the different family patterns of Eurasia versus the rest of the world in the case of Diamond, in comparison to Africa in the slightly more modest comparative sweeps of Boserup and Goody (Boserup, 1970; Diamond, 1997; Goody, 1976). Each and together, these three very different scholars testify to the general spatial potency of rural studies.

Globalization

Globalization has recently become *the* spatial concept à la mode. It is a notion in urgent need of analytical clarification and specification. Is globalization, or global integration if you want, a novel phenomenon, changing basic economic, social, and cultural parameters, and if so, how?

As a spatial concept, globalization may refer to an extension of the *reach* or *range* of social structures, cultures, and/or action, in brief, to an expansion of the significant social area. Secondly, it may refer to an extension or densification of the *connections* between resources and constraints, patterns of meaning and actors. Thirdly, it may also indicate a change of the *landmarks of* social *orientation* towards an inclusion of the globe as a whole.

Put briefly and crudely, tendencies to globalization are ancient, the predominant discourse on globalization is a highly ideological syndrome, and the most significant new features of globalization tend to get neglected.

Far-ranging imperial structures and worldwide imperial action are old. The Mongol Empire spanned the major part of Eurasia. The Spanish Empire ranged from the West Indies to the Philippines. The British Navy ruled the oceans of the planet, and the British Empire at its 19th century height either ruled or deeply penetrated all the five continents. The end of the Cold War has rather seen a de-globalization of political power.

Global structural interdependence through exchange and markets is also ancient. On the Baltic island of Gotland you find coins and objects traded a thousand years ago, from Bulgar and Kashgar on the Silk Route, from Herat, Baghdad, Constantinople, and from the British Isles. The voyage of Vasco da Gama took about ten years to depress spice prices at the long distance trade bazaar of Cairo. A world market, a global economic institution, emerged for grain more than a century ago.

Now, the computer screens of constantly trading financial markets are much faster. And the volume of gross financial transactions, in currencies and in various papers of value, has risen astronomically over the last decade. But, for ordinary people, the changes are much more modest, and the screams of global competition are not seldom fictional horror stories, either of neo-liberal calls for adaptation or of anti-neo-liberal calls for resistance.

World exports constituted less than a tenth of the world product in 1956, the best estimates range between 7 and 9 per cent, in any case lower than in 1913 and in 1929. The OPEC oil cartel moved it upwards, to 16 per cent in 1974, where around it oscillated till the mid-nineties, when it climbed up to 22 per cent in 1996 (IMF, 1988, pp. 50-51; IMF, 1996, p. 160; OECD, 1996c, table 6.12).

What Max Weber called 'world religions' developed about 1,300-1,700 years ago. Hinduism spread from Northwestern India across the whole subcontinent and beyond to the Southeast Asian archipelago. Buddhism spread from northeastern India to Central, South, and East Asia. Islam spread from the Arabian deserts to Portugal and Spain, sub-Saharan Africa, to Iran, to current Pakistan, and to Southeast Asia, to meet Christianity in the Philippines. Christianity became the religion of the Roman Empire, and entered Ethiopia, Armenia, Kerala, and Tang China etc. The concept of world literature launched almost 200 years ago, by Göthe. Now, we are beginning to talk about world music. There is also the spread of agriculture and foods. Of noodles from China to Italy, of maize and paprika from America to Eastern Europe via India, thanks to the Portuguese, or potatoes from the Andes via then Spanish Belgium to Northern Europe and Ireland (Jordan, 1996, pp. 247).

Least acknowledged, latest developed, and most novel is globalization in the sense of concerted worldwide action in favour of human rights, the global climate, the position of women and of children, and in connecting local non-élites across the world. Women and women's groups from virtually every country and corner of the world came together in Beijing for the UN conference. Peripheralized, native peoples, of the Scandinavian, the Russian, and the Canadian Arctic, of the South American, African, and Asian jungles, of the Australian deserts have found forms to connect and to visit each other. Black American rap has become a local mode of expression of urban youth on all the other continents as well.

There are two images of globalization. The dominant one sees the world as a *stock exchange*, full of screaming and gesticulating, intensely competitive young men, into which all other social institutions and considerations have to feed. This vision has been fuelled by the tremendous expansion of financial markets over the past decade, given a shrillness of fear by the ongoing tilt of the world economy, from the North Atlantic to the Pacific Rim, and a cocksureness by the post-Cold War idea that the market is the only game worth playing.

The other image pictures the globe as one *village*, with common forests and waters, private plots all dependent on the same climate and the soil, with different families and their typical family traits, but also with common institutions of deliberation, worship, of festivals and of mourning.

The global village concept was left too easily to McLuhan and the mass communications. But global reporting has not done much to global violence and global exploitation. Only the connectivity among the people outside the trade floor can do anything about them. The village, with its cultures and its people, presents a vision of globalization, one which is quite different from that of the stock exchange. Between the two, there is no integration, but conflict, perhaps battle.

Spatial relations

The book theme refers to a broader class of issues, to spatial relations. Spatial relations are those of, centre-locality, centre-periphery, global-local, regional-local, regional-global, regional-national, and, as a special substantive case, urban-rural.

Let us now leave the issue of urbanity-rurality and concentrate on the more general one of centre-locality. The important sociological lesson here is that centre-locality is not a zero-sum game. I learnt this a score of years ago from studying the Swedish trade union movement in a comparative perspective. A further look at Swedish municipalities, and at French administrative history taught that this was not a lesson of labour history but of spatial relations. Centralization and powerful local units may very well be combined, operating at different levels.

The notorious French State centralization, e.g., of school curricula, coexisted in fact with enormous local differences of speech, cultural differences, and socioeconomic conditions. The powerful centralization of funding and of decision-making in the national Swedish trade unions was accompanied by a concerted push towards strong local workplace organization, and an important local bargaining presence. Beginning in 1952 and then continuing for 25 years, Swedish municipalities were merged from above into a much smaller number of units. The Social Democrats and their program of social reform was the driving force. Municipalities should be large and resourceful enough to be able to sustain the new social services programs.

Amalgamation was pushed with a view to getting municipalities of equal strength to sustain the national programme of social reform. At the same time trade union locals were pushed to merge in order to be able to provide equal membership services.

Both examples show a complex dialectic of centre and locality. Swedish trade unions have a local plant implantantion you do not find elsewhere. No plant manager can afford to neglect their presence and their bargaining power. On the other hand, local union organizations have always and everywhere stayed loyal to centrally defined aims.

The municipalities, originally grown big so as to live up to central expectations, have become increasingly independent of national politics. Their resource base, which includes powers of taxation, adds a specific, local municipal dimension to Swedish politics.

Let us finally try to bring together a few of these threads of centre-local relations. The conventional centralization-decentralization discussion often goes astray for ignoring the multi-dimentionality of centre-local relations. At least, we should distinguish three of them.

One is *jurisdiction*, defining - de jure and de facto - where the recognized power to do X resides. This is the Weberian perspective of public administration and of the sociology of law. A second dimension is resources, mainly economic but may also include symbolic *resources*, both the flow of them - i.e., their redistribution - and the stock of them. This is the key interest of core-periphery system analysis. Thirdly, there is the patterning of *social capacity* between centre and locality, that is, the distribution of knowledge about the relevant world and of the capacity for action, collective or aggregate individual.

Most of the politico-ideological and of the socio-analytical debate has concentrated on either one of the two first dimensions, their relative importance and their empirical adequacy to given cases. But spatial relations also have a third aspect, one that is irreducible to the other two. That is local versus central capacity to act, determined by pertinent cognitive competence and by social skills to interact with relevant others. It is this third dimension which, in my opinion, is the key feature of determining the prospects of 'local responses to global integration' in the current world.

Here, there has been a tremendous change. Perhaps most dramatically underlined by the capacity of the Chiapas Zapatistas: the mass communicative wit of subcomandante Marcos, the computerized communications system, the collective discipline of armed but non-violent action, of radical-cum-flexible demands. Just compare this movement to the well-known peasant jacqueries.

I do not want to romanticize the Zapatistas of Chiapas. They are no more than a regional minority of one nation. But that much is clear, modernity has advanced far outside the metropolises, and the localities of the earth do not have to, and are not likely to take urban diktat lying down. And local capacities to respond are increasing.

This means that the global village, the idea that in relation to the planet Earth we are all villagers, still stands a chance, as another global modernity, thriving from local responses rather than from central fantasies of power.

Conclusion

Rural studies are making specific contributions and are offering important out-of-the-ordinary vantage points to general social science. Here, I have focused on rural and agrarian perspectives on space, spatial formations and spatial relations, from local-central to global, and on change and time. Recent general concepts like modernity and globalization may help us make sense of the rural world, but what is also clear is that rural and agrarian analyses shed new light on the world routes to modernity and on different and alternative forms of globalization.

References

Augustinos, G. (1991), *Diverse Paths to Modernity in Southeastern Europe*, Greenwood Press: New York.

Berger, J. (1979), *Pig Earth*, Writers and Readers: London.
Boserup, E. (1970), *Women's Role in Economic Development*, George Allen and Unwin: London.
Diamond, J. (1997), *Guns, Germs, and Steel*, Jonathan Cape: London.
Goody, J. (1976), *Production and Reproduction: A Comparative Study of the Domestic Domain*, Cambridge University Press: Cambridge.
IMF (1988), *International Finance Statistics*, Supplement on Trade Statistics, Washington D.C.
IMF (1996), *Direction of Trade Statistics Quarterly*, September.
Jordan, T. (1996), 3rd edition, *The European Culture Area*, Harper Collins: New York.
Lhomel, E. (1997), 'Structures agricoles en Europe centrale et orientale: une transformation inachevée', *Le Courier des pays de l'Est*, no. 416.
Mendras, H. (1995), nouvelle edition, *Les sociétés paysannes*, Gallimard/Folio: Paris.
OECD (1995), *A Review of Farm Household Incomes in OECD Countries*, non-printed report, OECD: Paris.
OECD (1996a), *Territorial Indicators of Employment*, OECD: Paris.
OECD (1996b), *OECD Economies at a Glance*, OECD: Paris.
OECD (1996c), *Historical Statistics 1960-1994*, OECD: Paris.
Therborn, G. (1992), 'The Right to Vote and the four World Routes to/through Modernity', in Torstendahl, R. (ed), *State Theory and State History*, Sage: London.
Therborn, G. (1995), 'Routes to/through Modernity', in Featherstone, M., Lash, S. and Robertson, R. (eds), *Global Modernities*, Sage: London.
Wallerstein, I. (1974), *The Modern World System*, Academic Press: New York.

3 Towards a Theoretical Understanding of the Generation of Diversity in Rural Areas

GASTON REMMERS

Introduction

Several scholars have observed that despite the homogenizing forces that are attributed to the process of the global integration of localities and to the project of agricultural modernization in particular, heterogeneity continues to exist and sometimes even seems to be enhanced by this very integration. Van der Ploeg (1994) makes this point when demonstrating how in a time-span of some 15 years (mid sixties - early eighties), different European regions have responded differently to modernization policies. In the mid-sixties, the scale (i.e. ha/labour unit) and intensity (i.e. output/labour unit) of farming did not vary much among European regions, while at the end of the seventies, this cluster had exploded in all directions. Some regions were intensifying their output per labour unit while others sought their future in amplifying the scale of their farming enterprises. Also, the well-known Arkleton study on rural change that covered most of the eighties in 12 European countries observed the growth of diversity in the ways rural people managed to make a living (Bryden, 1995).

Surprisingly, most research and policy activities seem to ignore this phenomenon, especially those that understand globalization (in financial, cultural or political disguise; Waters, 1995) as a process to which different localities should inevitably adapt. For instance, they conceive of GATT negotiations as imperative for the organization of local economies (Ramos and Romero, 1994), or seem to qualify the agribusiness complex as a determining factor for the development of regional farming (Bonanno et al., 1994). Localities would have no other option than to *respond* to global integration.

Now, although I certainly do not deny the influence that these 'superstructures' exercise on local situations, I think that insisting on them blinds our capacity to see things differently, and consequently, to conceive of other development perspectives. In short, this *'globalization/regulationist/food regimes' point of view*, as Buttel (1994, p. 19) qualified it, *seriously cripples our design capacity for the future of rural and agricultural areas*. This view is not able to appreciate fully the *selective appropriation* of global elements by local actors. These are transformed and adapted to local circumstances and accommodated into a local plan. By doing so, local actors are able to *localize* development, customize it - to a certain extent - to their own needs, thereby diverging and re-channeling the course the so-called globalizing forces are apparently heading for.[1] Localization is an ongoing process, and it is at the heart of the generation of diversity; yet it is badly understood.

What I propose to do in this chapter is to come to a better theoretical understanding of the continued (re)emergence and (re)surfacing of diversity, and I coin this as a step towards the enhancement of the design capacity regarding the future of rural areas. I will do so, after a brief review of some current efforts to explain diversity, by elaborating on Giddens' structuration theory, introducing plan, context and performance as new central notions. It leads up to recognize that imperfections are crucial to diversity and to the reproduction of life. Then, the link between diversity and creativity will be explored. I will finish with some remarks about the theoretical and practical implications of the theoretical model I propose. The ideas developed in this chapter draw from a PhD on endogenous development in a marginal region of Southern Spain, from which empirical data will be also included (Remmers, 1998). Although I draw my examples from agricultural production, I think that the ideas I put forward are relevant for other areas as well, like development policy.

Current efforts to explain diversity: on room for manoeuvre and autonomy of being

Long and van der Ploeg (1989) maintain that an important reason for the continued generation of diversity lies in the *room of manoeuvre* that is implicit in very interaction. This idea strongly opposes the claim on the makeability of society, inherent to the unilinearity of most rural and agrarian policies. Long and van der Ploeg ascertain that this is an unjustified claim, as it excludes the meaning that social agents give to these policies by interpreting them. That is why, they say, interventions cannot be conceptualized as 'a discrete and clearly localized activity (i.e. as a 'project')', because:

> Interventions are always part of a chain or flow of events located within the broader framework of the activities of the state *and* the actions of different interest groups operative in civil society (1989, p. 228; italics in original).

In the interface between the 'state' and the 'citizen', or between 'agricultural extension' and 'farmer', there always exists room for manoeuvre that is configured by the different agendas managed by both parts. Giddens (1984, p. 16) here highlights the existence of the 'dialectic of control', that refers to the power (as a transformative resource) possessed even by the most subordinated and with which they 'can influence the activities of their superiors' and so interfere in the course of things. This space is used by a farmer and by social agents in general, to adapt an external message, extract from it what seems convenient to incorporate in their own particular reality, thereby continuously configuring new localities.

Another possible explication for the continued generation of diversity could be what some authors call the *autonomy of being* (Amin and Thrift, 1994, p. 7), which we could define as an intrinsic drive towards the continuity of one's identity and existence. This autonomy is based on the particular coming together of different cultures in a certain locality. Amin and Thrift refer to Pred, who affirms that 'the historical unfolding of local civil society has a certain degree of autonomy' and this, because of the

> Locally singular combination of presences and absences, the locally peculiar sedimentation of practical and discursive knowledge, of common sense, of behavioural dispositions and coping mechanisms (Pred, 1989, p. 218).

Van der Ploeg (1993, pp. 27-29) also recurs to the idea of a 'peasant resistance', citing Pernet (1982) and Scott (1985). Sevilla Guzmán (1991) introduces the same notion when he speaks about the potential for struggle of social movements, much in the same vein as does Hadjimichalis (1994). It is, in effect, the stubbornness ('eigengereidheid' in Dutch) and waywardness ('eigenzinnigheid') of social agents that make new situations and new localities continuously being created, that continuously reset and reorganized relationships, and that allow new forms of bringing about farming to be continuously conceived. Thus, I agree with Massey (1993), that the local is not best seen as the locus of 'being', but as the locus of 'becoming'.

A new proposal: on plan, context and performance

As I think we can extend our theoretical understanding of the generation of diversity, in this chapter, I propose to do so by using key aspects of Giddens' structuration theory (1984). This theory purports to solve the eternal tension between actor and structure. In it, all social acts, all action, are an art of production and of reproduction. In a social act, an actor mobilizes a repertoire of *rules* and *resources* (that include rules of interpretation, normative rules and power). Usually s/he does so automatically, without reflecting on the usefulness or truth of these rules and resources; therefor, they constitute 'taken-for-granted-knowledge'. The recursively organized body of rules and resources is what Giddens calls *structure*. When this body is mobilized, it is reproduced at the same time and so all actors construct the rules of interaction together. This is why Giddens uses the word *recursive* to identify *structure*; the rules and resources only exist in the moment that they are called upon. And this occurs in social interaction through what he calls *social practices*. These consist of the relations between individuals and/or collectivities that are reproduced in time and space. Giddens reserves the word *system* for that.

Now, the use of this repertoire of rules and resources, be it discursive or practical, explicit or implicit, is an intended one. However, *intended action* can have *unintended consequences*. For example, Giddens advances as an example a man who goes home and upon arriving switches the light on. This is an intended action. At the same moment, he discovers a man stealing anything he can get hold of. This discovery was unintended. On the cutting edge, between the production and reproduction of rules and resources, the unintended consequences are born. The reproduction will never be an exact copy of the original. For example, the man that found the thief upon arriving home now may think that his neighbourhood is not as safe as he thought of while approaching his house. I think that here we may find the seed of learning processes, of progress and of continued generation of diversity, in short, of life.

So, essentially, production and reproduction are synonyms, as the process of reproduction always includes a new element, and that is why the result of this reproduction is a production. Reproduction - and production - are essentially contextualized processes in which a new element from the context is added to what is being reproduced. This context may be sensorial (visual, oral, audible, tactile), cognitive and/or emotional (the latter two comprise the social, economic, political, environmental and personal), both from the present and from the past. The result is a new product. In a following interaction, a new element from the context is added to this product and so an ongoing creating chain comes into being, a chain of kaleidoscopic and changing meanings.

This chain is visualized in Figure 3.1. In it, I introduce three basic notions: *plan, context* and *performance*. Plan and performance are initially derived from Richards (1989; 1995), who used the words to describe his dissatisfaction with the glorification, since the early eighties, of local agronomic knowledge as the deposit of great agri-ecological wisdom accumulated over years, if not centuries, of popular experimentation. About a complex arrangement of crops that can be found in the farmers' plot, he observes that,

> The crop mix - the layout of different crops in the fields - is not a design but a result, a completed performance. What transpired in that performance, and why, can only be interpreted by reconstructing the sequence of events in time. Each mixture is an historical record of what happened to a specific farmer on a specific piece of land in a specific year, not an attempt to implement a general theory of inter-species ecological complementarity (as plant ecologists might suppose). Researchers, then, are looking at the wrong problem. They are looking for the combinatorial logic in intercropping where what matters (...) is sequential adjustment to unpredictable conditions. It is important therefor not to confuse spatial with temporal logic - not to conflate plan and performance (Richards, 1989, p. 40).

Richards stresses that instead of focusing on agri-ecological knowledge hidden in time and space bounded configurations of agricultural resources, we had better focus on the *factors* that make people perform *at all* under difficult circumstances;

> Outsiders tend to undervalue the capacity to keep going under difficulties, and to treat the coping strategies as 'muddling through', not skilled achievements. But in truth - in the appalling, and rapidly deteriorating, environmental and economic conditions faced by many small-scale farmers in the African tropics - even to reproduce the status quo is oftentimes a brilliantly innovative achievement (1995, p. 70).

He then calls for an 'ethnography of performance'. Now, while this seems to be valuable, I think that Richards' focus on 'performance factors' pays too much tribute to accidental events or circumstances. It gives the performance an ad-hoc character and underestimates the strategies people develop (despite Richards' interest in coping strategies) to be able to arrive at a performance, strategies that establish coherence between different performances and that link them in time and space.

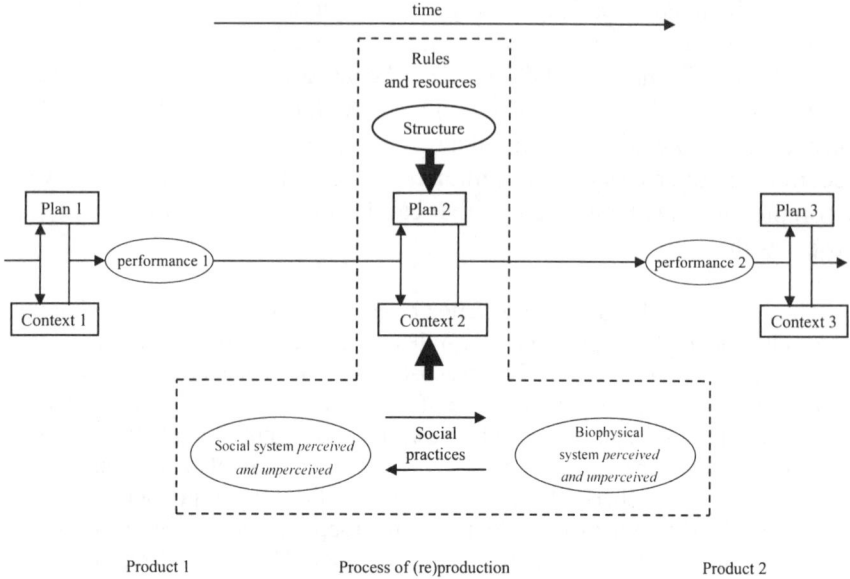

Figure 3.1 Interaction between plan and performance, and the (re)production of diversity, associated to concepts from Giddens' structuration theory

The idea of coherence in strategy is the essential notion that underlies the concept of styles of farming (van der Ploeg, 1994). A style of farming is defined by the *cultural repertoire on which it is based,* that is, the culturally shared notions about how to farm your land. Second, the internal *organization* (that is, within the farming household) of the elements of this cultural repertoire *exhibits a coherence.* Third, the cultural repertoire defines a mode of interpretation and modelling of *external relations*, with respect to *markets, available technology* and *authority* with its specific *policy* and *administrative management.* A style of farming thus entails a set of ideas about how to develop a farm, about how to pilot it into the future.

But are we not here glorifying the plan again? Where does the performance join in? Are we not conflating plan and performance as Richards said? I do not think so. With his notion of performance, Richards highlights above all the farmers' capacity to adapt, to experiment and to create. The concept of performance signals the capacity to incorporate and re-elaborate unforeseen things within a broader scheme, in other words, within *a farm development project.* The more difficult the conditions are, the more basic the project: survival. But even then, patterns of conduct remain inspired by local cultural equipment that is locally contested. These are the initial configurations from which a farmer departs; these are his/her 'plan'.

Between plan and performance, there exists a clear link. Each performance somehow embodies a previous plan. Every performance thus encloses a cumulus (although not always complete) of historical experience and knowledge. A performance is a plan materialized in practice in interaction - confrontation - with a context. As contexts differ, so do performances and thus do plans. The three change continuously. Each interaction between two of them generates conditions for other interactions, conditions that are to some extent unacknowledged. That is why continuously new situations are created and diversity emerges.

The notion of *context* requires specification. In my opinion, context is everything that surrounds an actor. Crucial in this is *that* part of the context with which an actor maintains, has had or could establish an interaction. This refers to the part of the context that: 1) has contributed to the configuration of the plan in the past; 2) contributes to it at present; or 3) might do so in the future. *The context, thus, can be relevant or not relevant, known or unknown.*

With what or whom are interactions established? Following Giddens' notion of a *social system*, these include only relationships with individuals and/or collectivities, humans in any case. I think, however, that we should include interactions with biological and physical objects as well. Our perception of these objects is mediated, in part, through social interaction; it is through social contacts that 'land', 'rock', or 'tree' acquire their meaning. These meanings go from the very concrete to the very abstract: what is for one person an *oak,* for another one is only a *tree.* While a third only sees a *plant,* a fourth perceives a *living thing,* for a fifth it is an *obstacle,* for an eighth it represents *anguish* etc. In the end, every object is turned into a subject in some way. The context is thus, at least in part, an accumulation of meanings; the fact that different actors attribute different meanings to the same thing implies, above all, that the knowledge about the context is always *partial.*

So, at least part of the biophysical environment is included in the social system. However, I am not saying that this biophysical environment only has life through social interaction. Instead, we can still speak about a *biophysical system.* The elements of the biophysical system also engender relations and create their own emergent properties, but these elements, relations and emergent properties are not necessarily mediated through human perception, because they are not known. This is another source for the partiality of an actor's knowledge about the context. If I include the biophysical environment in the social system, I only want to make it clear that it is the perception of a human being - his/her plan - that influences what is known or not known, what is changed or not changed, what is undertaken or is not undertaken.

The interactions engendered by an actor are, thus, constituting his/her context. It is in these interactions, that the rules and resources are constituted. With these, an actor elaborates his/her plan. A *plan* then, is the body of rules and resources (the structure) that an actor (re)constructs recursively and selectively in social interaction, i.e., with other human beings or 'subjectivated' objects. This does not mean, however, that everybody has the same plan. On the contrary, an actor is *selective* with regard to the type of interactions s/he establishes employing *specific* rules and resources, in a *specific* combination and with *specific* objectives. This, however, does not mean that every interaction is selected or desired by an actor; some interactions come to constitute unacknowledged conditions of intended action. So, in spite of the fragmentation of present day society (Bauman, 1995), we can still observe plans that are shared by different actors. This is precisely the origin of the notion of *style*.

So, *plan* and *context* are in a continuous process of bounce and rebound and their interaction forms the cutting edge between production and reproduction. This interaction process leads to the generation of the unintended consequences and crystallizes temporarily in a *performance*. In its turn, however, the performance generates unintended consequences in rebound with the initial plan, leading to an adjustment (or not) of the plan, in reference to the context. The context changes and is changed by the performance. From this new process of bounce and rebound between plan and context, a new performance is born, one that implicitly carries new unintended consequences. These, in turn, can come to constitute *unacknowledged conditions* that will be part of the context in future action. Therefore, the context is always known only to certain extent. In Figure 3.2, I have expressed my understanding of the process of the generation of diversity in a more graphical manner.

Each new position of the card differs a little from its previous position. These differences allow me to illustrate two things. First, this does not mean that position 5 can't be equal to position 3; there can be a return to a previous position, but position 5 is always different from the position that immediately precedes it, in this case number 4. In the second place, we can highlight the persistence of a relatively large surface that remains the same in all positions. With this I want to visualize the fact that, in the majority of interactions the structure is reproduced almost completely. Thus, the essence of the plan remains the same. This is also why a plan can be a project, a vision of the future, and why we can speak of a style of farming at all. When a card position can be identified with only a few or not even one single point in common with a previous position (as is almost the case with card 6 against card 5), then a change has been generated, one that was so drastic that we can speak of a paradigm change. That is to say a change in farming style which means a completely different organization of the farm labour process. This change will be produced not only when confronted with a radically changed context; above all, it requires a plan (a structure) that is *able to perceive* new possibilities to associate with its context.

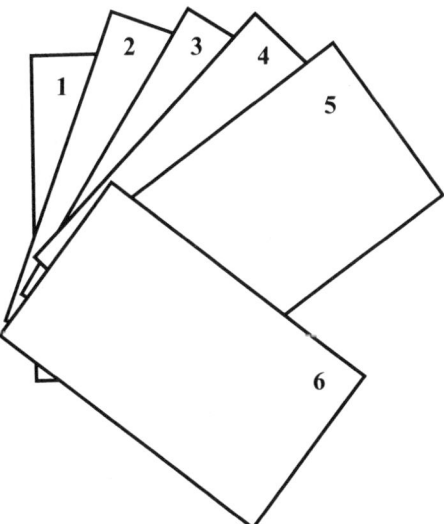

Figure 3.2 The generation of diversity as overlapping cards

Of plan and performance in wine production: a practical example

When I think of plan and performance, there are several images that I have in my mind. I think of a grape grower in the Contraviesa Mountains in Southern Spain (Remmers, 1998, pp. 159-165) who goes about pruning. The farmer has a general idea about how a vine should be pruned, knowledge that draws upon socially shared and constructed rules and resources. But each vine is different; it grows on a slightly different type of soil, with a different exposure to the sun, at a different stage of maturity, presenting a different vigorousness and - at least in the Contraviesa - it may be of a different variety.[2] A farmer will ask himself: is not the vine growing too fast for this particular type of soil? Is the balance between vegetative and reproductive growth at all right? Should it be forced to produce grapes (by leaving long shoots) or should the vine develop more 'wood' as the farmers say (by pruning it short)? So each grape constitutes a different context for the farmer and should be treated accordingly. This means that all vines require a specific *pruning performance*. Each pruning performance contributes to a growth performance of the vine over the season, an interplay between the genetic plan of the plant and the environment, its context.[3] This growth performance may revise the pruning plan of the farmer when faced with the vine in the following season.

The local pruning plan not only refers to a vision of vine development, but also implies a vision on farm development, a farming style. In the Contraviesa, vineyards are meant to produce a lifetime, 40-50 years. Optimizing growth is not the primary goal among those farmers that can be labeled as 'traditional wine growers'; sustained growth over time is considered more important. Grapes have been historically the most reliable income providers. As one farmer put it, 'the grapes are important for my food, and my almonds [a sometimes very rewarding crop, yet much more speculative and unreliable] allow me to cloth myself and do extra things'. One grows grapes for stability, related to an expanded time-horizon. The idea of stability fits with the continuous search for finding the right balance between productive and vegetative growth of the vines on the particular soils of the Contraviesa. It urges most farmers not to squeeze their vines to the maximum, by leaving only a few long shoots, because farmers' empirical expertise shows that it would shorten the productive life of the vine. This is why other pruning techniques - as e.g. those developed by a successful ecological farmer, who boasts on his fairly high *productive* and *economic performance* - are viewed with reservation. The eco-farmer leaves only 2 or 3 shoots, trying to lead them along a trellis of metallic wire. However, pruning in this way presses productive growth and shortens the lifetime of the vine to 20-25 years. It also makes ploughing with mules (common in the area) more difficult, as the mules can't go in between the vines. It asks for machine ploughing. But not only this; this particular way of pruning is linked to a different market orientation and demands a specialization on viti-viniculture, while locally the emphasis is put on a diversified farm (the so-called 'labrador' project). It demands a search for a higher added value and to some extent it demands a choice for a particular grape variety and taste. It is linked to selling the wine in 0.7 litre bottles in specific extra-local, urban based niche markets for ecological wine, whereas a 1.6 litre glass recipient is the usual way of selling the wine to local bars and restaurants. This extra-local market demands compliance with specific sanitary and fiscal regulations that are often difficult to align with family farm production. In other words, pruning differently in fact demands a profound reorganization of the labour process; let us say a shift from position 5 to 6 in Figure 3.2. The result is that local 'labrador' farmers have only selectively adopted elements of the project of the successful eco-grower, leading to slightly modified crop performances and hence to slightly modified farm development plans and performances. Gradually, new farming styles are evolving. Some 'labrador' farmers are specializing as vine-growers, but they do so using the more common pruning techniques. They do not change the characteristic taste of the wine and continue selling to their common local network, as the projects of these wine growers and local barmen interlock more easily: there is a shared understanding of the quality of the wine. Many barmen would not even want to deal with 'formalized wine', as they prefer to stay a little aloof of the legal fiscal web. Other farmers pick out the ecological element and focus on ecological production of their *figs*. Again, others do not specialize in wine growing but instead abandon it, because they fear that in the future they will not be able to comply with the fiscal-administrative regulations.

Nevertheless, this growing diversity of farming styles is hardly understood by the administration; its plan for the wine-sector consists of support only for those few farmers that will upgrade their 'bodegas' (wine production units for processing grapes) to sanitary and taste standards that make sale possible at the extra-local market. The *room for manoeuvre* for grape growers to develop their farm is in this way limited to administrative prescriptions and support lines. Because several farmers do not abide with it and continue to develop their own plan, they stay aloof, recurring in some occasions to illegal production as a relevant room for manoeuvre - an unintended consequence of intended administrative action. Thus, an administrative development plan that is prescriptive in nature and does not leave room for manoeuvre for several diverging development paths, is deemed to harvest unintended consequences and the actual *policy performance* will usually differ substantially from the original *policy plan*. The question then how an Administration can develop plans that suit the region better is very relevant, but at the same time it is too complex to deal with in this chapter. Suffice it to say for the moment that the administrative development plan is an outcome of the continued interplay between plans of different local actors; the challenge is to come to a *joint performance*.

Diversity, creativity and joint performance

One of the major conclusions of the previous theoretical inquiries may be that there are no perfect designs, that is, *plans* that can be translated integrally into a *performance*. A good plan, then, is *modest* in its conception; the rules and resources that interfere in social interaction should be flexible and adaptable. As a consequence, the social practices in which the structure is formed should be flexible and adaptable as well, to facilitate the generation of diversity, in short, the generation of life. Even more, imperfections are the very basis of diversity, of life itself.[4]

How can we then proceed to appropriately evaluate imperfections, or tensions between plan and performance, or two plans of two different actors? A joint performance implies creating something new and requires an ability of both actors involved to perceive relevance in the plans of each other. This makes me consider creativity in social action. I manage diversity and heterogeneity as synonyms and I understand them as a result of social action. Creativity would then be something that intervenes in the process of the production of diversity. So, when we speak about the production of diversity, essentially we speak about a *process of creation*; something new is produced, something changes and something is changed. When Giddens identifies a social act as a *transformative action* (1976, p. 110), with reference to the employment of power, I also wish to identify it as a *creative action*. *Creativity*, I think, just as *knowledgeability* and *capability*, are *formal properties* of each actor. This means that although in principle each actor possesses these properties, not every actor possesses them to the same degree (Munters, 1996, pp. 65-66). This differentiation between a *formal property* and a *substantial property* could help us to understand why apparently some actors manage to achieve their goals more easily than others.

At this point it seems fruitful to delve a bit in the psycho-sociological literature on creativity. Ochse (1990, p. 2) summarizes that, despite the existence of all kinds of different interpretations of the creative process, there are some common denominators. Creativity involves *bringing something into being that is original (new, unusual, novel, unexpected) and also valuable (useful, good, adaptive, appropriate)* (Ochse, 1990). It is clear that what is original for one person, or for a particular society, may not be so for others. For me (as the writer of this chapter), discovering this idea may suppose something original; but for you (the reader), it maybe not. The same we can tell about the value of the product of a creative action. However, instead of losing ourselves in all kinds of relativism, it is more interesting to observe that a creative process implies matters of *authorship* and *authorization*, as addressed by Schaffer (1994). He says that a discovery involves 'a lengthy process of hard work and negotiations within a set of complex social networks' (1994, p. 16). This idea is of great interest because it shows that a discovery not only comes into being by the one who had the idea, but also by the *social context* that authorizes the discovery. The social context has the capacity to facilitate the recognition of a 'discovery', to value it positively or to explicitly deny it or repress it. This leads us immediately to recognize that a process of authorization implies the exercise of power in a process of interaction. Consequently, *social interaction lies at the heart of any discovery*. I think that this is precisely where in many cases the organization of agronomic research and extension fails: there is hardly any interaction with farmers, it is de-contextualized from people and the agri-ecological peculiarities of a certain locale. Also, the Administration tends to suffer from blindness; it is often not able to recognize discoveries because it does not establish an interaction with its citizens. This is especially true for the so-called marginal European areas (see Remmers, 1996; 1998). Therefore, it looses design capacity for development.

An artisan cheese dairy, again in the Contraviesa area in Spain (Remmers, 1996; 1998), may serve as our example. Cheese was made of milk from sheep and goats kept by the same dairy, and it was sold without intermediaries at the local market. Once, they had twenty fresh pieces of cheese, but they sold only seventeen. The three remaining pieces were not thrown away, as would have been the case in industrial dairies, but they were kept on a shelf without paying them much attention. After some time, they discovered that the cheese had not become unsound, but instead, it had transformed to another type of cheese. Discussing with fellow cheese-makers in the area they had - unconsciously - rediscovered a very old technique of making and preserving cheese that crucially depended on the quality of the milk. Of course, this made it possible for them to capitalize on the fresh cheeses that could not be sold. However, Spanish sanitary regulation did not provide rules with regard to the new type of cheese. The administrative context was very reluctant to recognize this 'fresh-cheese-transformed-into-another-cheese' as a discovery and to authorize it as a contribution to the endogenous development potential of the area, which it paradoxically was so much interested in fomenting. Current Spanish sanitary regulation does reflect, above all, the interaction with the industrial sector, but it has very little to do with the artisan, small scale, family farm production. In this respect, it is not a very facilitating context for discoveries.

I wish to recall here the concept of *vivencia*, that was coined, according to Fals-Borda (1991, p. 4), by the Spanish philosopher Ortega y Gasset. The Colombian Fals-Borda elaborates this concept in order to conceive of a type of research called 'Participatory-Action-Research' (PAR). In this approach, he brings together the Ortegan and existentialist concept of 'experience' with the concept of 'commitment'. Fals-Borda writes that,

> Through the actual experience of something, we intuitively apprehend its essence; we feel, enjoy and understand it as reality and we thereby place our own being in a wider, more fulfilling context. In PAR such experience, called *vivencia* in Spanish, is complemented by another idea: that of authentic commitment (1991, p. 4).

The insertion of an external agent in a rural community (or of an agronomist in a group of farmers) permits this 'vivencia'. Fals-Borda thinks that the generation of the 'dialectic tension' that is established by the resulting interaction, 'can be resolved only through practical commitment, that is, through a form of praxis'. I think that Fals-Borda's 'praxis', as the sedimentation of the commitment in interaction between two actors (individuals or collectivities) with different rationalities, is a *joint performance* where two different plans interact with two different - and partially opposed - contexts. This joint performance engenders a renovation of both plans and consequently of both contexts, thus giving birth to a new performance. It is clear then that in Fals-Borda's perspective, social interaction also appears as a key element to engender creativity, necessary for what he calls 'social transformation', in short, to engender new forms of conceiving and materializing rural development.

Now, while the creative process of acclaimed geniuses like Einstein, Picasso and Gandhi inspired several scholars (Ochse, 1990; Gardner, 1994) to carry out research in order to know under what conditions creativity is unlashed, with the implicit or explicit objective to arrive at principles that might help to improve the design of educational programmes, the functioning of enterprises etc., little is known about the creative process among 'common people'. Their discoveries may not be as moving as those of the 'geniuses', but, yes, they are there, they are small and continuous and they have been accumulated in the cultural, historical and environmental patrimony of a society. They have been constructed in a continued and subtle process of contextualized interactions, implying slow processes of authorization. Such processes of authorization also constitute processes of validation for the discoveries which include physical artifacts as well as different types of conduct, ways of speaking etc., in brief, social artifacts as

Towards a Theoretical Understanding of the Generation of Diversity 55

they are socially constructed discoveries. *Precisely because of this, they are probably the most solidly founded discoveries, more solid even than scientific ones.*

The notion of *joint performance* translates easily into an image in which multiple chains of plans, contexts and performances weave threads that occasionally cross each other when establishing a joint performance. The image appears of a tangle of chains that constitute and are constituted by joint performances. This myriad constitutes a network. In some occasions, a joint performance can attain more importance and develop into a project in which more actors intervene. In this respect, Long and van der Ploeg (1989) speak about interlocking projects (see Figure 3.3).

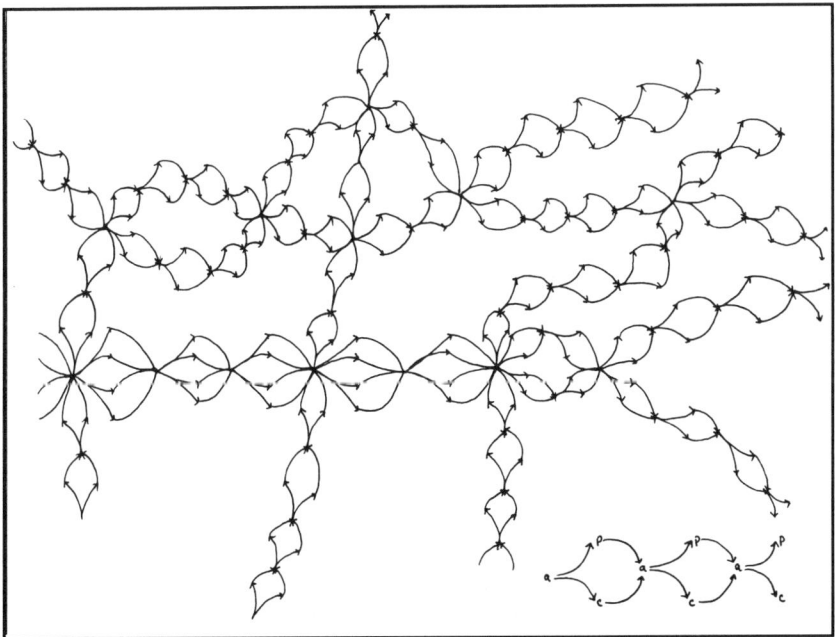

Figure 3.3 **The network: chains of plans (p), contexts (c) and performances (a) in interaction, establishing joint performances**

Let us go back to the cheese dairy. Obviously, it did take quite some time until the cheese makers and the local administration came to a *joint performance*. Finally, after a substantial struggle, the administration backed up the newly 're-created' cheese, after having imposed some technical adaptations in the production process. Their projects (plans) interlocked;

they were able to see each other as a relevant context. This is not the case with the grape growers. Not only the administration sees no worth at all in maintaining illegal and unwarranted - from a sanitary and fiscal point of view - wine production units, but also the grape growers themselves see little worth in trying ways to please the administration's worries about public health. There is no joint performance. Of course, their cat and mouse game is a joint performance, as a socially constructed phenomenon,[5] but it is not of the type I am interested in at present, i.e. social interactions in which two or more actors decide to embark upon a joint operation.

An attempt to estimate the implications of the theoretical model

Although undoubtedly the theoretical model needs through examination, it is above all its theoretical and practical implications that I am not finished in working with.

First, I would see that it helps us to understand a farming activity - any activity - as a chain of events connected in time and space: they are linked and bear *coherence*. Farming (and living in general, I would say) is a constructive activity: *it builds on*. At the same time, this coherence is in constant move; it slightly changes in a continued fine-tuning, and sometimes resets the objectives of an actor.

Second, the model can be seen as an action-theoretical frame that situates the *room for manoeuvre* of actors, i.e. the different ways actors touch upon, investigate, taste, stay aloof of and appropriate the context according to their plan. It situates the tension between plan and context, as well as the birthplace for the skilled social achievement that a performance is.

Third, and following the former two points, I think that plan, context and performance are concepts that can be used *analytically* to understand the *synthesizing* (compositional) capacity of actors.

Fourth, it questions what it is that we study when we do research. Are we examining plans or performances? What is valuable to us, or to the person whose plans or performances we study? I would say, paraphrasing Richards (1995), that most agronomic research conflates plan with performance in that it takes a performance as a plan, and by doing so, it disqualifies some performances as being 'poor' (or 'irrational'), whereas they may be skilled achievements to combine a plan (a rationale) with a context (the circumstances).

In the same vein, if we are not able to distinguish plan from performance, we will have difficulties in perceiving experimentation.

Performances include experimentation, as oscillations around a development path. If we take a performance as a plan disconnected in time and space from previous plans and contexts, we miss the point.

Fifth, I think it shows that diversity is not something given, but something that continuously arises and fades away. Given the sterility with which the word is used these days (parallel to its spread over powerful 'global' institutions), speaking about a 'loss of the diversity' then makes little sense; what matters is the loss of the capacity to reproduce. This implies, as I pointed out, coming to terms with the unintended consequences of intended action, with precisely what we do not want, what is considered 'a waste' or 'inefficient' (Grabher, 1994) from the perspective of a certain plan we have developed. How do we cope with them? What type of unintended consequences (ignoring for a moment that they are conceptually impossible to forecast) are vital and which are destructive to our reproduction?

Sixth, I think it urges us to look anew to what creativity is. In my view, it is a capacity to juxtapose different things (that can be - elements of - plans, contexts, or performances) in a new arrangement, in a way that makes sense, i.e. that is coherent. Immediately, it urges us to ask for our *scientific* and *political* capacity to relate, to establish *new coherence*, in other words, to *design*. It asks for our capacity to perceive the tension between plan and context as a *creative* one. I think that this is very much related to our capacity to learn (see also Remmers et al., 1998), to reinterpret, and to revalue unintended consequences, redundancy, illegality, waste. Can we give them new meaning?

Seventh, this creativity will be of much importance in establishing *innovative joint performances* between farmers, Administration officers, scientists and other actors in the rural scene. Are there ways to enhance this creativity? Are there ways to confront these actors in such a mode that a *learning process* is fostered (see Engel, 1997, for his ideas on innovation as a social capacity)?

Eighth, I think the model challenges the primacy of theory over practice, of concepts over empirical data, in most teaching and research. It coins action (that we would understand as the process in which a plan and a context are fused in a performance) as an essential (although not the single) activity of all learning processes. It says that confronting theory with empirical data, in other words, confronting plan with context in a performance, can lead to new theory and a new context. A good plan, in the form of a good theory, is something that *could* be true, not something that *should* be true.

This, unfortunately, is what happened to modernization thinking about rural and agrarian development. Although development in a context (in a specific locality, with a specific interaction between plan, context and performance) in which it probably was suited (this means that it corresponded to the local context), it came to constitute the normative truth for other contexts (localities) as well. The problem is that modernization thinking has been so powerful that it has been rearranging linkages between local plans, contexts and performances in such a way that different contexts (specific localities) were moulded to the modernization plan. In doing so, strong wishful thinking has led, at least in part, to a desired reality. To the same degree, institutional blindness developed towards alternative development strategies that either were left undisturbed by the process of modernization or were triggered in response to it and that might contain valuable alternatives for rural development.

Enhancing our design capacity regarding rural and agrarian development stems from becoming sensitive to these deviating, uncommon development paths people have developed and are developing. The continued surfacing of diversity is a constant source for renewal of development perspectives and policy. As a prerequisite to perceiving this source, I would coin that we should understand localization as a process that occurs continuously and which is as ordinary as the process of globalization.

Acknowledgments

I am grateful to Norma Romm (Centre for Systems Studies, University of Hull), Kris van Koppen (Department of Environmental Sociology, Agricultural University of Wageningen), Jan van Tatenhove (Department of Environmental Policy Sciences, University of Nijmegen), René de Bruin, Henk de Haan and Henk Oostindie (Agricultural University of Wageningen), for their encouraging comments on earlier drafts of this paper. This Chapter draws from chapters 1 and 7 of my PhD thesis, while I greatly benefited from the comments of my two supervisors, Professor Jan Douwe van der Ploeg (Department of Rural Sociology, Agricultural University of Wageningen) and Professor Roelof Oldeman (Department of Ecological Agriculture, Agricultural University of Wageningen). The final responsibility is, of course, mine.

Notes

1 I understand globalization *and* localization both as *processes in which the rules of interaction between localities are defined*. Localization then, occurs when a non-dominant locality ('the local') is able to exercise a decisive influence over a dominant locality (a globality, or 'the global') with respect to the issue at stake (Remmers, 1998, pp. 1-17).
2 In the Contraviesa, it is possible to find up to 15 varieties in one vineyard.
3 This case shows that the terminology developed here has possibilities for transcending the conceptual boundaries between the natural and the social sciences. It is possible, for example, to speak here about a *genetic plan* and a *phenotypic performance*. More arguments that sustain this possibility can be found in Remmers, 1998, pp. 82-83.
4 The idea that imperfections are basic to the generation of diversity and life is of increasing concern also in the natural sciences. For a discussion on the parallels between natural and social sciences see Remmers, 1998, p. 36.
5 By definition, every performance is a joint performance, in the sense that it is established in interaction with another actor or element from the biophysical environment. In other words, the performances of the different actors shape and mould each other mutually.

References

Amin, A. and Thrift, N. (1994), 'Living in the Global', in Amin, A. and Thrift (eds), *Globalization, Institutions and Regional Development in Europe*, Oxford University Press: Oxford.

Appadurai, A. (ed) (1995), First edition 1986, *The Social Life of Things: Commodities in a Cultural Perspective*, Cambridge University Press.

Bauman, Z. (1995), *Life in Fragments: Essays in Postmodern Morality*, Blackwell: Oxford and Cambridge.

Bonnano, A., Busch, L., Friedland, W., Gouveia, L. and Mingione, E. (eds) (1994), *From Columbus to ConAgra: The Globalization of Agriculture and Food*, University Press of Kansas.

Bryden, J. (1995), 'Pluriactividad Rural en Europa: el Proyecto *Rural Change in Europe*', in Ramos Real, E. and Cruz Villalón, J. (eds), *Hacia un nuevo Sistema Rural*, Serie Estudios 99, MAPA: Madrid.

Buttel, F.H. (1994), 'Agricultural Change, Rural Society and State in the Late Twentieth Century: Some Theoretical Observations', in Symes, D. and Jansen, A.J. (eds), *Agricultural Restructuring and Rural Change in Europe*, Wageningen Studies in Sociology 37, Wageningen Agricultural University: Wageningen.

Engel, P. (1997), *The Social Organization of Innovation. A Focus on Stakeholder Interaction*, Royal Tropical Institute, CTA, STOAS: Amsterdam.

Fals-Borda, O. (1991), 'Some Basic Ingredients', in Fals-Borda, O. and Rahman, M.A. (eds), *Action and Knowledge: Breaking the Monopoly with Participatory Action Research*, Intermediate Technology Publications: London.
Gardner, H. (1994), 'The Creators' Patterns', in Boden, M.A. (ed), *Dimensions of Creativity*, MIT Press: Cambridge.
Giddens, A. (1976), *New Rules of Sociological Method: A Positive Critique of Interpretative Sociologies*, Hutchinson and Co: London.
Giddens, A. (1984), *The Constitution of Society: Outline of the Theory of Structuration*, Polity Press: Cambridge.
Grabher, G. (1994), *Lob der Verschwendung: redundanz in der Regionalentwicklung, ein sozioökonomisches Plädoyer*, Wissenschaftszentrum Berlin für Sozialforschung, Edition Sigma: Berlin.
Hadjimichalis, C. (1994), 'Global-local Social Conflicts: Examples from Southern Europe', in Amin, A. and Thrift, N. (eds), *Globalization, Institutions and Regional Development in Europe*, Oxford University Press: Oxford.
Hobart, M (ed) (1993), *An Anthropological Critique of Development: The Growth of Ignorance*, Routledge: London.
Long, N. and Ploeg, J.D. van der (1989), 'Demythologizing Planned Intervention: An Actor Perspective', *Sociologia Ruralis*, Vol. 39, No 3/4, pp. 227-249.
Long, N. and Ploeg, J.D. van der (1994), 'Heterogeneity, Actor and Structure: Towards a Reconstitution of the Concept of Structure', in Booth, D. (ed), *Rethinking Social Development: Theory, Research and Practice*, Longman Scientific and Technical: Essex.
Munters, Q.J. (1996), 'Kwetsbare aspecten van het actorperspectief', *Sociologische Gids*, Vol. 43, No 1, pp. 60-68.
Ochse, R. (1990), *Before the Gates of Excellence: The Determinants of Creative Genius*, Cambridge University Press: Cambridge.
Pernet, F. (1982), *Resistances paysannes*, INRA: Grenoble.
Ploeg, J.D. van der (1987), *De verwetenschappelijking van de landbouwbeoefening*, Wageningen Studies in Sociology nr. 21, WAU: Wageningen.
Ploeg, J.D. van der (1993), *Over de betekenis van verscheidenheid*, Inaugurele rede bij de aanvaarding van het ambt van hoogleraar aan de LUW, LUW, Inaugural lecture, Agricultural University Wageningen.
Ploeg, J.D. van der (1994), 'Styles of farming: An Introductory Note on Concepts and Methodology', in Ploeg, J.D. van der and Long, A. (eds), *Born from Within: Practice and Perspectives of Endogenous Development*, Van Gorcum: Assen.
Pred, A. (1989), 'The Locally Spoken Word and Local Struggles', *Environment and Planning D: Society and Space*, Vol. 7, pp. 211-233.
Ramos, E. and Romero, J.J. (1994), 'La Crisis del Modelo de Crecimiento y las Nuevas Funciones del Mundo Rural', in Junta de Andalucía, *El Desarrollo Rural Andaluz a las Puertas del Siglo XXI*, Consejería de Agricultura y Pesca: Sevilla.

Remmers, G.G.A. (1993), 'Agricultura Trandicional y Agricultura Ecológica: Vecinos Diatantes', *Agricultura y Sociedad*, Vol. 66, pp. 201-220.
Remmers, G.G.A. (1996), *Hitting a Moving Target: Endogenous Development in Marginal European Areas*, Gatekeeper Series n. 63, IIED: London.
Remmers, G.G.A. (1998), *Con Cojones y Maestría: Un Estudio Sociológico-agronómico acerca del Desarrollo Rural Endógeno y Procesos de Localizatión en la Sierra de la Contraviesa (España)* (With Balls and Mastery: A Sociological Agronomic Study of Endogenous Rural Development and Localization Processesin the Contraviesa Mountains, Spain), Wageningen Studies on Heterogeneity and Relocalization, n. 2, Circle for Rural European Studies, Thela Publishers: Amsterdam.
Remmers, G.G.A., Stamataki, E. and Gadanaki, M. (1998), 'Do it Sistimatika: On the Learning Paradigm of Cretan Organic Olive Growers Seeking for a Rural Future', *European Journal of Agricultural Education and Extension*, Vol. 5, No 3, pp. 193-210.
Richards, P. (1989), 'Agriculture as Performance', in Chambers, R., Pacey, A. and Thrupp, L.A. (eds), *Farmer First: Farmer Innovation and Agricultural Research*, IT Publications: London.
Richards, P. (1995), 'Cultivation: Knowledge or Performance?' in Hobart, M. (ed), *An Anthropological Critique of Development: The Growth of Ignorance*, EIDOS, Routledge: London.
Schaffer, S. (1994), 'Making up Discovery', in Boden, M.A. (ed), *Dimensions of Creativity*, MIT Press: Cambridge.
Sevilla Guzmán, E. (1991), 'Una Propuesta de Desarrollo Rural Endógeno para Andalucía', *Revista de Estudios Regionales*, No 31, pp. 251-264.
Waters, M. (1995), *Globalization*, Routledge: London and New York.

4 Changing Spaces: The Effects of Macro-Social Forces on Regional Australia

GEOFFREY LAWRENCE, IAN GRAY AND DANIELA STEHLIK

Introduction

European-derived agriculture in Australia has always had a global focus - with most of what has been produced leaving Australia's shores as raw, unprocessed, primary products such as wool, sugar, beef and wheat. Up until the mid-1970s, such production and distribution occurred under a mantle of protection, subsidization and state regulation – something which has largely disappeared in recent decades. Rural communities were, to a limited extent, 'planned' communities, with Federal and State governments providing infrastructural support for railways, roads, schools, law courts, police stations and other facilities and services. Such state involvement was consistent with ideologies of decentralization, state-assisted economic growth (expansionism) and egalitarianism (social equity). Commitment to such ideals has now been replaced with a more narrow focus on free markets, 'user pays' and 'self help' - as part of what we might term 'neo-liberalism'.

Giddens (1994) has argued that, following the collapse of the socialist state system in Europe and the emergence of a more interconnected world economy, neo-liberalism - which acts, specifically, to foster global competition - has emerged worldwide to challenge (and eventually to defeat) conservative and socialist ideologies. He believes that while neo-liberalism may retain a vestige of conservatism (attachment to the nation, religion, and to patriarchy in gender and family relations), it has become the most radical approach to economic management and social arrangement, leaving conservatives to lament the passing of older forms of privilege and order, and socialists to defend the welfare state against the forces which undermine it.

64 *Local Responses to Global Integration*

Ideologies which have emerged in Australia over the past two decadeshave influenced the right wing forces (the Liberal/National Party Coalition, currently in government) as well as those of the center/left (the Australian Labor Party - which ruled from 1983 to 1996). Importantly, the Federal bureaucracy is heavily populated with economists trained in neo-liberalism (see Pusey, 1991) and the National Farmers' Federation (the peak farm body in Australia) has been dominated by groups whose members export their produce and in whose interest it is to see freer world trade (NFF, 1993).

Globalization, the farm problem and agri-food restructuring

For most Australian neo-liberal economists, the move to a more globalized world in which freer trade prevails is viewed as essential if Australian agriculture is to prosper. It is currently seen *not* to prosper because of a combination of factors such as the specific nature of traded agricultural commodities, low commodity prices, unfair world competition, and the way assets are 'fixed' in farming (see Malcolm et al., 1996 for a discussion of this issue). A severe and continuing drought has been an additional factor during the past decade (Stehlik et al., 1996a). The text book approach to understanding the 'farm problem' focuses on the inevitable 'pressure' that continued economic growth - viewed as essential for Australia's well-being - puts on the farm sector:

> The essence of the 'farm problem'...is that economic growth causes net incomes in agriculture to increase less than those in the non-agricultural sector. The problem arises partly because of the nature of the demand farmers face for their output. Demand for agricultural products does not respond a great deal to falls in prices, nor to rises in consumer's incomes. As an economy grows and national income increases, there is a decline in the proportion of extra income spent on food. Inevitably then, the share of national income going to agriculture declines relative to the share going to the rest of the economy. In addition, the supply of agricultural commodities increases more rapidly than the demand because of technological change. The result of supply outstripping demand is that prices fall and farmers have to increase output to maintain income, which they do by adopting new technology, and the cycle goes on (Malcolm et al., 1996, p. 57).

Furthermore, many farmers cannot be 'enticed' from farming because of a combination of lifestyle considerations and their inability to obtain fulfilling and well-remunerated full-time off-farm employment (the main reasons for which are the declining work options in rural regions - not only for the poorly educated, but increasingly so for the better educated). The best they can do is to produce more output per input of labour largely by utilizing new technology and/or by increasing the scale of their operations.

> The... economic forces that farmers confront add up to the conclusion that, with economic growth in the community in general, there will eventually either have to be fewer farmers... or poorer farmers. The third option is for farmers to be subsidized by taxpayers and consumers. This option has been widely adopted in the USA and Western Europe (Malcolm et al., 1996, p. 58).

For most of Australia's neo-liberal economists only the first two scenarios are to be countenanced: the third is anathema because it involves state intervention, considered to be a market distortion (see Gow, 1994). This is despite the facts that: the intensification of agriculture as well as persistent low income in agriculture has been implicated in continued environmental degradation in Australia (see Conacher and Conacher, 1995; Vanclay and Lawrence, 1995); that stress levels and general social malaise are a feature of contemporary farming (Gray et al., 1993); and, that there is only faint hope of persuading competing nations to remove all forms of subsidization from farming and of moving to a so-called 'level playing field'. Instead, the main instrument of state 'intervention', the Rural Adjustment Scheme, which operated from 1988 to 1997, provided grants for the least efficient to leave agriculture, and helped many of the marginally efficient remaining to increase the scale and efficiency of production via farm build-up loans. At the industry level, greater emphasis has been given to the removal of any market distortions, which might prevent 'adjustment' from occurring in line with overseas price regimes.

For neo-liberalists, social arrangements are seen to flow logically and advantageously from the market. It is inefficient to prop up producers who are not economically viable, nor is it desirable to seek to 'save' country towns whose economies are in decline. While there are some differences in the ways State and Federal governments react to this, they generally accept that changes are in line with economic realities. If market forces dictate that towns or regions must shrink, then so be it. That is the 'natural' outcome which will move resources into more appropriate endeavors. In some functional way, 'failures are part of a steering mechanism that directs an economy toward prosperity' (Gow, 1994, p. 11). It will be the efforts of entrepreneurial local people, discovering new opportunities for themselves, which will create growth.

The above argument, in a modified form, is what currently holds sway in Australia. It is one which overlooks a number of factors: that the 'free market' is a myth (and that for most nations economic decisions which influence industry are greatly tempered by political and social considerations); that the attempts of governments to further expose Australia's industries to international competition is - in a world of continuing protection abroad - hampering, rather than enhancing the prospects for growth of those industries; that the 'level playing field' is a 'lie' promulgated to justify industrial restructuring, although it results in de-industrialization; and that economic 'signals' are only one set of signals which producers will take into consideration when making decisions about location and resource use (see Rees et al., 1993; Stewart, 1994).

One way to understand the nature of change in agricultural policy is to 'graph' the various dimensions relating to state regulation, the free market, and to social welfare (see Almås, 1994). The diagrams below provide a summary indication of the ways in which policy has changed since the Second World War.

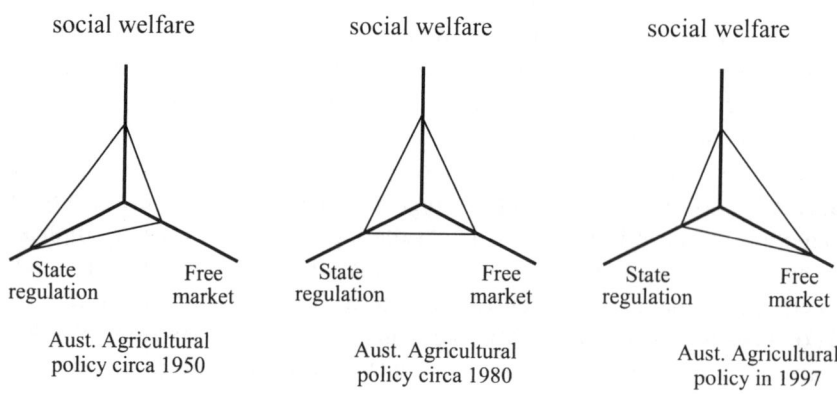

Figure 4.1 Australian agricultural policies since the second world war

Source: After Almås, 1994.

What is captured in Figure 4.1 is the extent to which state regulation - and desires to have farm families enjoy the benefits of secure incomes, through vehicles such as concessions, subsidies and price support - has given way to the free market as the major determinant of farm prosperity and farm-family welfare. It also points to the 'shrinking' of the state's role in both regulation and welfare support activities (see Almås, 1994 in relation to Norway; and, Lawrence, 1987, for an outline of changes in rural policy in Australia). What has happened in Australia is somewhat different from what has occurred in a European nation like Norway. In the latter, state regulation and social welfare both declined significantly in concert with the emergence of free market policies. In Norway, although the social welfare dimension has shrunk, state regulation has remained of great importance. Almås considers that there is something pendulum-like about policy change:

> When agriculture gains more freedom, there will be diversification, segmentation and anarchy in production. This will bring the regulators out...(who) will demand more planning and control of the development as well as greater national investment. And then the policy cycle may start all over again (1994, p. 24).

It remains to be seen whether this will occur in Australia, and especially in an era of growing world 'regulation' which may preclude or undermine attempts by nation states to return to regulatory solutions to agricultural problems (see McMichael, 1996).

As demonstrated by Almås (1994) and by recent theorists of globalization, it would seem desirable to move beyond the farmyard economics of orthodox agricultural economists and the questionable assumption of the New Right, to concentrate instead on a broader picture - one in which rural producers are now but a declining part. It is the postmodern consumer, the role of transnational corporations (TNCs), and the changing regime of regulation to which attention should be drawn. 'Agri-food restructuring' or more broadly 'rural restructuring' are the terms used by sociologists in an effort to grasp what forces are at work in altering the trajectory of rural areas of the developed capitalist world.

Agricultural/rural restructuring is concerned with an understanding of the place of local agriculture within the wider system of food production and distribution (see Symes and Jansen, 1994, p. 7) and of rural settlement within the wider global economy (Marsden et al., 1993). Farmers are linking more directly (such as with contracts) than in the past with TNCs (and the TNCs themselves are becoming more prominent in agricultural marketing and supply); most continue to produce bulk commodities, no longer for stationary marketing boards, but for the TNCs; others are seeking ways to 'value add' and 'niche market' their products; they are becoming increasingly pluriactive, and are working off the farm in greater numbers; they are beginning to respond to the demands of the so-called 'green consumer'; and they are being required by the state to become more sustainable (see Gray et al., 1993; Ferguson, 1997; Lawrence, 1995; Burch et al., 1999). Thus, alongside predominant tendencies toward efficiency and productivity - the driving forces predicted, and lauded, by neo-liberalists - smaller rural producers have found opportunities to remain in agriculture via the niche marketing of exotic fruits, or native species, or by tapping into 'post modern' phenomena like eco-tourism or farm stays. New communication facilities have provided farms and towns with direct links to the global marketplace and to global culture.

As retirement, leisure and recreation begin to figure increasingly as post-modern options, some rural locations (and operators) are setting up businesses to take advantage of this demand. In some locations, the provision of, for example, retirement homes, wetland tours, heritage festivals, or the staging of local cultural events, has allowed towns to move away from their usual dependence on agriculture and to develop their 'service' industries (see Stayner and Reeve, 1990; Beer et al., 1994). Countervailing tendencies of the withdrawal of services by the state appear to have limited the extent to which these post modern forms of economic activity have provided the bases for new economic growth. As Marsden et al. (1993) indicate, restructuring is not occurring evenly throughout rural space. Some locations, advantaged by climate, proximity to coastal beaches, or on the 'tourist' path between (or close to) capital cities, appear to have benefited differentially.

The response of the state to global forces

In line with global structural tendencies and neo-liberalist doctrine, the state in Australia has sought to withdraw from the direct support of industry (the winding back of tariffs, removal of direct subsidies, and other forms of subsidization/protection). Australian rural regions have been viewed as having 'de-industrialized', something which is part of a wider tendency within the nation (see Stilwell, 1992; 1993). According to Stewart:

> Regional policy has long occupied a prominent place in the political strand of industrial policy. In Europe and Canada, although less so in the United States and Japan, a considerable proportion of the funds spent on industry policy is actually allocated to developing particular regions or to preventing them from becoming de-industrialized. OECD figures show that in all the European industrial states, and in Canada, regional development - a form of regional equity - was one of the major objectives of policy. Only in Japan and Australia did... regional expenditures (at the national level) contribute a minor proportion

of total subsidies devoted to the structural adjustment of the economy (1994, p. 28).

By deregulating the financial market, reducing support for industry, and selling off government assets, the state has actively sought to expose producers to global trade regimes, ones based largely on the needs and interests of TNCs. The TNCs, in turn, have argued that they are not likely to invest in Australia (or have consciously moved their operations overseas) because of the 'high' cost of labour. The state's response under the Labor Government was to develop an 'accord' with industry and labour - the result of which was to reduce real wages for workers (see Stilwell, 1986) and, under the Coalition, to argue for wage deregulation and enterprising bargaining as the basis for any wage 'improvements'. The Coalition's policies are viewed as an attempt to break unionism and to allow differential wage conditions to prevail - something which some rural regions see as a potential 'boon' in helping to lure manufacturing industry, but which might also produce growing spatial income disparities (see Stilwell, 1993; Hamilton, 1996).

In terms of agriculture and rural manufacturing industry, the state has sought to ameliorate some of the worst effects of the falling market power of commodity trade by endorsing the formation of regional bodies to 'exploit' new options. With only limited funds provided and regional bodies having no formal legislative endorsement or statutory powers, the state is fostering cooperation between business and local government at a level 'between' State and Local Government (Rural Local Government in Australia has been notoriously 'backward' in seeking new production options and the regional bodies are viewed as providing a local impetus). Since the state does not want to 'interfere' in spatial economic activity, its endorsement of regions might be viewed as recognition, at least, of the new ways TNCs are beginning to deal with areas within nation-states, which have opened their doors to foreign capital. In a globalizing world economy where capital is highly mobile, the 'region' within the nation-state is likely to increase in prominence as firms bypass traditional Federal and State structures to locate in desirable regional spaces. However, while many Australian regions are desirable in terms of natural resources, labour costs are still very much higher than in the developing economies to Australia's north. So, rather than locating in regional Australia, many TNCs are taking produce and sending it overseas for second or final stage manufacture. The 'regional' solution to Australia's problems appears to be no solution at all unless, of course, wage deregulation (the lowering of wages) can provide rural/regional Australia with a comparative advantage over regions abroad.

The state has also sought to address current account deficits (arising largely because Australia imports most of its manufactured goods, but continues to pay for these from raw materials whose value is decreasing, in relation to imports, over time), as well as demands from taxpayers and industry for tax relief, by rationalizing service provision and infrastructural investment. Many services available to rural people have been provided by the state. With state revenues growing slowly and capital cities expanding in size and importance, state-directed economic activity has been re-centralized. This has resulted - often on *per capita* criteria rather than on 'need' - in a reduction of personnel in the regions such as school teachers, members of the police force and judiciary, state planners, social workers, taxation office workers, extension officers, and a host of other people on the public payroll. Government funds tertiary education in the regions and tertiary education is often seen to be a catalyst for future economic growth in those locations. With reductions in funding and the move to more private funding, the contribution that the universities and colleges can make, in direct economic terms as well as in terms of research, may decrease. The most obvious manifestations of the withdrawal of state support are described in the coming section.

Finally, the state has played - and continues to play - an important role in addressing issues of environmental degradation. It funds a number of important initiatives such as Landcare, involving approximately 4,300 farming/community-based groups throughout Australia in practical measures to restore the environment or overcome existing degradation (see Campbell, 1994; Lockie and Vanclay, 1997; Mues et al., 1998), and catchment management, through specially designated Federal funds (see Natural Heritage Trust, 1997). The extent to which Landcare and catchment management are simply ideologies which obscure practices which are unsustainable has been raised by a number of authors (see Vanclay and Lawrence, 1995; Bailey, 1997; Lockie, 1997; Howarth, 1997). Others believe that some government commitment to better environmental practices - and any attempt to bring rural producers closer to the other users of catchments - are more desirable than no commitment at all (see Campbell, 1994; Carr, 1997).

The state regulates tree-clearing and the use of rivers. It also provides quarantine and other services and advice to producers. In an era when overseas customers are becoming increasingly aware of and concerned about chemicals in agricultural production, the state - with industry - monitors pesticide and other levels in a number of exported products. It continues to play a role, albeit weaker than in previous periods, in monitoring and regulating agriculture. This is coming under scrutiny in an

Changing Spaces 71

era of 'user pays' principles and as *de*-regulation of all variety of government services is in vogue, in line with the New Right ideology.

Local social effects

Global economic forces, in concert with domestic neo-liberalist policies, appear to be, at least in part, responsible for the following five social outcomes:

i) Exacerbation of the trend toward long term population decline in inland areas

During the decade starting in 1985 and ending in 1995, one in every twelve rural properties disappeared. In most cases, they merged with one or more other properties in an effort to increase viability. In 1994-95, Australia had 115,368 viable rural properties - defined as those producing $20,000 worth of on-farm produce in anyone year (see *Australian*, 25 June, 1997, p. 3). Among commodity groups, the dairy industry experienced the greatest decline in numbers (3,100 farms lost at an average annual rate of 2.2 per cent). This was followed by wheat and other 'broad-acre' crop properties (numbers of farms dropping from 82,430 to 70,883 or by 1.7 percent per annum) (*Australian*, 25 June 1997, p. 3). The decline was greatest in the coastal strip in NSW (where farmlands were taken up for housing development) and in areas of inland Australia (where farm viability was undermined by continuing drought).

Some years before the recent figures emerged, it had been reported that:

> Areas of declining population were mainly in provincial, rural or remote areas. Reasons for decline included unemployment, the rural recession, contraction of government services and a drift of families and young people to capital cities for secondary school or tertiary education...With the loss of young people, many country regions...(suffered)...problems associated with an aging population profile and the need for more services for elderly people (Kelty, 1993, pp. 15-16).

The rationalization of private services is yet another factor in the downward spiral. With governments withdrawing services and with many branches of firms downsizing or closing, people are moving out of country towns. Those moving are those most likely to find work elsewhere, leaving already-disadvantaged groups, such as the aged, to cope with the declining services (see Stehlik and Lawrence, 1996). Data from the 1996 Census indicate that the rural shires which show growth above the national average all border on the sea. The previously well-defined trend for inland Australians to move toward the coast (mainly to regional cities close to the metropolis) is confirmed in the latest Census. The regions with the greatest fall in population were all rural and most were inland (see *Australian*, 16 July 1997, p. 8). Some inland mining towns provided per capita incomes equal to or above those in the wealthy suburbs of Melbourne or Sydney but, more typically, the income levels of rural dwellers do not compare well with those in the cities. According to Fitzgerald (1996, p. 42), rural life is generally characterized by 'poorly performing local economies...; declining employment opportunities; low and often inadequate household incomes; out-migration of youth; negative health outcomes associated with stress and low incomes; ...and reduced access to services resulting from rationalization...'. It has also been reported (see Stehlik et al., 1996b) that the quality of life of rural people is deteriorating. In view of other evidence that mining or other 'special purpose' communities are experiencing growth, it makes it difficult to draw definitive conclusions about the degree to which some uniform 'rural decline' is realistic or generalizable.

ii) Decline in social capital in rural regions

People's ability to work together to develop community structures is crucial for social and economic progress. Social interaction, developed through trust, and often occurring in a spontaneous and/or voluntary manner, is seen by some (see Cox, 1995; Gain, 1996) to be a major component in the success of both individuals and the community. If collective social capital is the basis of a democratic community (see Cox, 1995), its diminution might be viewed as threatening to or at least undermining democracy.

There has been a strong cultural tradition in rural society based on the maintenance of family-farm relations and viable local businesses. The degree to which voluntary community associations have been a fundamental plank of economic and social life in rural communities has been well described by Wild (1983), Poiner (1990) and Gray (1991). As farm-family members increase the extent of their off-farm work, as their incomes from agricultural production fall, as rural dwellers lose jobs, and as those with more opportunity for geographical mobility leave, the ability of rural communities to take collective action is lessened (see, for example, Stehlik et al., 1996b). Social capital is believed, in such circumstances, to have deteriorated, severely limiting the ability of communities to do the very things expected of them by neo-liberalism, that is, to be resourceful, 'self-reliant', and to provide the intellect with which to catalyze their own future growth.

Once, it was thought that the 'inevitable' processes of farm amalgamation and community decline would not affect the larger regional centers in a negative way (Beer et al., 1994). These centers were, after all, sheltered because they provided education and other services for the region. But, with the decline in government service industry workers, the belief that growth in the regional capitals will still occur has been questioned (see Chisholm, 1997). In Rockhampton (pop. 65,000), for example, which has based its growth on public service provision (and where some 40 percent of all registered voters are public servants), in one year alone lost 400 state and Federal jobs; most capital works - including the provision of public housing and elderly care facilities - have ceased; housing prices remain depressed; and unemployment has remained at a high level (Schwarten, 1997). Public servants are an intellectual resource for such cities and their removal leaves a 'void' which is not easily filled. Importantly, if a city the size of Rockhampton is under pressure to contract, what hope might there be for smaller towns within the regions?

The point here is this: neo-liberalist ideologies and policies are both justifying, and leading to the demise of social capital in certain sections of inland (rural) Australia *at the very time* those ideologies and practices demand responses which require that social capital is maintained and enhanced. Rural regions, unable to provide the necessary leadership or economic enterprise might then be labelled as 'backward', not because of any intrinsic backwardness, but because the state has seen it fit to remove some of the very people whose social capital might have contributed to regional economic growth. According to Gray et al. (1997), if rural communities are to be expected to gather sufficient collective resources to deal effectively with global processes, their social capital must be developed to a level sufficient for social action. Yet, government policies, which promote competition and allow/encourage involvement of national or international firms in local decision making, threaten conditions of cooperation at the local level. Similarly, bureaucratic stringencies, which are imposed on regional areas create divisions in local communities (see Gray et al., 1996). Both lead to a weakening, rather than a strengthening, of community social resources.

That many rural communities are 'going backward' in economic and social terms indicates the need, according to some policy analysts (see Fitzgerald, 1996; Gain, 1996; Dale and Bellamy, 1998), for the state to develop and implement 'interventionist' policies which will build the capacity of communities to formulate plans for integrated development.

iii) The de-traditionalization of rural society

Whether one considers the decline in rural tradition to be a major concern, or a great blessing, is not the point. What is occurring is that global processes are undermining older, more stable, forms of social interaction, calling into question the bases for future collective action. De-traditionalization can be best understood as the dis-embedding of patterns of communal authority and customary practices by the intensification of, in particular, consumer culture - itself a product of globalizing tendencies (see Heelas, 1996; Morris, 1996). For Giddens,

> Globalizing influences have been directly bound up with far-reaching changes happening in the tissue of social life. They have helped set in play pervasive processes of detraditionalization (which) in turn means an acceleration of the reflexivity of lay populations (1994, p. 42).

In a world of intensified social reflexivity, Giddens suggests 'Keynesianism...could not survive' as it presumed 'a citizenry with more stable lifestyle habits than are characteristic of a globalized universe of high reflexivity' (1994, p. 42). Globalization 'manufactures uncertainties', and the New Right has grasped the opportunity of linking further progress to deregulation. When pursued in a policy sense, deregulation is but another factor contributing to de-traditionalization (1994, p. 43).

The argument here is that traditional practices have been spatially-specific and generally stable. With time/space compression, what occurs within particular settings is 'collapsed' (Luke, 1996) to such an extent that change does not occur along prescribed lines, but along new, if poorly defined, lines. For Luke,

> Systems of direction and meaning, once provided by tradition...lose their spatial referents and action zones as space is reconfigured to suit the designs of state bureaucracies, accumulated capital, and technical experts...Sets of conventions or rules that regulate cultural and social life...become problematic or contested as the technics of space change (1996, p. 125).

In the mid 1980s - and following the impact of a 'rural crisis' in Australia - it was clear that farming and rural people were greatly confused (and annoyed) at what many perceived to be the inability of the state to restore a stable 'regime' of profit for rural/regional Australia (see Lawrence, 1987). Some were rejecting New Right-style policies, but did not have the capacity to organize meaningful resistance. Work undertaken by Gray et al. (1993) in four regions of rural Australia provides evidence of the extent of farmer confusion and dissatisfaction with the state's role in agricultural policy and their uncertainty about the future. The social structures of farming - the roles and relationships which had been created and maintained within the system of family farming and which provided it with stability - were being threatened by wider social and economic forces, as well as by the responses of farmers to those forces, specifically, the taking of off-farm work. Off-farm work helped to keep the producers on the land, but also altered the capacity of people to engage in voluntary associations, increased stress in marital relations, and altered the social status of producers. Further, it placed new (and unfamiliar) demands on family members (undermined 'conventional' and familiar roles of farming couples) and, for some, led to a run down in farm capital and to environmental deterioration. These produced, in turn, anxiety about the future of the farm as a viable economic entity (see Gray et al., 1993, pp. 73-77). Later work by Gray et al. (1995) confirmed the extent to which external pressures produced conflicting requirements in family farm reproduction, undermining the cooperation which had, hitherto, been the foundation for action at the community level.

In the sugar growing area of Mackay, Queensland, agricultural restructuring included 'continuous crushing' and moves to extended daily hours of production which were found to have a negative impact on lifestyle and community interaction (Passfield et al., 1996). In circumstances where there is an intensification of work, and/or where people are increasingly exposed to wider forces of rationalization, social life may be altered in a manner which renders previous patterns of social involvement increasingly tenuous. In some regions which have undergone 'restructuring' social activities are curtailed. For example, sporting contests are often scaled down or abandoned, with the sense of belonging, social cohesion and local identity either diminished or becoming increasingly problematic (Passfield et al., 1996; Montford, 1997). It is clear, as well, that the availability of new communication and other technologies, which link regional Australians to wider networks of actors and to consumer culture, contributes to the demise of older forms of authority, for better or worse.

iv) Acceptance of an ideology of 'self help' in regions undergoing restructuring

As successive State and Federal Governments have reduced expenditures by cutting services and curtailing infrastructural investment in regional Australia, there have been vocal - but not well coordinated - efforts to politicize the impact on regional communities. Given that voting patterns still suggest that regional Australia is important in helping to decide which party will win an election, and in an effort to minimize regional disaffection, governments have set up various 'task forces' to seek to understand the regional problem and its possible solution. The Kelty Report, commissioned by the former Federal Labor Government, examined the problems of the regions. Kelty and his co-authors concluded that public and private investment was the key to regional growth and recommended a 30-year infrastructure investment strategy which would target virtually all of the main areas of activity/employment in regional Australia (transport, communications, agriculture, culture and welfare, energy, etc.) (see Kelty, 1993).

Kelty also suggested that a necessary part of such a policy would be measures which 'empowered' the regions. While this had a certain appeal - it appeared to give local people an opportunity to develop plans for their own destiny - there was very little said about exactly who would be empowered, by whom, in what way, and to what extent. As Guille (1994, p. 26) noted at the time, the notion that regions should control their own destinies 'can become an excuse for inaction by central governments'. An organizational structure for the coordination of regional activities, the Regional Economic Development Organizations (or REDOs), was proposed, and some developed throughout the nation.

In the summary of the conference on rural social policy in 1996 (see Council of Social Services of NSW, 1996, p. 6), it was argued that the success of regional strategies depend upon the mobilization of a 'wide range of members of local and regional communities...(and) empower(ing) individuals and groups in leading their communities forward'. The model here, though still of the interventionist kind, was promoting an integrated regional development policy which included state provision of basic infrastructure and special assistance to disadvantaged regions.

With the arrival of the present Coalition government, however, such interventionism was seen to be out of line with free market logic. As the Deputy Prime Minister said at a conference looking at the future of rural Australia,

> I am fed up with people saying nothing is being done for the bush. It is, but the bush also has to have the leadership and the motivation to respond (reported in *Daily Advertiser*, 3 July 1997, p. 1).

The Coalition has set policies in motion, which withdraw state-funded economic activity from the regions. The REDO programme, for example, has been abandoned, but what is being retained is the ideology of self help.

Now, it becomes essential that communities develop their own plans in order to become, 'business ready'. Thus, what governments could/should do is to provide those communities with 'the tools' for competitive advantage - with little said about the infrastructure which might be required. At the same conference on rural Australia, authors began building upon the emergent new self-help ethos. Lawler (1997) highlighted schemes among Aboriginal groups in NSW, Roberts (1997) spoke about 'community based regional development' in the Riverina region of NSW, Watkins (1997, p. 92) argued that revitalization 'requires vision, strategy, leadership, partnership, and action, driven at the local level and utilizing the breadth of community resources'. Noteworthy - given the extent to which rural women have been expected to carry the burden of structural change in rural communities - was the degree to which initiatives taken by women's groups would be crucial to the success of rural Australia (see Broad, 1997; Campbell, 1997; Fisher, 1997). Women will, in other words, be working even harder to make up for the ground lost as agencies involved in planning, welfare and social security reduce their impact in rural Australia.

One of the most important initiatives in promoting 'self help' has been that of Landcare. Here, community members join forces to develop local responses to environmental degradation. It has been viewed by some (see Campbell, 1992) as a largely non-bureaucratic approach to land management where people take control. It epitomizes the new approach to the state's attempt to address the problems, which have occurred over generations by overgrazing and overcropping (land and water mismanagement). According to Lockie the intent of the National Landcare Programme is,

> surprisingly consistent with the economic rationalist doctrine that has dominated government over the last two decades... The neo-liberal political philosophy underpinning economic rationalism promotes small government, minimal regulation, and... market solutions to social and environmental problems (1997, p. 232).

Lockie believes that for the present Coalition government 'to provide direct funding for on-ground works on private land seem(s) inconsistent' with economic rationalist policy. He predicts that sufficient funding to address the full extent of degradation will not be forthcoming (Lockie, 1997, p. 233). If this is so, there will be more pressure on landowners and community members to fund, from their own resources, strategies to overcome land and water degradation. Without a major commitment from government, it is unlikely that the potential of Landcare will be reached. As has been shown (see Morrisey and Lawrence, 1997), leadership is something of a scarce commodity in local Landcare groups, and asking such groups to take initiatives without any real economic incentives may be unrealistic in times of economic stress.

As we have written elsewhere (see Gray et al., 1997), the promotion of self help as an ideal in circumstances where productivist 'solutions' to falling prices are adopted may be harmful both to producer and to farm. While laudable traits, hard work and perseverance are not necessarily going to provide solutions to structural problems. In the absence of positive economic outcomes, they may, instead, produce personal failure and/or further damage to the environment.

The point here is not that local 'self help' is an unimportant ingredient in regional development or that local initiatives aimed at correcting previous environmental abuse are not to be praised. As many studies have shown, local initiatives - backed up by state or industry support - can be a catalyst for change (see Kelty, 1993). It is, rather, that the ideology of 'self help' has emerged with a new vigor seemingly directly proportional to the speed at which the Keynesian welfare state is dismantled. It is as if rural people now accept that it is their responsibility, alone, to develop the conditions for their future success of their farms and communities *at the same time that governments appear to be abrogating their own commitment to rural regions*. In structural terms, there is scant evidence to suggest that local initiatives, of and by themselves, bring anything of lasting substance to rural regions (local populations are often unaware of market knowledge and wider 'rules' which need to be known and incorporated into development planning - see Shaffer, 1994). And, when it is realized that the state's continued withdrawal of funding further threatens community growth, it would seem that the capacity of those remaining to do something positive is, accordingly, limited.

v) Scapegoating of racial and ethnic minorities for economic uncertainty/decline

A most disturbing feature of social change in rural (and, it is important to note, wider) Australia is the extent to which present economic problems associated with restructuring are being attributed to ethnic and racial minorities.

All of Australia's non-Aboriginal peoples have come from overseas since the time of white settlement, some two hundred years ago. Racism linked to the supposed inferiority of the Aboriginal population was a feature of early colonial rule and continues to exist today (see National

Inquiry into Racist Violence in Australia, 1991). Aborigines have been considered, via the doctrine of *terra nullius*, not to possess land - a convenient means of dispossessing the black population of the basis for social and economic reproduction. Racism accompanied the goldrushes in the 1850s, when the Chinese diggers were regularly beaten, or run out of settlements. From the time of the Federation of the States in 1901, an informal policy of 'White Australia' led to the passing of the Immigration Restriction Act, deliberately used to exclude non-Europeans (see Castles and Miller, 1993). Although Australia took displaced migrants in very large numbers after the Second World War, virtually all were from Europe.

By the early 1970s, however, the proportion of largely English speaking, but non-white, migrants coming to Australia began to burgeon in line with the policies of multiculturalism, and the need in Australia for trained workers. As economic trade with Asian nations displaced that with Britain (and paralleling Britain's entry into the EU), the numbers of migrants entering from locations such as Hong Kong, Vietnam, India, the Philippines, Sri Lanka and Taiwan began to rise at the same time that those from Ireland and Britain fell. Since the 1980s, a number of prominent Australians have attacked what they have seen to be the 'Asianization of Australia' (see for example, Blainey, 1984). While this has been shown to be a nonsense (Asians as a proportion of the total population actually fell during the last Census period) (see *Australian*, 18 July 1997), it has not stopped political opposition to Asian migration (see Davidson, 1997) or prevented the growing Aboriginal protest about two hundred years of racism from becoming prominent in Australian political discourse - and with a particular vitality in rural Australia.

For the Aboriginal population a key element in their latest moves to obtain justice has been the so-called 'Mabo ruling' (named after a prominent Torres Strait Islander who mounted the case). In June 1992, the High Court of Australia overturned the doctrine of *terra nullius*, thereby admitting that colonization did not extinguish the rights of the original inhabitants - and that, therefore, native title was a reality. Following this, Aboriginal and Torres Strait Islander groups have made various land claims, leaving pastoralists, farmers and miners fearing that their lands might be taken away. The recent Wik decision (in which the High Court found in favor of the Wik people's claim that they have rights over currently leased/freehold lands) means that native title can coexist with other land titles. For the grazers, this is viewed as intolerable (see *Australian*, 17 May, 1997, p. 21). The media have made much of these concerns, despite the fact that most land claims have been for Commonwealth owned (and leased) land, or for National Park land. Quite strict, negotiated, procedures (such as through the Native Title Tribunal) are to be put into place for Aboriginal peoples to have access to lands currently being utilized - and only for the protection and enjoyment of traditional Aboriginal laws and customs (see *Australian*, 14 May 1997, p. 14).

The actions of Aboriginal people (who, with South Sea Islanders, are the most disadvantaged group in Australian society) (see Mullins, 1996) - together with the presence, and activities, of Asians in the inner cities of the larger state capitals - may be viewed as being partly responsible for the rise in individuals and parties aimed at halting the supposed deterioration of the Australian Way of Life (Davidson, 1997). Fish shop-owner, and member for the Federal seat of Oxley, Pauline Hanson, has founded her One Nation party on the belief that Aboriginal people receive too much welfare, and that Asian migration to Australia is too high. She complains that Australian jobs are being taken by Asians, and demands an immediate halt to further migrant intake from Asia. Her speeches in rural Australia have been very well attended (although, at times, with as many people protesting outside as are listening to her reportedly racist speeches inside the venues) (see *Australian*, 17 May 1997, p. 6). While its policies are not so blunt, the Coalition is viewed as promoting a 'quiet Hansonism'. Opinion polls indicate that she is likely to have a great deal of electoral success, as voters - especially rural voters - grow increasingly disillusioned with the two traditional political groupings, the Labor Party and the Coalition.

Hanson's Party - and Hanson's attitudes - should not be viewed in isolation. Other new political parties/groups - such as Australia First - have also derided Australia's multicultural policy, have condemned the pro-Aboriginal verdicts from the High Court, and have opposed the tightening of gun laws. The League of Rights - an organization which has made its base in rural Australia, and which promotes, among other things, a Jewish conspiracy theory about globalization and banking - is another. Anti-racist literature from the US is also being distributed in rural communities in north Australia (although, by whom is uncertain). The Returned Services League, while not a political party as such, lobbies to have Asian migration reduced and is uncompromising in its dedication to the Australian flag and the Queen of England - powerful symbols of white Anglo-Saxon rule in this country.

While many social commentators have applauded Australia's general tolerance to ethnic difference and its keenness to embrace multiculturalism, its most liberal attitudes and policies coincided with a period of economic growth, starting after World War II and up to the 1980s (see Castles and Miller, 1993; Davidson, 1997). It is too early to tell what direct effects will result from the apparent proliferation of racist and anti-ethnic ideologies among Australians. At this stage and without further detailed study, it is only possible to say that a more vocal racism and intolerance of 'difference' appear to be emerging in rural Australia. Ironically, this is occurring at a time rural Australians appear to be benefiting from such postmodern developments as Asian student intake into regional universities, Asian (and especially Japanese) tourism, and the 'commoditization' of Aboriginal culture, by Aboriginal people, as the basis for future financial independence. The economic backdrop to the fear and anxiety obviously shown by those looking for new solutions is one, however, of declining job opportunities for rural people, economic disparities between rural and urban living, uncertainty in relation to the future of agriculture, and the supposed likelihood of an Aboriginal 'land grab'.

Conclusion: uncertain times in rural Australia

In this chapter we have, in a 'broad brush' fashion, attempted to paint a picture of an Australian state which is progressing enthusiastically down the globalization path. Its policies have been fashioned by neo-liberalist thinking, and have led to the cutting of tariffs, the removal of support from industry, and to deregulation of financial markets. The state is withdrawing from economic activity, literally leaving decisions to the marketplace. Given that that marketplace is a global one, this means leaving decision making with the large TNCs, which dominate global trade.

At this time, it appears that Australia - and particularly its rural areas - have not seen a surge of economic activity so much desired by the state and predicted by those neo-classical economists wedded to notions of comparative advantage. Instead, the Coalition government is blaming existing 'inefficiencies' in production as a deterrent for capital, and has highlighted the need for labour market reform as a key element in securing the interests of the corporations. At the time of writing, the Coalition is proposing that many areas in or around the State capitals should become Free Trade Zones. If this were to occur, it would be likely that they mirror what has happened overseas: they will be areas free from trade union influence, where minimum wages prevail, where work is of a production or assembly-line (low skilled) type, where the state's infrastructure is provided on a subsidized basis, and where the TNCs can trade freely with their own affiliates without incurring trade penalties (see, for elaboration, Crough and Wheelwright, 1982).

The rural social consequences of the 'globalization' of Australian agriculture and rural society have not been hard to describe, and include:

- exacerbation of the trend toward long term population loss in many of Australia's inland rural areas combined, increasingly, with the development of post modern services and activities (recreation, leisure, retirement) in the more climatically favorable and coastal rural regions
- decline of social capital in rural regions, leading to a situation in which many country towns and rural areas do not appear to have the same political or economic 'clout' which they had in earlier times
- the de-traditionalization of rural society - leading to uncertainties about change and direction, and to the demise of some social (sporting, club and other) institutions
- the growing acceptance of an ideology of 'self help' in regions undergoing restructuring (and, associated with this, an implicit acceptance of responsibility if the local community is not able to compete successfully on economic terms), and
- the scapegoating of racial and ethnic minorities who are blamed for the economic problems of the nation.

It should also be acknowledged, however, that there are some positive sides to these tendencies. For example, the de-traditionalization of rural society facilitated through, for example, the introduction of new satellite, computer and other technologies has the potential to bring rural society closer to metropolitan Australia in terms of tastes, values and social and economic expectations. At the same time as local culture and power structures might wane, new opportunities exist - at least for those who can afford the new technologies - for the growth of cooperation through links with wider culture. The ideology of 'self-help' and the associated realization that the state is unwilling/unable to act to assist rural towns might provide the impetus for regional/global connections - the very links which some writers (see Lash and Urry, 1994; Featherstone et al., 1995) have suggested are crucial for future development within nation states. Finally, a number of post-modern developments have the potential to assist rural-based populations. These developments include: the growth of tourism (especially cultural and eco-tourism); the capturing of (overseas) niche markets for primary products; evidence that consumers at home and abroad have an increasing demand for fresh, clean and green foods; and, the re-definition of rural space as a place of consumption.

What, exactly, this will mean for rural Australia remains unclear. Changing spaces appear to herald uncertain times for rural Australia.

References

Almås, R. (1994), 'The Rise and Fall of Agricultural Policy Cycles: From Planned Economy to Green Liberalism', *Journal of Regional Studies*, Vol. 10, No 1, pp.15-25.
Australian 14 May 1997; 17 May 1997; 12 July 1997; 16 July 1997; 18 July 1997; 25 July 1997.
Bailey, M. (1997), 'Landcare: Myth or Reality?', in Lockie, S. and Vanclay, F. (eds), *Critical Landcare*, Key Papers Series 5, Centre for Rural Social Research, Charles Sturt University: Wagga Wagga.
Beer, A., Bolam, A. and Maude, A. (1994), *Beyond the Capitals: Urban Growth in Regional Australia*, Australian Government Publishing Service: Canberra.
Blainey, G. (1994), *All for Australia*, Methuen/Hayes: Melbourne.
Broad, L. (1997), 'The Untapped Resource', paper presented at the *Rural Australia: Toward 2000 Conference*, Charles Sturt University, Wagga Wagga, 2-4 July.
Burch, D., Goss, J. and Lawrence, G. (eds) (1999), *Restructuring Global and Regional Agricultures*, Ashgate Publishing Company: Aldershot.
Campbell, A. (1992), *Taking the Long View in Tough Times: Landcare in Australia*, Third Annual Report of the National Landcare Facilitator, National Soil Conservation Programme: Canberra.
Campbell, A. (1994), *Landcare: Communities Shaping the Land and the Future*, Allen and Unwin: Sydney.
Campbell, A. (1997), 'Ducks on the Pond: the Management Challenges of Women Running Farms', paper presented at the *Rural Australia: Toward 2000 Conference*, Charles Sturt University, Wagga Wagga, 2-4 July.
Castles, S. and Miller, M. (1993), *The Age of Migration*, Macmillan: Melbourne.
Conacher, A. and Conacher, J. (1995), *Rural Land Degradation in Australia*, Oxford: Melbourne.
Council of Social Service of NSW (ed) (1996), *Rural Communities Looking Ahead: Papers, Abstracts and Notes from the NSW Rural Policy Conference*, Dubbo, June 1995, NCOSS: Sydney.
Cox, E. (1995), *A Truly Civil Society: The 1995 Boyer Lectures*, ABC Books: Sydney.
Crough, G. and Wheelwright, T. (1982), *Australia: A Client State*, Penguin: Sydney.
Daily Advertiser, 3 July 1997.
Dale, A. and Bellamy, J. (1998), *Regional Resource Use Planning in Rangelands*, Land and Water Resources Research and Development Corporation: Canberra.
Davidson, A. (1997), *From Subject to Citizen: Australian Citizenship in the Twentieth Century*, Cambridge University Press: Cambridge.
Featherstone, M., Lash, S. and Robertson, R. (eds) (1995), *Global Modernities*, Sage: London.
Ferguson, A. (1997), 'A Case Study in Decentralisation and Rural Economic Development: An International Air Freight Export/Import Terminal at Parkes,

NSW', paper presented at the *Rural Australia: Toward 2000 Conference*, Charles Sturt University, Wagga Wagga, 2-4 July.

Fisher, M. (1997), 'Valuing Rural Women', paper presented at the *Rural Australia: Toward 2000 Conference*, Charles Sturt University, Wagga Wagga, 2-4 July.

Fitzgerald, R. (1996), 'Sustainable Development and Rural Structural Adjustment', in Council of Social Service of NSW (ed) (1996), *Rural Communities Looking Ahead: Papers, Abstracts and Notes from the NSW Rural Policy Conference*, Dubbo, June 1995, NCOSS: Sydney.

Gain, L (1996), 'Equity in Social Policy', in Council of Social Service of NSW (ed) (1996), *Rural Communities Looking Ahead: Papers, Abstracts and Notes from the NSW Rural Policy Conference*, Dubbo, June 1995, NCOSS: Sydney.

Giddens, A. (1994), *Beyond Left and Right: The Future of Radical Politics*, Stanford University Press: California.

Gow, J. (1994), 'Farm Structural Adjustment - An Everyday Imperative', *Rural Society*, Vol. 4, No 2, pp. 9-13.

Gray, I. (1991), *Politics in Place: Social Power Relations in an Australian Country Town*, Cambridge University Press: Cambridge.

Gray, I., Lawrence, G. and Dunn, T. (1993), *Coping with Change: Australian Farmers in the 1990s*, Centre for Rural Social Research, Charles Sturt University: Wagga Wagga.

Gray, I. Phillips, E., Ampt, P. and Dunn, T. (1995), 'Awareness or Beguilement? Farmers' Perceptions of Changem', in Share, P. (ed), *Communication and Culture in Rural Areas*, Key Papers 4, Centre for Rural Social Research, Charles Sturt University: Wagga Wagga.

Gray, I., Stehlik, D., Lawrence, G. and Bulis, H. (1996), 'Impacts of the Drought on Australian Rural Communities: Is it Socially Binding or Socially Divisive?', paper presented at *Windows on the World: 28th International Conference of the Community Development Society*, Melbourne, 22-24 July.

Gray, I., Stehlik, D. and Lawrence, G. (1997), 'Economic Management, Social Contradiction and Climatic Disaster: Drought Policy in the 1990s', paper presented at the *Rural Australia: Toward 2000 Conference*, Charles Sturt University: Wagga Wagga.

Guille, H. (1994), 'Regional Development: A Critique of the Kelty Report', *WISER 1*, No 2, pp. 23-28.

Hamilton, C. (1996), 'Globalization and the Working People: The End of Post-war Consensus', paper Presented at the *ANZAAS Conference*, Canberra, 3 October.

Heelas, P. (1996), 'On Things not Being Worse, and the Ethic of Humanity', in Heelas, P., Lash, S. and Morris, P. (eds), *Detraditionalization: Critical Reflections on Authority and Identity*, Blackwell: Massachusetts.

Kelty, B (1993), *Developing Australia: A Regional Perspective*, A Report to the Federal Government by the Taskforce on Regional Development, Vols. 2, National Capital Printing: Canberra.

Lash, S. and Urry, J. (1994), *Economies of Signs and Space*, Sage: London.

Lawler, R. (1997), 'Hidden Treasure - Aboriginal People and Two NSW Rural Communities', paper presented at the *Rural Australia: Toward 2000 Conference*, Charles Sturt University, Wagga Wagga, 2-4 July.

Lawrence, G. (1987), *Capitalism and the Countryside: The Rural Crisis in Australia*, Pluto: Sydney.

Lawrence, G. (1995), *Futures for Rural Australia: From Agricultural Productivism to Community Sustainability*, Inaugural Address, Central Queensland University, RSERC, CQU: Rockhampton.

Lockie, S. (1997), 'What Future Landcare? New Directions under Provisional Funding', in Lockie, S. and Vanclay, F. (eds), *Critical Landcare*, Centre for Rural Social Research, CSU: Wagga Wagga.

Lockie, S. and Vanclay, F. (eds) (1997), *Critical Landcare*, Centre for Rural Social Research, CSU: Wagga Wagga.

Luke, T. (1996), 'Identity, Meaning and Globalization: Detraditionalization in Postmodern Space-Time Compression', in Heelas, P., Lash, S. and Morris, P. (eds), *De-traditionalization: Critical Reflections on Authority and Identity*, Blackwell: Massachusetts.

McMichael, P. (1996), *Development and Social Change: A Global Perspective*, Pine Forge: California.

Malcolm, B., Sale, P. and Egan, A. (1996), *Agriculture in Australia: An Introduction*, Oxford: Melbourne.

Marsden, T., Murdoch, J., Lowe, P., Munton, R. and Flynn, A. (1993), *Constructing the Countryside*, UCL Press: London.

Montford, L. (1997), 'The Influence of the Commercialization of Sport on Rural Communities', paper presented at the *Leisure - People, Places, Spaces Conference of the Australian and New Zealand Association for Leisure Studies*, Newcastle, NSW, 9-11 July.

Morris, P. (1996), 'Tradition and the Limits of Difference', in Heelas, P., Lash, S. and Morris, P. (eds), *Detraditionalization: Critical Reflections on Authority and Identity*, Blackwell: Massachusetts.

Morrisey, P. and Lawrence, G. (1997), 'A Critical Assessment of Landcare in a Region of Central Queensland', in Lockie, S. and Vanclay, F. (eds), *Critical Landcare*, Centre for Rural Social Research, CSU: Wagga Wagga.

Mues, C., Chapman, L. and van Hilst, R. (1998), *Landcare: Promoting Improved Land Management Practices on Australian Farms*, Australian Bureau of Agriculture and Resource Economics: Canberra.

Mullins, S. (1996), *After Recognition: Access and Equity for Australian South Sea Islanders*, RSERC, CQU: Rockhampton.

National Farmers' Federation (1993), *New Horizons: A Strategy for Australia's Agri-food Industries*, National Farmers' Federation: Canberra.

National Inquiry into Racist Violence in Australia (1991), *Report of the National Inquiry into Racist Violence in Australia*, AGPS: Canberra.

Natural Heritage Trust (1997), *Guide to Community Group Applications*, Natural Heritage Trust: Canberra.

Passfield, R., Lawrence, G. and McAllister, J. (1996), 'Not So Sweet: Rural Restructuring and its Community Impact - the Mackay Sugar District, Queensland', in Lawrence, G., Lyons, K. and Momtaz, S. (eds), *Social Change in Rural Australia*, RSERC, CQU: Rockhampton.

Poiner, G. (1990), *The Good Old Rule: Gender and other Power Relations in a Rural Community*, Sydney University Press: Sydney.

Pusey, M. (1991), *Economic Rationalism in Canberra*, Cambridge University Press: Canberra.

Rees, S, Rodley, G. and Stilwell, F. (eds) (1993), *Beyond the Market: Alternatives to Economic Rationalism*, Pluto: Sydney.

Roberts, M. (1997), 'Integrated Community Based Regional Development in the Riverina Region of NSW', paper presented at the *Rural Australia: Toward 2000 Conference*, Charles Sturt University, Wagga Wagga, 2-4 July.

Schwarten, R. (1997), *1997 Budget Speech - 4 June* (Reproduced from Hansard), Issued by the Member for Rockhampton in July.

Shaffer, R. (1994), 'Rural Communities and Sustainable Economic Development', in McSwan, D. and McShane, M. (eds), *Issues Affecting Rural Communities*, Proceedings of the Conference on Issues Affecting Rural Communities, Rural Education and Development Centre, James Cook University.

Stayner, R. and Reeve, I. (1990), *'Uncoupling': Relationships Between Agriculture and the Local Economics of Areas in New South Wales*, The Rural Development Centre, University of New England: Armidale, NSW.

Stehlik, D. and Lawrence, G. (1996), 'A Direction Toward Sustainability? Australian Rural Communities and Care for the Aged', *Journal of the Community Development Society,* Vol. 27, No 1, pp. 45-55.

Stehlik, D., Bulis, H., Gray, I. and Lawrence, G. (1996a), 'Rural Families and the Impact of the Drought of the 1990s', paper presented to the *Family Research Pathways to Policy Conference*, Brisbane, 27-29 November.

Stehlik, D., Bulis, H., Gray, I. and Lawrence, G. (1996b), 'Communities in Crisis? Towards a Concept of Quality of Life in Australian Rural Communities Which Have Experienced the Drought of the Early 1990s', paper presented at the *World Conference on Quality of Life*, University of Northern British Columbia, Canada, 22-25 August.

Stewart, J. (1994), *The Lie of the Level Playing Field: Industry Policy and Australia's Future,* The Text Publishing Company: Melbourne.

Stilwell, F. (1986), *The Accord and Beyond*, Pluto: Sydney.

Stilwell, F. (1992), *Understanding Cities and Regions*, Pluto: Sydney.

Stilwell, F. (1993), *Reshaping Australia: Urban Problems and Policies*, Pluto: Sydney.

Symes, D. and Jansen, A. (eds) (1994), *Agricultural Restructuring and Rural Change in Europe*, Wageningen Agricultural University: Wageningen.

Vanclay, F. and Lawrence, G. (1995), *The Environmental Imperative: Eco-social Concerns for Australian Agriculture*, CQU Press: Rockhampton.

Watkins, W. (1997), 'Revitalizing Rural Communities', paper presented at the *Rural Australia: Toward 2000 Conference*, Charles Sturt University, Wagga Wagga, 2-4 July.
Wild, R. (1983), *Heathcote*, George Allen and Unwin: Sydney.

Part II

Farmers and Farming Women

5 Grounding Globalization Theory: Local Responses to Global Processes in the Light of the Global-Local Links Debate in Rural Sociology

LUIS LLAMBÍ, ELIÉZER ARIAS AND GERMÁN FREIRE

Introduction

An important debate is currently taking place in rural sociology about how to understand the links between globalization and local rural restructuring. This debate confronts two prominent theoretical perspectives in the social sciences: on the one hand, those who, anchored in neo-Marxian political economy, emphasize the impact of global agents and processes on current rural restructuring; on the other hand, those who from a post-modernist perspective perceive globalization as a continuously re-negotiated process in which a large array of actors participate, but in fact stress the agency of local actors in face-to-face relationships and local encounters. We wish to contribute to the debate by building on our own research experience in Latin America. We contend that most of the theoretical insights and methodological suggestions contained in these theoretical perspectives are complementary rather than contradictory, although we argue that a new critical synthesis is necessary. To contribute in that direction is the main objective of this chapter.[1]

The point we want to stress is that current globalization processes and particularly country-specific structural adjustment programmes (SAPs) to cope with them, not only have an impact upon local agricultural systems and rural livelihoods, but also generate a large variety of responses from agents located at different spatial scales - including rural localities - which in turn have a feedback in the opposite direction. At the local/rural level, we perceive two basic sorts of coping mechanisms that agents display in pursuing their goals or adjusting their lives to changes in their (economic, political, cultural, and natural) environment. On the one hand, there are the so-called adaptive responses by which agents learn to live with the new situation, designing strategies with the purpose of taking advantage of them. On the other hand, there are non-adaptive responses by which people try to modify, resist, or even subvert these conditions to make them fulfill their goals. Furthermore, we propose to approach these links as bi-directional and mediated by various layers of social agency and emergent (economic, political, and cultural) patterns and conditions.[2] We hope that by approaching global-local (rural) restructuring in this way, we are overcoming some of the shortcomings of both one-sided political economy and post-modernist perspectives.

The chapter is organized into three parts. The first provides a theoretical and epistemological reading of the current global-local links debate in rural sociology. The second is an abridged summary of the empirical findings of a comparative research agenda on the impact of structural adjustment programmes in two horticultural communities in the high valleys of the Andes: Pueblo Llano (Venezuela) and Cerrito (Colombia). Finally, in the conclusions, we propose one possible research strategy and some theoretical hints to bridge the gap between global and local rural studies.

The global-local links debate in rural sociology

To a large extent, political economic theories of globalization, anchored in world-systems theory and the 1970s 'regulation theory' school, emerged as a response to the mainstream economic theories of comparative advantage in world trade and the self-regulation of markets. More recently, however, a new interloper emerged within rural sociology: the post-modernist critique to the globalization of agriculture and food, under the guise of actor-oriented, actor-network theory, or social constructivist approaches.

The debate has been nourished with the contributions of a large number of authors writing from different perspectives.[3] In this chapter, given space constraints, we decided to illustrate the debate through the analysis of two leading positions: On the one hand, the contribution of Phil McMichael, who, anchored in a political economy perspective, emphasizes globalization as the political project of a powerful global elite, although he finds multiple expressions and challenges in rural localities all over the world. On the other hand, the work of Norman Long who gives priority to the meanings which for local agents assume so-called global or external processes.

It is important to emphasize, however, that despite their different epistemological underpinnings, substantive priorities, and expository styles, both approaches have been getting closer in the course of the debate. They coincide, for example, on the need to overcome previous theoretical perspectives, which gave undue emphasis to the homogenizing effects of globalization processes to the detriment of their differentiating effects. They also concur on the need 'to ground' (historically in McMichael's perspective, ethnographically in Long's view) abstract constructs, which tend to reify formerly conceived polar concepts: e.g. the global versus the local. Both perspectives also agree in overcoming former determinist readings of social processes, opening theoretical space to both necessity and contingency in the explanation of social events. Lastly, they coincide in giving variable explanatory weight to the strategies of social agents, although embedding them in the framework of structural regularities and behavioral patterns. In the following paragraphs, we will only stress, however, their still presumably contradictory theoretical and epistemological perspectives.

McMichael's PE approach: the globalization project and its local rural expressions

For Phillip McMichael, the analysis of the links between globalization processes and local rural restructuring provides an excellent opportunity to develop a proper historical specification of both global and local dynamics as theoretical constructs. For him, there is more than just one global dynamic, but there is only one ideologically and politically coherent globalization project. Conversely, there are also many local dynamics because globality is internally differentiated. Thus, the real epistemological challenge is to specify our concepts in their historical concreteness. A false opposition between globality and locality emerges in our research agendas whenever our concepts are not constructed relationally and historically. As such they tend to be endowed with agency becoming reified levels of analysis. McMichael's methodological proposal is to jointly analyze the local expression of global processes and empirically contrast the validity of the theoretical construct beyond specific case studies.

The bottom line, however, is that there is one hegemonic globalization project, i.e. a 'set of institutional and ideological relations constructed by powerful social forces' (McMichael, 1996, p. 26), which is assumed 'to be consequential' throughout the global economic and political system. This project emerged out of the eviction of the national developmentalist project of the postwar era, but it currently grows out of the need 'to stabilize capitalism through global economic management' (McMichael, 1996, p. 31).

McMichael is also adamant in specifying the social entities endowed with a purpose to which he attributes a 'global reach' or agency: the managers of international agencies, the Group of Seven (G-7) states, state managers embracing liberalization elsewhere, and some academic ideologues. They constitute a 'new global elite', or even an 'incipient global ruling class', who respond to the interests of new financial and transnational corporate groups (McMichael, 1996, pp. 26, 32, 41).

Paradoxically, the globalization project opens some space to 'localism', i.e. the mushrooming of local political cultural renewals, as it also engenders alternative responses from relatively disempowered social agents. As global economic management and national structural adjustments erode the former social and agrarian protections created during the postwar era, marginalized local communities strive not to be left out altogether either by finding new niches in the emerging global economy, or through new social resistance movements. McMichael finds in the Zapatista rebellion, starting in Chiapas (Mexico) in 1994, a sort of empirical paradigm of new social movements in the emerging global scenario. 'Cosmopolitan localism', an assertion of local cultural and economic specificity as a universal right, is for him the Zapatistas' response to the globalist project.

But the reference to the Zapatista uprising serves McMichael with another purpose: to show the potentially recursive effects of these local processes to alter global dynamics. The Mexican *peso* currency crisis of December 1994, which engendered the so-called *tequila effect* in global financial markets, a financial bailout of the Mexican economy in 1995, and the creation in 1995 of an IMF global emergency fund to rescue bankrupt national economies are also considered by McMichael as indirect effects of the global waves created by the Zapatista rebellion.

Long's actor-oriented approach: a post-structuralist critique to 'centrist' approaches to globalization

Long's actor-oriented approach owes much to the post-structuralist gist of Anthony Giddens and the social constructivism of authors such as Bourdieu, Knorr-Cetina, Callon and Latour. The common thread linking these authors is their insistence on the need for social science to be open to a world full of contingencies. Long, in particular, argues against neo-

Marxist attempts in political economy to propose, more than to test heuristically, the argument that there is an immanent logic in the capitalist system which would make the actions of social agents predictable. He does not adopt, however, an extreme indeterminacy position. For him, it is possible to accept that some rural restructurings are the result of the impacts of external structural forces (such as the state or the market), but he insists that these forces are always necessarily mediated and transformed by the interpretations and strategies of local agents, thus opening space to multiple contingencies.

Following his long-standing empirical research agenda in rural social change, particularly in Latin America, Long's current interest is to discuss rural transformations in the context of 'the complex dynamics between the processes of globalization and localization' (1994, p. 7). He specifies globalization as an accelerated flow of commodities, people, capital, technologies, images and knowledge through and beyond national borders. In contrast to former globalization theories, for him there exists no singular global order but multiple social networks involving people who were previously isolated by spatial, political and cultural barriers. In an attempt to overcome the reification of structures by outdated structuralist approaches, he appeals to metaphors such as flows and networks to substitute for notions such as structures and structural effects or impacts. By contrast, the notion of localization, particularly in rural contexts, helps him to understand in the everyday life of local rural people meanings of processes such as the increased commoditization of agrifood chains, new state policies and interventions, and new technical and scientific discourses.

Instead of McMichael's epistemological strategy to ground theory in history, Long proposes to ground his conceptual apparatus in detailed ethnographic accounts on how people conceptualize these processes as they experience them, on how they formulate their strategies to cope with them, and on how they finally fulfill their actions. His main objective is therefore 'to explore the ways in which "external" notions and "conditionalities" are translated into localized meanings and actions' (Long, 1994, p. 14).

Long's main criticism to political economy (PE) theories of globalization, particularly in rural sociology, is that they are biased by what he considers a centrist and hegemonic view of power relations, providing scant or nil ability to local rural agents. For him, it is not completely evident, for instance, that transnational corporations, state executives, or even rural extension workers, have the ability to shape rural people's lives and determine their actions. To assume the overwhelming strength and power of these so-called external institutions, tends to obscure the reality when these 'external' agents only represent a small subset of a vast and more complex universe of actors (1994, p. 8). For him, the advantage of an actor-oriented approach is that it draws the attention to how all agents, and particularly local (individual or collective) agents, try to create space to fulfill their own projects, frequently independently and occasionally opposed to the so-called external actors.

This leads to a definition of societal power in which all actors exhibit some freedom of maneuver. Social processes are never imposed 'from above' by structural forces or the purposive actions of global agents, but they are always reinterpreted, manipulated, and transformed by local agents striving to push their own life projects ahead. Social change, in sum, is always the result of a continuous struggle and negotiation among agents who are bestowed by different world-views and frequently by opposed interests (1990, p. 17).

As we may now perceive, the debate is full of theoretical and epistemological insights calling to bridge the complex of relations, which extend from the global to the local, and vice versa. In our view, however, it still raises more questions that propose concrete guidelines on how to achieve this goal adequately. The next section will attempt to problematize further on the theoretical and empirical construction of global contexts and local scenarios, by drawing on our own Latin American research agenda.

Grounding globalization theory in our Latin American research agenda

This part of the chapter sketches some of the findings of a collaborative research agenda that we started at the beginning of the 1990s. For reasons of space, we will need to skip most of the narrative, the historical and ethnographic richness of the research, to proceed with a mostly theoretical and epistemological reading of the results.

The project researched into the way people in two rural Andean communities, Pueblo Llano in Venezuela and Cerrito in Colombia, are responding to the changing conditions affecting their livelihoods. First, we introduce the reader to the basic traits of SAPs in both countries. Then, we provide a brief overview of the recent trends affecting the agricultural systems in both rural localities. Finally, we report the responses of Pueblo Llano's and Cerrito's farmers to the shifting economic scenarios introduced by SAPs and economic openings, as well as the responses of Colombian immigrants to shifting labour market and political conditions in Venezuela.

Grounding globalization in national political economies: SAPs in Colombia and Venezuela

Structural adjustment is the most visible face of globalization in Latin America. SAPs, however, have varied substantially in different countries of the region. National governments, depending on their ideological orientations and variable 'margins of maneuver' have been trying to re-arrange these programmes (although with different degrees of success) to make them suitable to their own purposes. Adding a comparative perspective to our research agenda was important because we wanted to assess the relative weight which had to be assigned to national and sub-national factors vis-a-vis supranational forces in local rural restructuring, as well as to obtain a more clear specification of the causal links between agents and social structures located at various scales. Our main hypothesis was that rural and agrifood restructuring, although unquestionably subject to global forces (such as in McMichael's globalist project) is a highly contested process whereby, despite their often narrow room for maneuver, national governments, and rural local actors can significantly alter some of its outcomes.

In the late 1980s, Colombia and Venezuela started a series of macro-economic policy reforms aiming, among other objectives, to relocate their economies in the emerging global markets. In 1989, however, after over thirty years of an explicitly inward-oriented economic growth model, the Venezuelan government implemented an 'orthodox' IMF-sponsored 'shock' therapy. The cornerstone of the adjustment package was the devaluation and floating of the national currency. The depressive nature of the adjustment contributed to a deterioration of real income and a sharp increase in unemployment. In February 27th, 1989, the announcement of the first measures contained in the adjustment package was greeted with four days of rioting and looting.

In contrast with the 'shock' policies applied in Venezuela, structural adjustment in Colombia has been a slower and more gradual process. This is explained, partly, by the fact that foreign debt has had less influence on Colombia's economy. It is also partially explained by the fact that the Colombian economy was far more diversified and open than Venezuela's during the previous import-substitution-industrialization (ISI) period. But perhaps the component of the economic opening policy which has had the greater impact on rural societies on both sides of the border has been the Bilateral Free Trade Agreement (FTA) signed in 1991 between Venezuela and Colombia. Another important factor has been the gradually greater divergence between the exchange rate policies followed by each country in the midst of their SAPs.

Both the Bilateral FTA and the exchange rate policies have had important effects on the direction and volume of the agri-food commodities traded between Colombia and Venezuela. The FTA initially generated a modest but visible revitalization of the agri-food systems in both countries. In March 1994, however, economic uncertainty caused the Venezuelan currency to drop sharply. As a consequence of the continuous deterioration of economic conditions in Venezuela, together with economic boom in Colombia, the agricultural economies on both sides of the border have been experiencing a series of transformations, which alter the commercial and migratory flows that have historically linked these two countries.

How these changes affected local agri-food systems and rural livelihoods in both countries was our next line of inquiry.

Grounding globalization in locality

a) Pueblo Llano and Cerrito: two parallel, but related stories For centuries the West-east Andean range crossing the border between Venezuela and Colombia has bolstered rather than hindered the long-standing ties between these two neighboring countries. A dense web of relations based on migratory flows, frequent intermarriage, economic ties and a common cultural and historical heritage has linked these regional societies to an extent not frequently found elsewhere in Latin America.

After 1989 the Pueblo Llano municipality experienced a renewed boom in horticultural production. Since then, labour shortages have increased in this rural municipality, not only because of the area's topographic characteristics,[4] but also because of the historical patterns of out-migration of the native population to other areas of the country in search for better standards of living. Colombian immigrants supply the majority of the labour force in the area. Surprisingly, one of the findings of the Pueblo Llano case study was that 62 per cent of these immigrants came from Cerrito in the Santander Department, near the border, a fact which facilitated the selection of our case studies.

On the initial stages of the project we realized that the historical migratory flow between the two countries was shifting. After 1994, social and political unrest caused the Venezuelan currency to drop sharply, reinitiating a period of severe economic crisis and producing a new reversal to the multilateral agencies' SAP initiated in 1989. By contrast, in Colombia, parallel to an economic upturn in large part the result of new oil discoveries and a booming drug trade, the chronic violence that has plagued the country since the 1940s was mounting. Guerrilla warfare, drug trafficking and a dirty civil war have conditioned a further displacement of the peasant population in the whole country. Therefore, on the process, the research objectives were modified to account for these new developments. The occasion was propitious for the study not only of the impact of former migratory flows on both sides of the border, but also of the effects of the reinsertion of former Colombian migrants into their communities of origin.

Up to the mid-1980s, the agriculture of Cerrito was basically cereals and potatoes destined for local trade and household consumption. The remittances sent by family members in Venezuela, or brought by them in their short visits to the homeland, became an important source of income for most peasant families. One of the main consequences of this trend was the rapid aging of the population pyramid, to an extent that for several decades labour shortages left agricultural cycles largely dependent on pre-colonial and colonial non-wage labour exchanges. Another consequence was that many farm plots were left fallow for indefinite periods of time.

By the mid-1980s, Colombian immigrants in Pueblo Llano developed new ways to recruit workers. Up to that time, the labour force had been supplied by the migratory network based on family ties and friends. But with the intensification of horticultural production at the end of the decade, the migratory flow became insufficient. This role as brokers, allowed pioneer migrants to exercise a great degree of control over the size of the labour force in Pueblo Llano's labour market. Taking advantage of this fact, they refashioned the traditional institution of sharecropping allowing them a higher degree of leverage when negotiating with Venezuelan farmers.

Today Cerrito is going through an agricultural boom similar to the one experienced by Pueblo Llano fifteen years earlier. A rather unexpected effect of the return migration has been the import of certified high-yield seeds for the production of new crops, and the transfer of technical know-how in modern sprinkle irrigation. Nowadays, irrigation is a generalized practice in Cerrito. As a result, a minimum of two annual cycles is harvested in the main trading crops. With the acquisition of new agricultural technology there are increasing yields and a decrease in the fallow land period. Cerrito is today the main producer of garlic and potatoes in the whole east Andean region of Colombia.

Trans-migrant flows have also introduced a whole array of consumer and trade items and cultural practices and rituals which tend to strengthen the historical links between these two Andean communities, without necessarily producing total cultural homogenization. A new sense of identity is also developing: 'We are all Pueblollaneros, Andinos, and not only Venezuelans or Colombians'.

b) Adaptive farmers' responses to their shifting market and policy scenario
After 1989, when the IMF-backed SAP started in Venezuela, Pueblo Llano experienced a renewed boom in horticultural production. An increased horticultural production together with a general trend toward the specialization in only two products (potatoes and carrots) may be regarded as a direct impact of the macroeconomic policies which have resulted in the increased profitability of these products, even in the context of the general crisis of the overall Venezuelan agricultural sector. The trend followed by the larger producers towards specializing in only these two crops may be explained as a response to the impact of economic policies in non-tradable products, in the context of relatively stable and growing markets. There is a countervailing tendency, however. Among the smaller farm owners, a more diversified crop pattern has arisen in search of an increased flexibility to face the high volatility of horticultural market prices.

Changes in crop patterns and market orientation have also been accompanied by changes in production techniques. The use of locally produced non-certified seeds instead of imported certified seeds is directly related to the continuous devaluation of the national currency within the context of the SAPs. The immediate result has been a reduction in yields. A related trend has been the use of chicken and goat manure in place of chemical fertilizers as a result of the elimination of subsidies for fertilizer, also a policy related to the SAP. It would be reasonable to expect that both the currency devaluation and the elimination of subsidies would have resulted in a reduced use of chemical pesticides. Two factors explain why this has not been the case. First, the trend toward single crop production has increased the crops' vulnerability to old and new pests. Secondly, the liberalization of trade with Colombia has increased the profitability of importing chemical pesticides from Colombia or from third countries.

Horticultural production has also been a highly labour-intensive activity since it was introduced in the area by the Canary Island immigrants in the 1960s. Since then, labour shortages have characterized the area, because of the area's topographic characteristics but also because of the historical patterns of out-migration of the native population to other areas of the country in search for better standards of living.

It is possible to argue that the general and unexpected result of all these developments is an increased environmental degradation in the area. This general trend is related to: 1) the increasing deterioration of soil and water resources as a consequence of erosion and increased debris on the watershed; 2) the increasing deterioration of the quality of water and soil as a consequence of the intensification in the use of agri-chemicals; and 3) the increasing pollution of horticultural products as a result of fecal and chemical residues in them.

Other unintended effects of agricultural intensification is a visible deterioration in the quality of life among Pueblo Llano inhabitants, despite a much celebrated increase in their agricultural revenues. This deterioration is a direct consequence of the responses adopted by local farmers to their new economic environment. We already mentioned the shifts toward organic manure in substitution for chemical fertilizers as a result of the elimination of subsidies. The use of manure led to a great proliferation of flies in the area, since the poor management of the manure creates the ideal conditions for nurturing larvae. The paradox is that Pueblo Llano, while increasing its rural revenues, has experienced a significant increase in mortality and morbidity rates stemming from gastrointestinal diseases as a result of poor sanitary conditions and the spreading of diseases through the flies.

c) Non-adaptive farmers' responses to threats in their livelihood styles In 1993 after the signing of the Bilateral Free Trade Agreement (FTA), Colombian potato exports flooded the Venezuelan market creating both a market drop and volatility in prices. The potato farmers' first reaction was to lobby the national government in Caracas, asking for protection and the modification of the treaty. As they had no success, they worked to create a regional organization of potato producers incorporating farmers from other Andean municipalities. Facing imminent bankruptcy, they took the decision - for the first time in a Venezuelan farmers' movement - to get in touch directly with the organizations of Colombian producers in order to manage the enlarged potato market together. As a result, in July 1993, these negotiations ended up in an informal agreement of shared 'administration' of the potato bi-national market through which the volume of imports in each direction will depend on supply deficits in each country, stemming from differences in production cycles. The Venezuelan and Colombian governments had no choice but accept this *de facto* modification of the FTA.

d) The Colombian immigrant responses to shifting economic conditions in Venezuela By the mid-1980s, in the midst of Pueblo Llano's horticultural boom, the migratory flows from Colombia became insufficient. In order to control the labour force that would give them the opportunity to better negotiate work and living conditions, some pioneer Colombian immigrants started to develop new recruiting networks in their places of origin. The pioneer Colombian immigrants would now go to their hometowns, whereby they would directly recruit new labourers to work for them in Venezuela. These 'non-traditional' migratory networks, and the control on the supply of labour force that was associated with them, provided these 'middlemen' with enough freedom of maneuver to negotiate with Venezuelan landowners an increased access to their agricultural lands.

There is a non-written common law in the Venezuelan Andes that land cannot be sold to 'foreigners', meaning any non-native of the region. During the last two decades, however, a particular form of sharecropping developed as the main access of Colombian immigrants to land. For years, labour shortages have created a sellers' market in which some Colombian immigrants control the supply of the labour force. Most Venezuelan farmers are thus forced to look for Colombian sharecroppers in order to gain access to both the sharecroppers' labour and to labour force in general.

But SAPs also meant state reforms, and specifically political and administrative decentralization in Venezuela. Since 1990, the creation of the *municipio* (the municipality) has meant a political entity that is closer-to-the-people. As a result, the valley of Pueblo Llano, originally administered from the far-away town of Timotes, became an independent municipality and, for the first time, its inhabitants gained the right to elect their own mayor and municipal counselors.

In this new scenario, the municipality became an increasingly relevant locus of political participation for the immigrants. The 1961 Constitution gave the immigrants the right to participate in the local elections provided they have more than five years of residence in the country. Yet, this right was seldom exercised since the former 'districts' were not a significant locus of political participation to foster their claims. On the other hand, within this new political scenario, the immigrants developed an increased consciousness of the political leverage that their numbers offered them to negotiate their votes in exchange for achieving their social demands.

A turning point was the creation, in 1992, of an Association of Colombian Immigrants in Pueblo Llano. The conditions were ripe in 1993, when Colombian immigrants, making use of their right to vote, actually decided the last municipal elections. As a result, a drastic change has taken place in the attitude of the present candidates in Pueblo Llano toward that group of voters. Among the most important concessions received by Colombian immigrants is the access to housing programmes via the Municipal Council. This has been an important achievement given the severe lack of housing in the area. Another important recent benefit for the Colombian population in Pueblo Llano has to do with the way illegal migrants have been treated in the last few years by local authorities, considering the fact that they are so essential to the economy of the valley. Arrests and deportations have not stopped, but they do not happen as often, and they are not initiated by the mayor's office.

Some preliminary conclusions

The global-local links debate in rural sociology is full of theoretical insights and methodological suggestions that are relevant not only for rural sociology, but for social science in general. It contrasts with the dull repetition of empiricist, small-scale studies, which for decades characterized much of the rural sociological literature. The debate has been healthy for the political economy of global agri-food systems inasmuch as it pinpoints some of its dangers: one-sided causal explanations, over-stressing the agency of global actors and minimizing the roles of local agents and histories in this global-local restructuring. It has been healthy for postmodern thinkers as well, because it shows some of its pitfalls: a tendency to fall into a raw empiricism by avoiding any formal theorizing; a diffuse notion of power and the insufficient attention it devotes to issues of social inequality. But it runs the risk of becoming unproductive navel-looking. We cannot substitute arguing about metaphors for substantive theorizing and knowledge building research about the urgent issues posed by structural adjustment and globalization processes.

McMichael's approach is to ground globalization theory in history, i.e. to specify its concepts in their historical concreteness, in order to set up the time and space validity of its theoretical generalizations. In practice, however, his grounding does not go far enough from the macro-historical processes, providing few theoretical and methodological clues as to how to go further and analyze more localized situations.

McMichael is also partially correct when he argues that there is some degree of ideological consensus among what he refers to as a global elite. But it could also be alleged that this global elite is not a homogeneous body but compounded by different agents representing strikingly dissimilar economic and political interests. At times, it is true, they exhibit some degree of ideological coherence, particularly when they rally behind relatively abstract principles such as the 'free' market and a 'level-playing field' in international trade relations based on comparative advantage; but differences arise when they try to turn these rather abstract goals into rules regulating the emerging global order, or when they attempt to re-interpret them as policies in their own national turf. The consequence is to portray global agents as a more unified and powerful force than they really are, whereby results a rather reductionist view of social agency.

Long's approach is to ground globalization in local ethnographies, bringing cultural and identity issues back into rural sociology. He is also in a reasonable path when he stresses the role of local elite groups or tries to expose otherwise invisible and relatively disempowered actors. His social constructivist approach is particularly healthy for rural social science inasmuch as it impels political economists to look toward micro-scale phenomena which also form part of current globalization processes. But we should not be deluded. Local producers and transnational corporations may be part of the same 'lengthened networks', but their material and non-material resource differentials, i.e. their power differences, should not be underestimated. Alternative social movements and projects are important, but when the actions of global agents interlock with long and wide 'networks of power', they can indeed render local rural agencies helpless and can undermine the alternative projects 'from below'.

What does all this mean for the new perspective on the links between global processes and local rural restructuring that we are proposing? This is probably best explained by having recourse again to our own theoretical and methodological saga.

Our initial focus was to adopt a political economic perspective to locate national agri-food systems and rural societies within the new global scenario. Yet, globalization viewed from 'the South', raises a lot of questions which tend to be overlooked when similar issues are looked at only 'from the North'. Looked at from 'the North', globalization tends to be seen as a matter of global market integration, the worldwide-reach of some transnational corporations, the struggle between the three superpowers emerging from the end of the cold war (US, EU, Japan), and the Westernization of patterns of consumption worldwide. A view from 'the South' gives a completely different perspective: nation-states struggling not to be left out of global markets and the political fora in which the new rules of the game are discussed; domestic economic interests trying to find their niches in shifting market networks; rural and urban citizens striving to survive in ever more pressing living conditions.

Thus, we share with Long a concern for the tendency in the political economy literature to magnify the power of transnational forces in shaping agri-food systems at the expense of national and local forces. We started with the assumption that rural and agri-food restructuring, while unquestionably subject to global forces (such as in McMichael's globalist project), is a highly contested process whereby, despite their often narrow room for maneuver, national governments and rural local actors can significantly alter some of its outcomes. Distancing ourselves from most post-modernist perspectives, we were not only seeking to document the agents' responses, but also to pose the proper theoretical questions to explain them.

How were farmers, and other rural dwellers, responding to the new economic and political environment created by structural adjustment programmes? Were farmers merely 'adapting to' or coping with these changes via, for example, strategic shifts in crop patterns and the adoption of new technologies? Or, were they actively resisting these changes and developing non-conformist strategies to them?

Our empirical material revealed some 'non-adaptive' responses among different categories of rural agents as they attempt to act upon the political and economic conditions, which they consider, are negatively affecting their performance. Pueblo Llano potato farmers upgrade their organizations to increase their bargaining power beyond their local scenario and learn to develop alliances with their former competitors beyond national borders when their traditional strategy of lobbying the national government fail. Colombian immigrants take advantage of the increased bargaining power provided by a stringent labour market and by administrative decentralization to promote their own demands, thus developing a new sense of citizenship at the local level. An unexpected result is that sometimes agents are not only trying to subvert or merely adapt to the conditions which they feel are negatively affecting them, but they also seek to reshape, manipulate or appropriate them to suit their interests. These responses to globalization may not possess the charm and global appeal of the Zapatista uprising, but are probably more representative of what is going on in a large number of rural localities throughout Latin America and elsewhere.

From this discussion, it should be clear now that current globalization processes require us to rethink some of the notions and metaphors that until recently have been rather a-critically used in the social sciences. Power is one of these troublesome concepts, which have proven most difficult to deal with. Our contention is that in most of the rural sociological literature anchored in political economy, there is still an economistic bias which tends to underscore issues such as the process of state-building, and the relationship between power, cultural values, and the 'natural' environment, to name just a few. By contrast, there is also a political bias among some political economic approaches which, paradoxically, has not been able so far to update and problematize with former theories of power and the state to account for the new challenges posed by globalization.

From political economy we have retained some sensitivity to issues such as the asymmetry of power in the new global order, and the inequality of access of different strata of the population to the use of economic, political and cultural resources. This supposes giving proper weight to the actions of agents located in the different scenarios formerly constructed, as social constructivist authors suggest. Even if we have stressed the responses of rural local agents in this chapter, we cannot overestimate their strength either by putting them on an equal footing with the global elites that have been so far participating in the supranational fora where the rules of the game for the emergent global order are decided.

An interesting question remains whether to ground theory in history, in daily life ethnographies, or in both? Our answer is: in both. We advocate the need for theorizing by developing new theoretical frameworks, which should be nourished by both detailed macro-historical narratives and daily life ethnographies. This does not necessarily mean, however, that we should develop 'grounded theories' by having recourse to blind empiricism, or that we should turn back to abstract and one-sided deductive theorizing.

As a result of the insights provided by our research agenda, a vision of globalization emerges that is full of intertwined multiple historical trajectories, the intended and unintended effects of purposive actions and the unintended effects of countervailing trends. To some of us, nurtured in the certainty of some 'historical laws of motion', this probably gives a sense of uneasiness and insecurity, but is not this what the current globalization processes are all about?

Acknowledgments

The authors would like to emphasize the important contributions of Lourdes Gouveia of the University of Nebraska at Omaha and our colleagues at the Pontificia Universidad Javeriana de Colombia, to the collective research projects on which this chapter is based. We are fully responsible for this version of the results.

Notes

1   The empirical material on which this chapter is based draws heavily on a series of research projects conducted at the Venezuelan Institute of Scientific Research (IVIC), Laboratory of Rural and Agrarian Studies, some of them in collaboration with other academic institutions. One of these projects, entitled 'Beyond NAFTA: The Restructuring of Agrifood Systems in Colombia and

Venezuela' emphasized the role of global and national agents in the rural and agrarian restructuring currently taking place in Colombia and Venezuela. This project was supported by a North-South Center research grant. This project gave us the opportunity to conduct a comparative fieldwork study on the impact of two national structural adjustment programmes (Colombia 1990-1995) and Venezuela (1989-1995) on local rural restructuring. Another project, entitled 'Cross-Border Links: Migrants' Strategies and Rural Restructuring in the Venezuelan and Colombian Andes', emphasized the role of local agents on both sides of the border in this same restructuring. This latter project was based on a bi-national fieldwork in Pueblo Llano, the Venezuelan receiving locality, and Cerrito, the sending municipality.

2   Both the results of the intended and non-intended effects of social actions.
3   A non-exhaustive list of the main theoretical contributions to this literature encompasses works such as: Arce and Marsden 1993; Bonanno et al. 1994; Buttel and McMichael 1990; Friedland et al. 1991, Friedmann 1982; Friedmann and McMichael 1989; Goodman and Watts 1994; Long and Long 1992; McMichael 1994; 1996; 1997; Marsden et al. 1993; Raynolds et al. 1993; van der Ploeg 1993; Whatmore 1993.
4   High and steep sites and a stony topsoil which hampers the introduction of mechanical technologies in soil preparation and harvesting.

References

Arce, A. and Marsden, T. (1993), 'The Social Construction of International Food', *Economic Geography*, Vol. 69, No. 3, pp. 293-311.

Bonanno, A., Busch, L., Friedland, W., Gouveia, L. and Mingione, E. (eds) (1994), *From Colombus to Conagra: The Globalization of Agriculture and Food*, University Press of Kansas: Lawrence.

Buttel, F. and McMichael, P. (1994), 'Reconsidering the Explanandum and Scope of Development Studies: Toward a Comparative Sociology of State-Economy Relations', in Booth, D. (ed), *Rethinking Social Development: Theory, Research and Practice*, Longman: London.

Friedland, W.H., Busch, L., Buttel, F.H. and Rudy, A.P. (eds) (1991), *Towards a New Political Economy of Agriculture*, Westview Press: Boulder.

Friedmann, H. and McMichael, P. (1989), 'Agriculture and the State System: The Rise and Decline of National Agricultures, 1870 to the Present', *Sociologia Ruralis*, Vol. 29, No. 2, pp. 93-117.

Friedmann, H. (1982), 'The Political Economy of Food: the Rise and Fall of the Postwar International Food Order', *American Journal of Sociology*, Vol. S88, pp. 248-286.

Goodman, D. and Watts, M. (1994), 'Reconfiguring the Rural or Fording the Divide? Capitalist Restructuring and the Global Agri-Food System', *The Journal of Peasant Studies*, Vol. 22, No. 1, pp. 1-49.

Llambí, L., Gouveia, L. and Arias, E. (1995), 'Global-Local Links in Latin America's New Ruralities: A Case Study in the Venezuelan Andes', in *Agrarian Questions: The Politics of Farming*, Proceedings, Vol. I, Wageningen Agricultural University: Wageningen.

Llambí, L. and Arias, E. (1996), 'Globalization, Structural Adjustment and Rural Transformations in Latin America: Comparative Case Studies in Colombia and Venezuela', in Benería, L. (ed), *Structural Adjustment in the Americas*, Cornell University Press: Ithaca.

Long, N. (1990), 'From Paradigm Lost to Paradigm Regained? The Case for an Actor-Oriented Sociology of Development', *European Review of Latin American and Caribbean Studies*, Vol. 49, pp. 3-24.

Long, N. and Long, A. (1992), *Battlefields of Knowledge: The Interlocking of Theory and Practice in Social Research and Development*, Routledge: London.

Marsden, T., Murdoch, J., Lowe, P., Munton, R. and Flynn, A. (1993), *Constructing the Countryside*, University College London Press: London.

McMichael, P. and Raynolds, L.T. (1994) 'Capitalism, Agriculture and World Economy', in Sklair, L. (ed), *Capitalism and Development*, Routledge: London.

McMichael, P. (1996), 'Globalization: Myths and Realities', *Rural Sociology*, Vol. 61, No. 1, pp. 25-55.

McMichael, P. (1997), 'Rethinking Globalization: The Agrarian Question Revisited', *Review of International Political Economy*, Vol. 4, No 4, pp. 630-62.

Raynolds, L., Myhre, D., McMichael, P, Figueroa, V. and Buttel, F.H. (1993), 'The "New" Internationalization of Agriculture: A Reformulation', *World Development*, Vol. 21, No 7, pp. 1101-21.

Van der Ploeg, J.D. (1993), 'Rural Sociology and the New Agrarian Question', *Sociologia Ruralis*, Vol. 33, No 2, pp. 240-260.

Whatmore, S. (1993), 'Global Agri-Food Complexes and the Refashioning of Rural Europe', in Amin, A. and Thrift, N. (eds), *Holding Down the Global*, Guidford: London.

6 Between Global and Local: State Mediation of Gender Relations in Farming

SALLY SHORTALL

Introduction

Farming throughout Europe and across the western world is marked by diversity. This is partly due to such factors as climate, soil, and distance from centres of consumption, but also to the fact that agriculture is a social construction. As Long and van der Ploeg (1994) note, the way agricultural practice is organized depends heavily on the actors involved in it, and the different social, economic, cultural and historical relations in which it is embedded. As a result, globalization has unfolded in many diverse ways as localities respond differently to the pervasive economic and social processes they encounter.

For women on farms, it is not only the globalization of agriculture that will affect their lives. Universal values about the position and treatment of women will also be of significance. The extent to which such values exist is of course debatable (Strassoldo, 1992; Pettman, 1997). Nonetheless, international women's conferences, International Women's Year, and UN declarations on women push for common responses to issues affecting women.

The increasing unacceptability of gender inequalities has led to a heightened awareness of the often under-valued and unrecognized work of women on farms. In this chapter, I want to look at three responses to the situation of farm women, all of which challenge the unequal position of women in farming. In three different national contexts, distinct forms of local responses have developed to the growing awareness of gender inequality within farming. I argue that these distinct responses are the result of political ideology and culture, the middle or 'meso-level' between the macro level of globalization and the micro level of local responses. This meso-level mediates between the macro effect of globalization, and frames the type of local response that evolves. Using the North of Ireland, Canada and Norway as case studies, I argue that a comparative analysis of the three political environments in which farm women are situated illustrates how political context influences the type of collective action and social change that emerges in each place.

I will argue that in order to understand the type of change that has occurred, and its impact on the way women organize, we need to consider how power is structured and distributed in the broad political sense. Focusing on the political environment in which farm women are situated is an important indicator of the type of collective action and social change that will emerge. Women in the same occupation, but in different political contexts, vary in their level of political organization and social rights. Following Jenkins and Perrow (1977), it is illustrated that concentrating on the political environment and available resources better illuminates the different situations of farm women in Norway, Canada and Northern Ireland.[1]

These three case studies have been chosen because they represent very different political contexts. They are all western countries, where family farming is the predominant system of farming. Women on farms in each place operate within a family farm and all face the gender issues this entails (Shortall, 1999). Yet local responses in each place are different, and I argue that the political context is an important explanatory factor. Norway is an example of a corporatist, social-democratic state, with a relatively strong commitment to gender equality. While Norway lagged behind other Scandinavian countries for a period with regard to gender equality, this situation has changed rapidly as a result of conscious policies (Karvonen and Selle, 1995). Most noticeably, Norway is different from the other two cases because channels to instigate gender equality policy are institutionalized, and hence terms such as 'state feminism', and 'woman friendly state'. Change in the situation of farm women is likely to be legitimated and guaranteed by the state. Canada represents a pluralist state, sympathetic of collective action and group rights, and it funds various lobby groups as organizations. One of the factors that distinguish Canada from Norway is that political space and civil society remain more bounded and interest groups and organizations lobby government from 'outside'. Organized protest groups are less likely to be incorporated within the political apparatus. Change in the Canadian context is linked to the organization, mobilization and resources of the Canadian Farm Women's Network, which I argue represent a new social movement, and which lobbies government from outside of institutional channels. I also argue that the Canadian political context fosters the development of new social movements. Northern Ireland is a contested region. Farm women's collective action is less likely given the political and religious divisions that exist and the likelihood of other primary identities. Furthermore, gender inequalities are less of a priority for a state whose stability is more closely tied to being seen to tackle religious discrimination. In addition, I will argue that the state in Ireland,[2] North and South, is based on a male breadwinner model, and consequently focuses primarily on women's role within the family. This has shaped the form of training provisions that have emerged for women. Each case study represents a very different political context. They provide a framework within which it is possible to consider the influence of the state and political ideology on the collective action of farm women and the type of social change that evolves. The focus then is *not* on farm women's lives or change in farming and how these impact on women,[3] but more specifically on the political context and how it influences the changes that have developed.

The chapter is structured around the three case studies. Each case study begins by outlining some of the relevant literature on the state, social movements and social change and relating it to the situation of farm women in that state. Then, the changes that have occurred altering the situation of women on farms are considered. The conclusions illustrate the importance of attending to the political context in which farm women are placed.

Norway, social democracy and farm women

The major distinguishing feature between egalitarian corporatist states and pluralist states, relates to the organization of political space *vis a vis* civil society. In a pluralist state, interest groups and lobbying bodies may be encouraged, but entry to political space may continue to be through formal specialized roles, in which case pressure groups remain outside the political apparatus. Alternatively, the legitimate boundaries between the public and the private, between the body politic and civil society may be more permeable, and it may be acceptable and legitimate for interest groups to occupy positions within the political space (Crouch, 1986). Norway is an example of the latter case.

The roots of Nordic egalitarianism has occupied many scholars (Esping-Andersen, 1990; Friis, 1981; Andren, 1964). Relative peace, stability and economic growth in homogeneous societies provided a favorable context. Norway is characterized by its commitment to economic, political and social equality. The standard of living is high, and it has a highly developed welfare state, with a high degree of government regulation. Norway's welfare state, like that of all social democracies, is couched within a broad egalitarian ideology (Esping-Andersen, 1988, p.170).

Of great significance to women's interest groups in Nordic countries is the institutionalized nature of interest demands nurtured by a corporatist social-democratic state. In other words, as in many other places, women do organize and mobilize around their interests. However, what is different about this political context is that these efforts are met with greater political support, and there are channels in place, which allow a more central political representation of these interests. The mobilization of women has influenced the institutionalization of subsequent equality policies. In this political environment, the mobilization of women is matched by political institutions and politics that are committed to equality and solidarity as social democratic values. In this context, the mobilization of women is strengthened by the legitimacy and guaranteed rights afforded women by political institutions (Karvonen and Selle, 1995). The structure of the state in Scandinavia, along with a strongly egalitarian civil society, has enabled demands from social movements including feminism, to influence the political culture, political institutions and political priorities (Siim, 1993). The boundaries between civil society and political institutions are permeable.

Norway's interest or pressure groups tend to be included within formal institutional channels, largely explained by its homogeneity, and the nature of its political system (Storing, 1963). Most usually then, interest groups have their concerns represented in parliament. This is apparent when we turn to women. Gender issues are more likely to be represented at a central state level rather than by representatives or autonomous feminist interest groups (Charles, 1992). In Norway, as in all Nordic Countries, public commissions were established in the late 1960s to examine the role of women. On the basis of their reports, advisory councils on equality between the sexes were formed within state bureaucracies. In this way, the state absorbed ideas about the position of women and tried to further equality by enacting legislation and other social policy measures (Haavio-Mannila, 1981). In an international context, women score well in terms of their social position, educational attainment, economic activity and political participation.

In short, the whole political system in Norway is imbued with an ideology supportive of gender equality. This has, and continues to be the basis of social change in Norway. Cognitive frameworks of acceptable social roles for women have changed significantly, and rapidly, in Norway.

State intervention in the farm sector occurs nearly entirely on behalf of the enterprise (Meyer and Labao, 1994). It tends to deal with farm business matters rather than farming culture. It is not surprising that the state which did dramatically intervene in customary farming practice was a social democratic Nordic state; Norway.

Farm women and ownership of land

The patrilineal line of inheritance is pervasive in the industrialized world, and for example, it has been documented for Ireland (Shortall, 1991; 1992; O'Hara, 1994), Britain (Gasson, 1984; Whatmore, 1991), Australia (Alston, 1990; James, 1982), Canada (Reimer, 1986; Ghorayshi, 1989) and the United States (Rosenfeld, 1985; Sachs, 1994). The typical passing of land from father to son is considered one of the key sources of inequalities in gender relations in agriculture (Gasson et al., 1988). The patrilineal line of inheritance is a central social structure in agriculture which powerfully reinforces the image of farming as a male occupation (Shortall, 1992). For the majority of women on farms, their entry is through marriage. Farming practice fashions sons rather than daughters as family 'successors' (Whatmore et al., 1994). Where women do own land, it is an important dimension of power (Salamon and Keim, 1979); however, the patrilineal line of inheritance makes this an unusual event. Inheritance laws in Norway are unique, as I will now consider.

A strong cultural commitment to gender equality brought forward a law of succession which gives the right to take over the farm intact to the eldest child irrespective of gender (Haugen, 1994; Jodahl, 1994). In spite of a strong male resistance to the new law, the state brought it forward as a matter of principle (Haugen and Brandth, 1994; Blekesaune et al., 1993). The ideological commitment to gender equality meant this policy was introduced by the state, despite resistance.

There is no doubt that formal political equality is of limited value if the traditional practice of unequal gender relations persists. Even so, legal changes may constitute the first step (Haugen, 1994). The allodial law has changed the context of women on farms in Norway, through challenging the patrilineal line of inheritance. It questions the basis of legitimacy of traditional gender-defined farming practice. This challenge came from the *State*. The social democratic nature of the state means that the organization of women around feminist issues is likely to be channeled through the state. The deep commitment to gender equality creates a situation where far reaching measures to advance equality in farming are taken. This is what has happened in Norway.

Canada, a pluralist state and farm women

While definitions of collective action vary, it is generally understood to mean the collective pooling of resources to a common end (Tilly, 1981b). Collective action covers a wide range of activity, from petitioning, parading to strikes and revolutions. Social movements are seen as a sub-area of collective action. What distinguishes social movements are their attempt to change existing social relationships, processes or institutions, rather than the political framework in which social groups and organizations operate (Gusfield, 1981; Tilly, 1981b). It is, of course, not always the case that social movements succeed in achieving change, and nor are social movements the only means of social change. This is clear in the analysis of the three case studies.

Research on social movements has focused on the microsocial-psychological aspects of movements, the importance of ideology, the culture of protest and a multitude of other important elements (McAdam et al., 1988). However, in this chapter, the social movement literature that considers the availability of resources and the political environment is the most pertinent. Prominent in resource mobilization literature is the argument that psychological factors are insufficient to understand social action. Psychological factors, a sense of injustice, and indeed social action are too pervasive to explain how and when a social movement will become active and when it is likely to achieve success. Instead, macro-analysis of resource mobilization and rational action, as it has been advanced by Tilly (1981b), suggests that key elements in collective action are the significance of the state, the structure of power, and the organization of routine politics (p. 21). Similarly, Jenkins and Perrow (1977) examine the success of farm worker insurgents compared with earlier periods and argue that rather than focusing on internal motivating factors of discontent, a focus on the external political environment and available resources better explains the success of the farm workers' protests in the 1960s. They argue that the altered political environment within which the challenge operated was a key element. They further hold that a 'powerless' group like farm workers require strong and sustained outside support if they are to be successful (p. 251). Challenges are more likely to be successful when there is intervention by liberal organizations. A similar argument is made by Gale (1986) who maintains that a political system that includes agencies already sympathetic to the movement is very important. Two other aspects of the social movement literature are relevant for the arguments advanced in this chapter. Frame alignment is the process of tying the aims of new movements to existing accepted values, which act as a legitimating frame and increase the likely success of the movement. Finally, the extent to which a group has ties and identities interwoven with other groups in a given population, reduces the likelihood of a distinct social movement arising (McAdam et al., 1988).

While Norway is a relatively homogeneous society, Canada is noticeably heterogeneous. Canada is characterized by multiculturalism and it attempts to accommodate native peoples, immigrants, and Quebecois. A distinctive feature of Canada is that it not only protects individual rights, but also the rights of individuals as member of certain communities (Kymlicka, 1994). The Canadian Charter of Rights and Freedoms protects minority-language rights, Aboriginal rights, affirms multiculturalism, and protects against discriminatory treatment on the grounds of sex or race (Taylor, 1992). Canada is characterized by difference, and it attempts to protect and accommodate difference. Indeed, failure to do so will result in its demise, as Quebec's referenda on separatism illustrate. Women are seen as another group to be accommodated, and debates about community and collective rights usually refer to women as well as ethnic groups and immigrants (see for example Baker, 1994). Canada is unusual in the level of resources made available to groups to organize around their interests and needs,[4] and it is in this pluralist, well endowed society that a farm women's social movement has emerged. It is one of a number of autonomous groups lobbying Government to implement change, alongside -for example- native peoples, immigrants, and environmentalists. The existence of these groups is a feature of a pluralist society (Charles, 1992). While there are many interest groups in Canada, they are not incorporated into the institutional channels to the same extent as interest groups in Norway.

Canada has a relatively active and visible feminist movement. It was influenced by the development of the American feminist movement in the 1960s, and the Canadian feminist movement has occasionally been more successful at achieving legal reform than its southern counterparts (Backhouse and Flaherty, 1992). The farm women's movement developed in the 1970s. While it did not develop out of the more general Canadian feminist movement, the organization of farm women was no doubt facilitated by its existence.

The first farm women's group in Canada was formed in 1975, and by 1991, there were forty two new farm women's groups (Shortall, 1993; 1994). Three key factors set the scene for the farm women's groups to develop. Firstly, women initially organized groups because of their concern about the 'farm crisis,' i.e., increased farm bankruptcies, financial difficulties and cutbacks in rural social services. Secondly, the women's movement meant that increasing attention was paid to the concerns and views of women, and increased state funding was provided for projects dealing with women's issues. Thirdly, a high profile divorce case, Murdoch v. Murdoch, caused a great deal of public debate about the value of farm women's work. Irene Murdoch worked on her husband's farm, and after an arduous legal battle, she was awarded one quarter of the ranch's value. More high profile cases followed the Murdoch case, and also raised the question about the appropriate division of land on divorce. This caused public debate about the value of the work women do on the farm and in the farm house (MacKenzie, 1992).

The farm women's groups then, came to being in a context where women and farm women received increased attention. In addition, farm women began to organize themselves following International Women's year, which had led to an increase in state funding to assist the organization of women (Bruners, 1985). This reflects a particular state response to a global women's event. The source of funding was primarily through the office of the Secretary of State, and women were encouraged to focus on feminist issues rather than farming issues, which the women involved considered an artificial distinction (Shortall, 1993). Nonetheless, it provided a frame with which the farm women could align, and by doing so, legitimate their activities and access resources. The Canadian Farm Women's Network (CFWN), a National umbrella organization for the scattered farm women's groups was formed in 1985. It is the CFWN, not the Canadian State, which has provided the main impetus for change regarding the status of farm women through lobbying, providing networks and proposing alternatives.

Farm women and ownership of land

While ownership of farm property is an issue that the CFWN has acted on, it is in a way very different from the Norwegian case. An Ontario women's group published (1987) and later revised (1994) a manual titled; *Cover Your Assets: A guide to Farm Partnerships* (MacKenzie, 1992; Teather, 1996). This booklet details both the benefits for the farm (tax advantages, loan entitlements), and the necessity for women to legalize their stake in their business partnership. The patrilineal line of inheritance is not questioned, rather women are encouraged to safeguard their legal position after entering a farm business, usually through marriage.

Representation in farming organizations

Farm women quickly realized that they met few women in farming organizations, in government farming bodies and committees, or on marketing boards. When they raised this issue, they were often told no suitably qualified women existed (Shortall, 1994). The CFWN decided to form a 'talent bank' of farm women; this is a directory of qualified farm women who can be proposed as vacancies arise in farming organizations. Provincial networks provide training for women who wish to sit on boards and councils. This strategy has had some limited success. Nonetheless, women continue to struggle to ensure adequate representation (Farm Living, November 9, 1995). Farm women have noted, too, that it is more difficult to include women in traditional grass-root type farming organizations, rather than in federal or provincial government farming organizations, boards and committees (Farm Living, October 23 1994). The CFWN has called for changed regulations regarding membership, and has also urged farming organizations to deliberately recruit, support and develop women at grassroots, district and regional levels.

The Canadian Farm Women's Network highlights the limited number of women in farming organizations. Through their talent bank and lobbying of organizations, they actively try to increase the representation of women. In doing so, they are questioning both previously taken for granted farming norms and the legitimacy of institutions that are unrepresentative on a gender basis.

The farming media

The CFWN, and most provincial farm women's networks, issue regular newsletters. This provides an alternative source of farming information for women. It also provides a forum where women can discuss and debate issues of particular relevance to women, such as partnership arrangements, the availability of credit for women operators, and the status of women's farm work. In addition, the farm women's networks provide training for farm women's groups to deal effectively with the media. Women have received training on public speaking and drafting press releases. In recent years, many provincial newspapers with farming supplements carry regular articles about the farm women's networks, and short pieces written by farm women.

The farm women's newsletters have a wide circulation amongst members. Although modest, there is increased representation of women in more main stream farming media. Again, the farm women's movement have acted as a key force bringing about change through providing an alternative form of communication, and training women to effectively deal with the general farming media.

Defining farm work

A key concern of the CFWN is how to define farm work and how to ascertain the value of farm women's work. It is a frequently discussed topic in the newsletters and at farm women's conferences. Since 1990, editorials in the CFWN newsletter have urged women to make their farm work visible by changing the title of their work so that it can be counted in the census of agriculture (Shortall, 1994). Newsletters feature articles by farm women that say discussion and dialogue has raised their appreciation of the often invisible and unrecognized work they do (CFWN newsletter 3, 4, 1991). One of the most significant achievements of farm women's network was their successful lobbying of Statistics Canada to change the Census of Agriculture questionnaire. Prior to 1991, it was only possible to cite one person as farm operator. Women argued that in instances of partnerships between men and women, it was usually the man who was cited in the census form as the farm operator, thus rendering women invisible. This practice was changed in 1991, and now up to three operators can be named. It is generally accepted that the change came about because of effective lobbying by farm women's network (Farm Women's Bureau, 1996). The change only increases the visibility of women in terms of the typically 'male' farm work that they do, but nonetheless, it marked a very important triumph for the farm women's network.

The liberal pluralist Canadian State responded to international events on women by providing more funding for women to organize. This, combined with its protection of group rights, provided a context for the development of the farm women's social movement.

The North of Ireland: a male-breadwinner state, conflict and farm women

Both the North and South of Ireland are, in many respects, 'male breadwinner' states. Strong male breadwinner states tend to draw a firm dividing line between public and private responsibility. While women participate in the labor market, this participation tends to be part-time, and there is a lack of childcare services. All of these criteria apply to Ireland, which Lewis (1992) advances as one of her examples of an historically strong male breadwinner state, her other example being Britain. Thus, in the North, although married women have, in a European context, a relatively high participation rate in paid employment, they are also more likely to be employed part-time and in low paid jobs. The UK has one of the poorest provisions of childcare services within the European Union, and until recently, the North had the worst provision within the UK (Welsh provisions have recently slipped below those in the North). Both the British and Irish states, albeit in slightly different ways, continue to advance a male breadwinner model (O'Connor and Shortall, 1999). It is in a context of a divided society where gender equality is of a lower priority than religious and nationalist identities, and one where a male breadwinner model is prevalent, that farm women in the North exist. The development of farm family committees, almost entirely made up of women, to deal with women's and farm family issues, neatly dovetails with Lewis' male breadwinner model. While men are exclusively organized around the productive, economic, elements of farming, the organization of women by farmers' unions, focuses on family and women's issues, both treated together and separately from economic concerns.

Considering whether or not the political environment in Northern Ireland is likely to foster collective action by farm women immediately signals the political tensions; the legitimacy of the state in Northern Ireland is a divisive political issue. The focus by the British State in Northern Ireland has tended to be on religious discrimination and political divisions, and it is argued that this focus on religious inequalities has shifted attention from gender inequalities (Kramer et al., 1996; Davies, et al., 1995; Maxwell, 1993). In addition, supporting McAdam et al.'s (1988) argument that collective action is less likely to emerge in a group with strong ties to other groups and identities, women's identity in Northern Ireland is fractured by politics and religion (Roulston, 1989; Rooney, 1995; McWilliams, 1993). This is not to suggest that women have not participated in collective action, or in women's groups in Northern Ireland. The contrary is the case. Many potential leaders of women's movements were key players in political and community activities. Where women did organize, the groups frequently divided on religious and political issues (Roulston, 1989). Many feminist issues are political, and divide along political lines (Meeney, 1993) - reflecting fractured identities. It is clear, then, that the political situation in Northern Ireland does not allow it to be the most supportive political context for women to organize, in terms of the prevalence of an ideology committed to gender equality, or the priority it will receive in the allocation of resources relative to religious equality. In addition, women's identity is closely connected to their religious and political context, and in the past it was in activities related to this that they have tended to organize.

Northern Ireland then, is a conservative region, where political and religious divisions are of paramount importance. Unlike Norway, where gender equality is a key political goal, in the North, religious inequalities are the key political concern. Unlike Canada, where state funding for women's groups (including farm women's groups) is widely practiced, women's groups in Northern Ireland receive less funding than in the rest of the UK (McWilliams, 1993). Gender issues are not of the same priority as political and religious issues. The role of the state and of the women's movement in mobilizing farm women is, thus, likely to be more restricted.

Women in agriculture

Almost all women on farms in Northern Ireland 'married into' their occupation. Few women farm independently, although some women have sole responsibility for the farm if their spouse has off farm employment. In general, women are very involved in their farms (Shortall, 1996).

The participation of women in agricultural education and training is low. For the year 1994/1995, 1,151 people enrolled in full and part-time agricultural courses in the three agricultural colleges in the North, of whom between one and four and a half per cent were women. On-going training is provided for adults in farming, consisting of short courses and discussion groups. Again attendance is almost entirely male and the discussion groups are colloquially known as 'the men's groups'.

The formation of farm women's groups

Four out of forty two agricultural advisers in Northern Ireland are women. One of these felt that farm business plans would be improved if women were more vociferous in stating their opinions and ideas when farm business plans were discussed. She was also aware that women were doing farm accounts and would benefit from a more complete understanding of the financial state of the farm. Despite repeatedly asking women to come along to existing training provisions, women did not participate. She decided to organize some training specifically for women, and discussed the idea with two of the other women advisers. Then, they actively solicited women on the farms with which they had contact. These three women advisers are responsible for the creation of the five farm women's groups.

The advisers formed the groups in response to a practical, technical problem. They thought that the farms with which they had contact would be more effective if the women on those farms were trained. In other words, the formation of the groups was not motivated by political, moral or feminist considerations. Clearly, there is a gender factor involved in the fact that it was women advisers who recognized the lack of training for women as problematic.

The farm women's groups

The change that has occurred in Northern Ireland is that some women are now receiving agricultural training. This change is not the result of the state, or a social movement/organization by women, and it is not even the result of a change in organizational practice. It rather emerged because of the action of a number of key individuals. Indeed, it is not clear that these individuals have organizational support. Colleagues of the women advisers continue to have difficulty accepting the training as such rather than as an additional provision for women. This relates to the difficulties conceptualizing women's work roles. In order to recognize the value of training, it is necessary to recognize the work. The training *is* gendered, it is for farm women and no doubt this exacerbates the problem as training for men, which is no doubt taken as the norm, is overtly organized around types of farming (dairying, tillage, etc.) and the virtual gender exclusivity is not formally stated.

Key individuals within an organization have made a difference. However, it is difficult to assess how sustained or extensive an exercise this can be without the institutional commitment of the state. The agricultural advisers were not concerned about changing the system of agricultural training, but rather with assisting farm women gain access to training. This leaves the existing model, based on the idea of the male farmer, intact. The provision for women is additional, and it leads to some irrational practices like duplicating sessions with the vet and meal representative for the women's groups and the men's discussion groups.

The training provided is a provision particularly for women. It is for women identified on the basis of their involvement in a family farm. The groups do relate to the intrinsic interests of women on farms in that they provide access to training, but the participation of women is tied to their membership of a family unit. Hence, the groups are known colloquially as the 'wives' groups or clubs. This reflects the male breadwinner ethos of the state.

In the last few years in Northern Ireland, forms of inequality and discrimination other than religious are receiving increased attention (McWilliams, 1993). A recent policy has brought all government departments under scrutiny to see if their policies are discriminatory under five headings, one of which is gender. This may provide a wider context of support for the farm women's groups. The groups are pointed to as one of the department of agriculture's provisions for women. This may not result in a great deal of change in gender and training patterns, however. Frequently, existing programmes are elevated for reasons of political expediency. The training groups were formed to provide women with access, not to question the gendered nature and structure of agriculture training. In addition, as it stands now, the provision only reaches a particular group of women. On a more positive note however, the formation of the training groups has flagged training for farm women as an issue, and in the current political climate it is possibly one that will receive increased attention.

The contentious nature of the state in Northern Ireland means that political and religious inequalities have priority status. In addition, the male breadwinner ethos means that men are viewed the primary earners. Both of these factors affect the way farm women organize; feminist issues are not a priority and farm men are seen as the breadwinners.

Conclusions

In Norway, Canada and Northern Ireland, particular aspects of farming culture that contribute to the absence of women from the public space of farming have altered. In order to understand the changes that have occurred in each place it is necessary to consider the meso-level of the state and political ideology that exists between, and shapes, the form in which globalization processes are adopted, and the type of local reaction that occurs.

Following Tilly (1981b), it is argued that key elements in collective action are the role of the state, and the structure of routine politics. In each case, the type of change that has occurred is reflective of the wider political context. In Norway, a state committed to gender equality directly changed the system of inheritance. In Canada, a pluralist society, sympathetic to and supportive of organized groups, funds the Canadian Farm Women's Network who have increased women's visibility in census of agriculture questionnaires, and who strive to increase women's presence in the farming media and farming organizations. The CFWN, however, lobbies from outside of institutional channels. In Northern Ireland, while the State appears to be obsessed with religious discrimination and has advanced detailed measures and policies to monitor such discrimination, it has also carefully ensured that such measures are restricted to religious discrimination. In Northern Ireland, change for farm women has not occurred because of central state intervention, or through the representation of a funded interest group, but rather through the concern of women agricultural advisers with a technical problem - women on farms are untrained. In addition, the state operates on the basis of a male breadwinner model. In other words, it treats women as though they were dependent on a male earner. The provision of training groups, colloquially known as 'the wives' clubs', fits in with this ideology.

Together, these case studies illustrate the multifaceted way in which farming culture affects the situation of women, and the many processes by which change can occur. For a long time women have organized around feminist issues. In addition to this micro activity, there is an increasing macro level acceptance that gender inequalities are inadmissible. It is argued in this chapter that an analysis of the political context illustrates the mediation of micro and macro events by the state. Norway, an example of a social democratic state, has an entrenched commitment to gender equality. It is this ideological commitment, combined with the inclusion of interest groups within the state apparatus that motivated the change in the allodial law. In Canada, the sympathetic political view to women's organizations meant the CFWN was able to access resources in the early stages of formation, and indeed continues to do so. In addition, the liberal Canadian State is quite receptive to organized groups, as is clear in this case where it is funding an organization to lobby the state itself. It is an example of the pluralist society described by Charles (1992) which supports autonomous feminist interest groups, while Scandinavian social democratic states are more likely to embody their interests at a central level, as in the case of Norway. In Northern Ireland, given the priority of nationalist questions and the related threat to stability, and the state's determination to develop anti-discrimination measures specifically for religion, gender issues are less of a state concern, and there are fewer resources available to support women's organization. In addition, the concept of organized activity to lobby the government is entirely different in Northern Ireland than in Canada, as in the former such activity frequently questions the legitimacy of the state. Women have fractured identities along religious and political lines. The training for farm women that has emerged is the result of key individuals reacting to a technical farming problem, and the women involved were approached on the basis of their identity as members of a family farm.

In all three cases, change has occurred. It could be argued that individual cases represent more or less deep-rooted change. The central argument advanced in this chapter is that the state mediates between global values on gender equality and the local response that occurs.

Notes

1. In the North of Ireland, interviews with agricultural advisers and farm women in training groups were carried out in 1994/1995. This is described in greater detail elsewhere (Shortall, 1996). Work with the Canadian Farm Women's Network was conducted between 1990-1992 (Shortall 1993; 1994). While the Norwegian case is built from secondary analysis, this is justifiable on a number of grounds; firstly the purpose of this article is not to establish myself as an expert on Norwegian agriculture and the lives of Norwegian farm women, but rather to pen a broad illustrative case of a different political context to that presented by the other two case studies. As the article illustrates, Norway provides an ideal example. Secondly, Norway has a very rich literature available in English on farm women and change (see Shortall, 1996, footnote i), and on gender equality, social democracy and the state, of which I have availed.
2. I recognize the difficulties of referring to the North of Ireland as a state, but I think it is justifiable for the purposes of this chapter (see O'Dowd, 1991).
3. There is a wealth of information on this topic for each of the three case studies. Interested readers should consult for Norway; Haugen, 1990; Haugen and Brandth, 1994; Haugen, 1994; Brandth, 1995; Brandth and Haugen, 1997; Verstad, 1998; Brandth and Haugen, 1998; Blekesaune, 1996. For Canada; Reimer, 1986; Shortall, 1993; 1994; Shaver and Reimer, 1991; Teather, 1994; MacKenzie, 1992. For Northern Ireland; Heenan and Birrell, 1996; Shortall, 1996; Kilmurray and Bradley, 1989.
4. For a discussion of the resources Quebec makes available to Jews and Greeks, see, for example, Rosenberg and Jedwab, 1992.

References

Adren, N. (1964), *Government and Politics in the Nordic Countries*, Almquist and Wiksell: Stockholm.

Alston, M. (1990), 'Feminism and Farm Women', *Australian Social Work*, Vol.43, pp. 213-234.

Alston, M. (1995), 'Women and Their Work on Australian Farms', *Rural Sociology,* Vol. 60, No 3, pp. 521-532.

Backhouse, C. and Flaherty, D. (eds) (1992), *Challenging Times: The Women's Movement in Canada and the United States*, McGill-Queen's University Press: Montreal.

Baker, J. (1994), 'Introduction', in Baker J. (ed), *Group Rights*, University of Toronto Press: Toronto.

Bell, J. and Pandy, U. (1989), 'Gender-role Stereotypes in Australian Farm Advertising', *Media Information Australia*, Vol. 51, pp. 45-59.

Blekesaune, A., Haney, W. and Haugen, M. (1993), 'On the Question of the Feminization of Production on Part-time Farms: Evidence from Norway', *Rural Sociology*, Vol. 58, No 1, pp. 111-129.

Blekesaune, A. (1996), *Family Farming in Norway. An Analysis of Structural Changes within Farm Households Between 1975 and 1990*, Department of Sociology and Political Science, University of Trondheim, Rapport No 6/96, Centre for Rural Research.

Bourke, J. (1993), *Husbandry to Housewifery - Women, Economic Change, and Housework in Ireland, 1890-1914*, Clarendon Press: Oxford.

Brandth, B. (1995), 'Rural Masculinity in Transition - Gender Images in Tractor Advertisements', *Journal of Rural Studies*, Vol. 11, No 2, pp. 123-133.

Brandth, B. and Haugen, M. (1997), 'Rural Women, Feminism and the Politics of Identity', *Sociologia Ruralis*, Vol. 37, No. 3, pp. 325-344.

Brandth, B. and Haugen, M. (1998), 'Breaking into a Masculine Discourse. Women and Farm Forestry', *Sociologia Ruralis*, Vol. 38, No 3, pp. 427-442.

Bruners, D. (1985), 'The Influence of the Women's Liberation Movement on the Lives of Canadian Farm Women', *Resources for Feminist Research*, Vol. 14, No 3, pp. 18-19.

Charles, M. (1992), 'Cross-national Variation in Occupational Sex Segregation', *American Sociological Review*, Vol. 57, pp. 483-502.

Connolly, C. (1995), 'Ourselves Alone? Clar na mBan Conference Report', *Feminist Review*, Vol. 50, pp. 118-127.

Crompton, R. (1995), 'Paying the Price of Care: Comparative Studies of Women's Employment and the Value of Caring', *Working Paper 4*, Demos: London.

Crouch, C. (1986), 'Sharing Public Space: States and Organized Interests in Western Europe', in Hall, J. (ed), *States in History*, Basil Blackwell Ltd: Oxford.

Davidoff, L. (1974), 'Mastered for Life: Servant and Wife in Victorian and Edwardian England', *Journal of Social History*, Summer, pp. 406-428.

Davies, C., Heaton, N., Robinson, G. and McWilliams, M. (1995), *A Matter of Small Importance? Catholic and Protestant Women in the Northern Ireland Labour Market*, The Equal Opportunities Commission: Belfast.

Duggan, C. (1987), 'Farming Women or Farming Wives? Women in the Farming Press', in Curtin, C., Jackson, P. and O'Connor, B. (eds), *Gender in Irish Society*, Galway University Press: Galway.

Elbert, S. (1988), 'Women and Farming: Changing Structures, Changing Roles', in Haney, W. and Knowles, J. (eds), *Women and Farming. Changing Roles, Changing Structures*, Rowman and Allanheld: New Jersey.

Esping-Andersen, G. (1990), *The Three Worlds of Welfare Capitalism*, Princeton University Press: Princeton.

Esping-Andersen, G. (1988), *Politics against Markets*, Princeton University Press: New Jersey.

European Commission (1988), *Women in Agriculture*, Supplement to Women of Europe: Brussels.

Farm Women's Bureau (1996), Circular March, Vol. 1, No 1.

Friis, E. (ed.) (1981), *Nordic Democracy*, Det Danske Selskab: Copenhagen.

Gale, R. (1986), 'Social Movements and the State: The Environmental Movement, Counter-Movement and Governmental Agencies', *Sociological Perspectives*, Vol. 29, pp. 202-240.

Gasson, R. (1984), 'Farm Women in Europe: Their Need for Off-farm Employment', *Sociologia Ruralis*, Vol. 24, No 3/4, pp. 16-29.

Gasson, R. (1992), 'Farmers' Wives: Their Contribution to the Farm Business', *Journal of Agricultural Economics*, Vol. 43, pp. 74-87.

Gasson, R., Crow, G., Errington, A., Hutson, J., Marsden, T. and Winter, D.M. (1988), 'The Farm as a Family Business: A Review', *Journal of Agricultural Economics*, Vol. 39, No 1, pp. 1-41.

Ghorayshi, P. (1989), 'The Indispensable Nature of Wives' Work for the Farm Family Enterprise', *The Canadian Review of Sociology and Anthropology*, Vol. 26, No 4, pp. 571-595.

Gusfield, J. (1981), 'Social Movements and Social Change: Perspectives of Linearity and Fluidity', in Kriesberg, L. (ed), *Research in Social Movements, Conflicts and Change*, JAI Press Inc.: Connecticut.

Haavio-Mannila, E. (1981), 'The Position of Women', in Friis, E. (ed), *Nordic Democracy,* Det Danske Selskab: Copenhagen.

Halsaa, B., Hernes, H.M. and Sinkkonen, S. (1985), 'Introduction', in Haavio-Mannila, E. et al. (eds), *Unfinished Democracy - Women in Nordic Politics*, Pergamon Press: Oxford.

Haugen, M. and Brandth, B. (1994), 'Gender Differences in Modern Agriculture. The Case of Female Farmers in Norway', *Gender and Society*, Vol. 8, No 2, pp.206-229.

Haugen, M. S. (1994), 'Rural Women's Status in Family and Property Law: Lessons from Norway', in Whatmore, S., Marsden, T. and Lowe, P. (eds), *Gender and Rurality*, David Fulton Publishers Ltd: London.

Haugen, M. S. (1990), 'Female Farmers in Norwegian Agriculture: From Traditional Farm Women to Professional Farmers', *Sociologia Ruralis*, Vol. 30, No 2, pp. 197-209.

Heenan, D. and Birrell, D. (1997), 'Farm Wives in Northern Ireland and the Gendered Division of Labour', in Leonard, M. and Byrne, A. (eds), *Women and Irish Society: A Sociological Reader*, Beyond the Pale Publications: Belfast.

Hernes, H. (1988), 'The Welfare State Citizenship of Scandinavian Women', in Jones, B. and Jonasdottir, A. (eds), *The Political Interests of Gender,* Sage Publications: London.

Hernes, H. and Hanninen-Salmenin, E. (1985), 'Women in the Corporate System', in Haavio-Mannila, E. et al. (eds), *Unfinished Democracy - Women in Nordic Politics*, Pergamon Press: Oxford.

Jenkins, J. and Perrow, C. (1977), 'Insurgency of the Powerless: Farm Worker Movements (1946-1972)', *American Sociological Review*, Vol. 42, pp.249-268.

Jodahl, T. (1994), 'Northern Europe: Farm Women in the Nordic Countries', in van der Burg, M. and Endeveld, M. (eds), *Women on Family Farms. Gender*

Research, EC Policies and New Perspectives, Circle for Rural European Studies: Wageningen.

Karvonen, L. and Selle, P. (1995), 'Introduction: Scandinavia: A Case Apart', in Karvonen, L. and Selle, P. (eds), *Women in Nordic Politics. Closing the Gap.* Dartmouth Publishing Company: Hampshire.

Kennedy, L. (1991), 'Farm Succession in Modern Ireland: Elements of a Theory of Inheritance', *Economic History Review*, Vol. XLIV, No 3, pp. 477-499.

Kilmurray, A. and Bradley, C. (1989), *Rural Women in South Armagh: Needs and Aspirations*, Rural Action Project: Belfast.

Kremer, J., Hallmark, A., Cleland, J., Ross, V., Duncan, J, Linday, B. and Berwick, S. (1996), 'Gender and Equal Opportunities in Public Sector Organizations', *Journal of Occupational and Organizational Psychology*, Vol. 69, pp. 183-198.

Kymlicka, W. (1994), 'Individual and Community Rights', in Baker, J. (ed), *Group Rights*, University of Toronto Press: Toronto.

Lewis, J. (1992), 'Gender and the Development of Welfare Regimes', *Journal of European Social Policy*, Vol. 2, No 3, pp. 159-173.

MacKenzie, F. (1992), '"The worse it got, the more we laughed": A Discourse of Resistance Among Farmers of Eastern Ontario', *Society and Space: Environment and Planning Development D*, Vol. 10, No 6, pp. 691-714.

Mann, M. (1986), 'A Crisis in Stratification Theory?', in Crompton, R. and Mann, M. (eds), *Gender and Stratification*, Polity Press: Oxford.

Maxwell, P. (1993), 'Equal Pay Legislation - Problems and Prospects', in Davies, C. and McLaughlin, E. (eds), *Women, Employment and Social Policy in Northern Ireland: A Problem Postponed?*, Policy Research Institute: Belfast.

McAdam, D., McCarthy, J. and Zald, M.N. (1988), 'Social Movements', in Smelser N. (ed), *The Handbook of Sociology*, Sage Publications: London.

McWilliams, M. (1993), 'The Church, the State and the Women's Movement in Northern Ireland', in Smyth, A. (ed), *Irish Women's Studies Reader*, Attic Press: Dublin.

Meaney, G. (1993), 'Sex and Nation: Women in Irish Culture and Politics', in Smyth, A. (ed), *Irish Women's Studies Reader*, Attic Press: Dublin.

Meyer, K. and Labao, L.M. (1994), 'Engendering the Farm Crisis: Women's Political Response in USA', in Whatmore, S., Marsden, T. and Lowe, P. (eds), *Gender and Rurality*, David Fulton Publishers Ltd: London.

O'Connor P. and Shortall, S. (1999), 'Does the Border Make the Difference? Women's Employment in Irish Society', in Breen, R., Heath A. and Whelan, C.T. (eds), *Irish Society North and South*, Oxford University Press: Oxford.

O'Dowd, L. (1991), 'The State of Ireland: Some Reflections on Research', *Irish Journal of Sociology*, Vol. 1, No 1, pp. 96-106.

O'Hara, P. (1994), 'Out of the Shadows - Women on Family Farms and their Contribution to Agriculture and Rural Development', in van der Burg, M. and Endeveld, M. (eds), *Women on Family Farms. Gender Research, EC Policies and New Perspectives*, Circle for Rural European Studies: Wageningen.

Ontario Farm Women's Network Newsletter (1991), Vol. 3, No 4.

Osborne, R. and Cormack, R. (1989), 'Fair Employment: Towards Reform in Northern Ireland', *Policy and Politics*, Vol. 17, No 4, pp. 287-294.

Pettman, J. (1997), 'Gender Issues', in Baylis, J, and Smith, S. (eds), *The Globalization of World Politics*, Oxford University Press: Oxford.

Reimer, B. (1986), 'Women as Farm Labour', *Rural Sociology*, Vol. 51, No 2, pp.143-155.

Rooney, E. (1995), 'Political Division, Practical Alliance: Problems for Women in Conflict', *Journal of Women's History*, Vol. 6, No 7, pp. 40-49.

Rosenberg, M. and Jedwab, J. (1992), 'Institutional Completeness, Ethnic Organizational Style and the Role of the State: the Jewish, Italian and Greek Communities of Montreal', *The Canadian Review of Sociology and Anthropology*, Vol. 29, No 3, pp. 266-287.

Rosenfeld, R. (1985), *Farm Women: Work, Farm and Family in the United States*, University of North Carolina Press: North Carolina.

Roulston, C. (1989), 'Women on the Margin: The Women's Movement in Northern Ireland 1973-1988', *Science and Society*, Vol. 53, No 2, pp. 219-236.

Sachs, C. (1994), 'The Invisible Farmers: Women in Agricultural Production', in van der Burg, M. and Endeveld, M. (eds), *Women on Family Farms. Gender Research, EC Policies and New Perspectives*, Circle for Rural European Studies: Wageningen.

Salamon, S. and Keim, A.M. (1979), 'Land Ownership and Women's Power in a Midwestern Farming Community', *Journal of Marriage and Family*, Vol. 41, pp. 109-119.

Saskatchewan Women's Agricultural Network (Swan) Newsletter (1995), Fall.

Shaver, F. and Reimer, B. (1991), 'Economy and Household: The Gender-based Division of Labour on Quebec Farms', *Research in Rural Sociology and Development*, Vol. 5, pp. 131-141.

Shortall, S. (1991), 'The Dearth of Data on Irish Farm Wives: A Critical Review of the Literature', *The Economic and Social Review*, Vol. 22, No 4, pp. 311-332.

Shortall, S. (1992), 'Power Analysis and Farm Wives: An Empirical Study of the Power Relationships Affecting Women on Irish Farms', *Sociologia Ruralis*, Vol. 32, No 4, pp. 431-451.

Shortall, S. (1993), 'Irish and Canadian Farm Women: Some Similarities, Differences and Comments', *The Canadian Review of Sociology and Anthropology*, Vol. 30, No 2, pp. 172-191.

Shortall, S. (1994), 'Farm Women's Groups: Feminist or Farming or Community Groups, or New Social Movements?', *Sociology*, Vol. 28, No 1, pp. 279-291.

Shortall, S. (1996), 'Training to be Farmers or Wives? Agricultural Training for women in Northern Ireland', *Sociologia Ruralis*, Vol. 36, No 3, pp. 269-285.

Shortall, S. (1999), *Women and Farming: Power and Property*, Macmillan Press: Basingstoke.

Siim, B. (1993), 'The Gendered Scandinavian Welfare States: The Interplay between Women's Roles as Mothers, Workers and Citizens in Denmark', in Lewis, J. (ed), *Women and Social Policies in Europe*, Edward Elgar: Hants.

Storing, J. (1963), *Norwegian Democracy,* George Allen and Unwin Limited: London.
Strassoldo, R. (1992), 'Globalism and Localism: Theoretical Reflections and some Evidence', in Milnar, Z. (ed), *Globalization and Territorial Identities*, Avebury: Aldershot.
Taylor, C. (1992), *Multiculturalism and 'The Politics of Recognition'*, Princeton University Press: Princeton.
Teather, E. (1994), 'Contesting Rurality: Country Women's Social and Political Networks', in Whatmore, S., Marsden, T. and Lowe, P. (eds), *Gender and Rurality,* David Fulton Publishers Ltd: London.
Teather, E. (1996), 'Farm Women in Canada, New Zealand and Australia Redefine their Rurality', *Journal of Gender Studies*, Vol. 12, No. 1, pp. 1-14.
Tilly, C. (1981b), 'Introduction', in Tilly, L. and Tilly, C. (eds), *Class Conflict and Collective Action,* Sage Publications: California.
Tilly, L (1981a), 'Women's Collective Action and Feminism in France 1870-1914', in Tilly, L. and Tilly, C. (eds), *Class Conflict and Collective Action*, Sage Publications: California.
van der Burg, M. (1994), 'From Categories to Dimensions of Identities', in van der Burg, M. and Endeveld, M. (eds), *Women on Family Farms. Gender Research, EC Policies and New Perspectives*, Circle for Rural European Studies: Wageningen.
Verstad, B. (1996) personal communication.
Voyce, M (1994), 'Testamentary Freedom, Patriarchy and the Inheritance of the Family Farm in Australia', *Sociologia Ruralis*, Vol. 34, No 1, pp. 71-84.
Whatmore, S. (1991), *Farming Women: Gender, Work and Family Enterprise*, Macmillan: London.
Whatmore, S. (1994), 'Theoretical Achievements and Challenges in European Rural Gender Studies', in van der Burg, M. and Endeveld, M. (eds), *Women on Family Farms. Gender Research, EC Policies and New Perspectives*, Circle for Rural European Studies: Wageningen.
Whatmore, S., Marsden, T. and P. Lowe (1994), 'Introduction: Feminist Perspectives in Rural Studies', in Whatmore, S., Marsden, T. and Lowe, P. (eds), *Gender and Rurality*, David Fulton Publishers Ltd: London.

Part III

Communities and Households

7 Social Identification with Local Communities and the Globalization Process in Rural Areas of Eastern Europe

PAWEL STAROSTA AND MARIANA DRAGANOVA

Introduction

The findings of community studies focused on the question of social bonds can be summarized in the form of different hypotheses, with the community-lost hypothesis being the best known (Kornhauser, 1960; Hunter, 1975; Wellman, 1979; Wellman et al., 1988). It assumes an almost complete disintegration of primary bonds and the disappearance of territory as a basis for the development of social bonds, a process, which can be observed in the contemporary world. According to the supporters of this hypothesis: 1) the non-territorial basis for the grouping of people is more important than the territorial (Wellman et al., 1988); 2) the vertical pattern of a community including 'the structural and functional relations of its various social units and subsystems to extra-community systems' (Warren, 1973, p. 242) is stronger than the horizontal pattern to be found in 'the structural and functional relations of its various social units and systems to each other' (Warren, 1973, p. 242); and 3) interrelationships between people both within the community and with the community tend to weaken and become impersonal (Jałowiecki, 1989).

Three causes are underlined in contemporary discussion of the factors determining the process of local community decay with their sources deeply rooted in the modernization process characteristic for advanced industrial societies. The first of them is the process of population growthconnected with industrialization and urbanization. According to Simmel (1975) and Wirth (1964), the growth of population and population density leads to the weakening of interpersonal contacts. The development of technology and means of transport leads to a greater spatial mobility and the diminishing significance of the territorial foundations of interpersonal bonds. Thus, the development of a mass consumption society leads to social atomization and the collapse of the role hitherto played by local communities as the basis for social integration. These industrialization and urbanization processes were carried out in Eastern European countries mainly in the 1950s (Musil, 1984). They were, however, not so deep as in Western societies, because of the shortage of capital and the shortcomings of applied technologies. Moreover, the rapid industrialization and urbanization processes in Eastern Europe were concentrated in time and not based on the internalization of industrial society's system of cultural values (Robertson, 1992). Its ultimate effect was not only urbanization but also sub-urbanization with all its social and cultural consequences.

The urbanization process in CEECs was progressing in a horizontal and extensive way with some negative effects on rural regions and their population. By turning private farming and land ownership into public (in Russia, for example, land was nationalized and in Bulgaria collectivized), farmers lost their links with the land and there was an increase in alienation from their place of dwelling. This intensified the migration process of large groups of villagers towards the industrial centres and weakened the affiliations of at least two generations with their places of birth. This process was a little different in Poland, where most agriculture remained private but rural areas did not escape the urbanization process.

The next source of the diminishing role played by local communities is the formation of contemporary national states and companies. The progressive centralization of political power and the concentration of locally generated surpluses of capital in political centres meant ultimately that the local systems were deprived of their former function as a resources distributor (Milofsky, 1989). In Eastern Europe the centralization of power was based both on the ideological and also on the political background. In this situation local communities became dependent on the metropolitan centres and lost their political and cultural autonomy. The centralization of power and capital took place both in Western mass consumption and in the totalitarian Eastern European societies. In Western countries political power was based on a concentration of private capital, whereas in the Eastern European countries - on state capital.

The third source of the declining importance of local communities was the development of the means of mass communication and mass culture in industrial society (Kloskowska, 1983). It is underlined that the development of mass culture has led to the unification and standardization of the transmitted content. As a result local communities have lost their function as the place in which systems of values are shaped. Consequently, the normative distinctness of the local systems has collapsed as well.

In the 1970s the project of modernity was replaced by the perspectives of global development (McMichael, 1996). The concept of globalization means 'both the diffusion of models of economic development, progress and marketization and the adoption of and/or resistance to cultural idioms of Westernization (or Japonization, Iranianization, etc.) upon local values' (Roninger, 1995, p. 277). Its fundamental assumptions are as follows: firstly, 'the global system is not reducible to a scene consisting merely of societies and/or other large-scale actors. Thus individuals, societies are to be treated in terms of one coherent analytical framework' (Robertson, 1992, p. 61); secondly, 'it is equally important to avoid reductionism in dealing with the analytical dimensions of the process of globalization. Thus far, the emergence of what some call the modern world-system has been discussed in either political or economic terms' (Robertson, 1992, p. 61). It is added also 'that cultural pluralism is itself a constitutive feature of the contemporary global circumstance and that conception of world system, including symbolic responses' (Robertson, 1992, p. 61). Moreover, it is underlined that local communities and the local level of social organization assume the growing importance of the global perspective as a one of the main forms of social life. As underlined by some authors, in the era of globalization 'people resist the process of individualization and social atomization, and tend to cluster in community organizations that over time, generate a feeling of belonging, and ultimately, in many cases, a communal cultural identity' (Castells, 1997, p. 60).

The growing importance of 'locality' is possible owing to the appearance of the following factors. The first is the restriction of those functions performed by the national state. As a result the importance of both supranational and local power centres has increased. The second is the economic factor. The saturation of the world market with basic goods means that it is not the quantity of production, which has become a leading economic problem all over the world, but rather its quality and the differentiation of goods not requiring mass production. The invasion of mass culture and the considerable spatial mobility of members of industrial societies mean that the individual loses a cultural sense of space (Bryden, 1993; Jałowiecki, 1989). Finally, 'the technological possibilities opened up by microelectronics, such as flexible automation, and the increasing diversification of demand contributed to the development of decentralized structures. This stimulated a resurgence of interest in small and medium-sized enterprises related to local milieu and of local and regional initiatives' (Stohr, 1992, p. 36). In this situation mass culture, mass production, mass consumption and great spatial mobility release in individuals a demand for a feeling of social identity determined by membership in specific temporal-spatial variables. As underlined by Giddens, 'regional identities become accentuated as a response to, and defense against, the growing impact of the "wider world" on our lives: at the same time, nation-states become in some ways weakened' (Giddens, 1993, p. 342).

In this context, local solidarity is becoming desirable social value as integral part of the processes of individuation (Barbic, 1996). However, it 'is not a presumed primordial given, but rather is more often socially constructed in interaction with other communities and institutions external to the local community' (Hunter and Staggenborg, 1988, p. 251). It is obvious that the construction of local community requires the mobilizing of local capabilities to act. What counts in this process, is not only the skills and knowledge of the local actors, but also their attachment to the place and their readiness to play citizen's role. The social identification with the place of residence is recognized as one of the prerequisites for the local involvement and for creating new conditions of life in the rural areas (Beggs et al., 1996). It is pointed out also that the existence within communities 'of common values and psychological identification should effectively stifle deviancy and disorganization, (these) and social unrest are among the basic problems confronting modern man' (Poplin, 1972, p. 23). This suggests that socio-psychological identification with local communities needs permanent exploration and examination. In the earlier community studies more attention was devoted to objective bonds than to man's psycho-social bonds with the local territory.

As a result of the opening of borders and the introduction of market economy principles the societies of Eastern European countries have been exposed to the impact of globalization processes with double force, not only on the European but also the world scale. The question which arises here is: whether and to what extent the processes of economic, political and cultural globalization (despite certain variations in them) produce the same consequences in relation to patterns of local bonding in countries with different cultural backgrounds, and what the local responses to global cultural tendencies in the Eastern European countryside are.

Conceptual framework and procedures

The contemporary debate about the role of the territory in social life as well as the controversies concerning the psychic bonds between the individual and the territory has induced us to undertake studies focussed on the extent and the determinants of social identification with local rural communities within the different cultural contexts of Eastern Europe.[1]

In this chapter, we shall try to answer the following questions:

1. To what degree do the inhabitants of rural communities in Bulgaria, Poland and Russia identify themselves with their rural and small town communities? In other words, how strong is their local identification and what is the degree of similarity between these countries?
2. Which are the most important factors determining social identification within rural and small town communities? Do these factors vary between countries?
3. Which empirical social identification types can be distinguished in the analyzed communities of the three countries? Do these types appear with an equal intensity or does their frequency vary depending on the country and community type?

If the strength of bonds with (and within) local communities is similar and if, despite variations in historical-cultural determinants, it appears that similar factors determine the strength of these bonds, then a conclusion can be drawn that global political, economic and cultural processes are producing similar effects.

The concept of identification means a psychological sense of identity of the individual with another person or, in other words, the individual's inclination to take over from another some characteristics as a basis for feeling and understanding their own ego. In sociology this concept has been introduced to describe the individual's psychic relations with social groups. Bertrand and Wierzbicki (1971, p. 91) underline that 'identification is understood to mean imitation or also the process of emotional identity with a given person, group or agent, as well as with a social role, and even the fact of ascertaining an object's identity'. As regards local community studies, an important distinction was introduced by Wilkinson (1963) who underlined that local identification is composed of two dimensions of the same phenomenon. The first is the individual's ability to determine the characteristic features of a given locality or the individual's interest in community issues, thus it is a cognitive skill by means of which the individual describes the characteristic features of a given place. In Wilkinson's approach this cognitive aspect is called 'identification of', while the other is called 'identification with', signifying the emotional bonds with a given territorial community as a whole. In research carried out in the 1980s and the 1990s the concept of local sentiment was employed for the description of social bonds feeling but the meaning is the same as that of the term 'identification' proposed by Wilkinson. Taking into consideration these and other theoretical proposals, through local identification we shall understand the individual's socio-emotional and cognitive relations with a given territorial community.

In order to provide answers to these questions we designed two scales for the cognitive-interest aspects and for the emotional aspects of local identification, and their sum provided a general scale of local identification.[2]

Empirical community studies have focussed on two issues from the last two decades: firstly, to attempt to verify the relevance of the 'community lost' hypothesis, secondly, the factors, governing the strength of local bonds were sought.

A set of independent variables has been delimited by theories and research findings, which emphasize the importance of such different factors as the determinants of the strength local bonds in the conditions of mass society.

The first of them, the so-called linear model, suggested that 'population size and density would most influence the bonds and sentiments' (Goudy, 1997, p. 2). According to supporters of this model (Wilson, 1985), an increased population size and density have a negative effect on the strength of psychic bonds with the local community. This idea explains inhabitants' psychic bonds with their place of dwelling through the theories of urbanization. The empirical indices from this theory in our studies were: 1) population size in a given community; and 2) frequency of trips made by a given locality's inhabitants outside the administrative district's area.

The second, a stratification model, assumes that the individual's position in the social structure determines the strength of social and psycho-cultural bonds with the local community. In this respect, people with a lower social position have a weaker feeling than those with a higher position (Boczkowski, 1990; Stinner et al., 1990). In our studies the indices from the stratification model were such variables as: 1) the respondents' education level; 2) the respondents' annual income; and 3) belonging to an occupational category with lower status (including skilled workers, unskilled workers, farmers, agricultural workers).

Many studies emphasize the significance of local roots as a theory to explain the strength of local sentiment (Kasarda and Janovitz, 1974; Goudy, 1990, Beggs et al., 1996). The number of 'dwelling years' as an index of local roots is frequently analyzed jointly with the remaining stratification variables. It is our opinion, however, that this variable cannot be an index of the individual's general social-class position, but it can be an important element of the individual's local community status (Barber, 1972). This variable was included in our analyses.

Another theory explaining the feeling of social bonding with the local community makes reference to the network concept (Wellman et al., 1988). The main argument in this concept is as follows: the wider and the more intensive the personal contacts maintained by the inhabitants of some territory, the bigger the strength of their psychic bonds with the local system (Kasarda and Janowitz, 1974; Goudy, 1990).

Some sociologists stress also the significant role played by such variables as local participation and local political alienation as psychic determinants of bonds with the place of dwelling (Poplin, 1972; Turowski, 1974). Poplin suggests that 'the key to psychological identification is involvement, that is, a willingness on the part of the individual to participate in local community affairs' (Poplin, 1972, p. 24). He assumes that the inhabitants' relationship with the local system can be a result of: 1) the ability of local leaders to mobilize the inhabitants to act on the local political scene and 2) feeling that democratic rules are observed in the operation of local structures of power. Our studies included both, a variable characterizing the level of respondents' political alienation and a variable of the level of their political participation on the local scene.

According to the questions formulated earlier we accepted a hypothesis that social identification with local communities continues to be quite strong in selected countries of Eastern Europe. Hence, we assume that the 'community-lost' hypothesis, with regard to the psychic aspect of bonds, does not find any significant confirmation. Secondly, we assume that psychic bonding with rural communities will be determined by the same set of stratification factors, such as income, education and occupational status.

The strength of social identification with rural communities in Bulgaria, Poland and Russia

The statistical data calculated for the total identification scale shows that in all the selected communities the mean values are located above the scale centre (see Table 7.1).

The highest level of local identification was recorded in the Russian communities (9.13 on the 0-12 scale), lower in the Polish (8.81) and lowest - although similarly high - in the Bulgarian communities (8.04). The variations in identification strength between particular countries are bigger than the variations between local communities within the countries under analysis.

140 *Local Responses to Global Integration*

Kotel is the only exception, where general social identification is much higher than the results from Gavrailovo and Byala (the difference is more than 0.5). This can be explained through cultural identity and the old and rich history of the town, its renaissance traditions and an active present-day cultural life. In the case of Kotel, general social identification could be interpreted in a wider sense as a cultural identification.

Generally, it could be an effect both of the stronger influence exerted by macro-social factors of cultural unification, and of the great similarity in the socio-economic conditions prevailing in the localities situated within single regions of Bulgaria, Poland, and Russia. The variation between the local identification level in Russia and Poland is smaller, however, than between the Polish and Bulgarian communities.

Table 7.1   Strength of social identification by country and community

Areas	Mean	Std Deviation	N	Min	Max
Russia	9.13	1.960	400	0	12
Luch	9.21	1.975	198	0	12
Illinskoye	9.05	1.947	202	0	12
Poland	8.81	2.013	617	0	12
Poddêbice	8.90	2.018	293	0	12
Dobroñ	8.67	2.093	186	0	12
Siemkowice	8.82	1.894	138	0	12
Bulgaria	8.04	2.287	599	0	12
Gavrailovo	7.80	2.602	200	0	12
Byala	7.76	1.981	199	0	12
Kotel	8.56	2.154	200	0	12
Total	8.60	2.153	1616	0	12

Source: Authors' research survey.

On the other hand, the results of the regression equations for particular countries and for the analyzed populations appeared quite surprising. The data in Table 7.2, show that the general level of local identification in the communities under survey is determined primarily by two types of variables: 1) of local political participation and alienation; and 2) length of residence in a given locality. Hence, it seems that the theory of social mobilization within the local system and the theory of local roots gives the best explanation. Consequently, the more effective the population's mobilization for political participation and, simultaneously, the stronger the roots, the higher the degree of local identification. And, thus, the basis of the global impact is the effectiveness of local authorities. Hence, it can be said that localism and the quality of local policy has become a global problem (Robertson, 1992).

Table 7.2 Regression models of social identification in selected Eastern European countries

	Model 1 Bulgaria		Model 2 Poland		Model 3 Russia		Model 4 Total sample	
R. Square	.305		.203		.223		.203	
F	5,27		7,09		4,10		14,37	
Sig.	,000		,000		,000		,000	
Independent variables	Beta	t.	Beta	t.	Beta	t.	Beta	t.
Length of residence	0,412	4,449	0,022	0,404	0,274	3.391	0,141	3,515
Community population size	0,084	1,041	0,081	1,457	-0,019	-0,242	0,141	3,390
Frequency of trips outside local district	-0,004	-0,041	0,073	1,242	0,094	1,137	0,120	2,736
Level of local political participation	0,217	2,311	0,245	4,064	0,227	2,791	0,218	5,173
Level of local political alienation	-0,182	-2,069	-0,259	-4,431	-0,206	-2,538	-0,224	-5,413
Number of friends	0,161	1,937	0,110	1,979	0,037	0,474	0,098	2,440
Annual income	0,032	0,339	-0,030	-0,522	0,026	0,316	0,033	0,737
Level of education	0,092	0,993	0,043	0,681	0,136	1,564	0,103	2,513
Occupational lower status	0,138	1,788	0,034	0,620	-0,001	-0,012	0,066	1,716

Source: Authors' research survey.

From Table 7.2 it can be seen that alongside factors determining the local identification level in all analyzed countries there exist also determinants specific for a given country. The most transparent layout of factors determining local psychic bonds was observed in the Polish communities. The identification of Polish respondents with their places of dwelling is determined solely by the degree of participation in local political life or their level of local alienation. Thus, local policy is a basis for developing local psychic bonds.

In the Russian communities the model explaining the strength of psychic bonds with the place of dwelling is composed of two types of variables. They legitimate both the theory of social mobilization (feeling of local political alienation) and the theory of local roots (length of residence). It should be noted that the strength of the main explanatory variables is similar in both Poland and Russia. On the other hand, a more complicated situation exists in the Bulgarian communities, where length of residence in a given community is of primary importance for the character of local psychic bonds.

The indices connected with the theory of social mobilization rank second and the index characterizing the frequency of contacts with friends third. The variables connected with the stratification and the urbanization models were statistically not significant.

The above models of social identification with local communities both in Bulgaria and Russia point towards a complete matching of the first and second most important factors. The first, 'length of residence' has been traditionally important in these two countries where the population, especially in rural areas, is not very mobile and bonds with the place of dwelling are stable and lasting. Unlike this, Poles were more mobile, even during the 'socialist' period, and more independent and free to travel abroad. There is a rational explanation for the second factor, the 'level of local political participation', as well. The frequent elections in the two countries in the years after the changes and increased political and civil activity may be the reason for increased political participation.

Close social connections and contacts among the inhabitants from the studied communities are the third factor both for Poland and Bulgaria.

The high level of local political participation registered in all three countries could be interpreted as consequences of the positive political changes in the late 1980s. The latter caused a wave of social and political activity and awakened civil conscience. They started deciding who is going to govern them, they solved their local problems alone and started thinking of themselves as a factor in many problems. However, this is a long two-way process dependent on the necessity for total change in the present clumsy and totalitarian administrative structures. Therefore, disappointment resulting from the higher expectations of political democratization (mainly among Poles and Russians) is shown in the higher value of local political alienation - a factor, which negatively influences the level of general social identification with the local community.

Types of social identification with local rural communities in Bulgaria, Poland and Russia

Emotional attitudes towards the local community and the interest displayed in local community issues constitute two of the dimensions of local identification analyzed in this chapter. Five empirical types of social identification with both rural and small town communities have been distinguished on the basis of a cluster analysis including both cognitive and emotional variables.

The first type is characterized by a relatively high level of interest in community issues and a low level of emotional bonding with a given locality. About 207 respondents displayed these kinds of attitudes, 12.8 per cent of the whole sample. The second by a high level of knowledge about the community and, simultaneously, a high level of emotional bonding (548 respondents - 33.9 per cent). The third by a low level of knowledge about the community and a high level of emotional bonding. It is the opposite attitude to the first (230 respondents - 14.2 per cent). The fourth is an attitude characterized both by a low level of knowledge about the community and a low level of emotional bonding. This was represented by only 158 respondents (i.e. 9.8 per cent). Finally, the fifth by an average level of knowledge and interest displayed in community affairs, and by an average level of emotional bonds with the local community (473 respondents - 29.3 per cent). Thus, two identification types characterized by contrasting emotional and cognitive aspects and three types by converging emotional and cognitive aspects were distinguished, and at three levels: low, medium, and high (see Table 7.3).

A more detailed analysis revealed that the first identification type (characterized by a high level of interest shown in community affairs and a low level of emotional bonding) was displayed mainly by the Bulgarian (43 per cent) and the Russian respondents (31 per cent). Such attitudes are more frequently displayed by respondents from small towns with over 7,000 inhabitants. Respondents affiliated to the Orthodox Church and those not affiliated to any church primarily display this type of attitude. Other characteristics include: secondary school education, relatively frequent trips outside their rural administrative district, the highest level of political alienation, an age of 41-50, and belonging to the occupational category of managers. These have a small number of friends - usually one or two. Most of them are married.

The second type (a high level of knowledge and a high level of emotional bonding) is represented mainly by Polish (42 per cent) and the Russian respondents (34 per cent). Such attitudes tend to predominate among the inhabitants of small towns (below 7,000 inhabitants) and very small towns (2,000 to 5,000). Most declare affiliation to the Orthodox Church and the Catholic Church, they have a higher level of education and make trips outside their administrative district several times a month. Those displaying a high level of knowledge and of emotional bonding are a little older than those belonging to the first type. They are characterized by the lowest level of political alienation and a greater number of friends and include mainly managers, specialists and farmers. Most of them are married.

The third type (a low level of knowledge and a high level of emotional bonding) is represented mainly by Polish respondents (52 per cent), by those affiliated with the Catholic Church and the inhabitants of villages and small towns. This type of attitude is dominant among the old, and widows and widowers. Most almost never make trips outside their administrative district, moreover, most had only primary school education and were characterized both by a high and a low level of political alienation. With regard to their occupational status, most were unskilled workers and pensioners, characterized by a high degree of social isolation, and this category included the greatest number of those having no friends at all.

The fourth type (a low level of knowledge and a low level of emotional bonding) is represented mainly by Bulgarian respondents (63 per cent) and is primarily typical of the inhabitants of the smallest analyzed communities (below 2,000 inhabitants). Among them unmarried respondents aged 20 to 30 were dominant and most have only vocational school education. They are characterized by the highest spatial mobility and the highest level of political alienation and represent the greatest of those not affiliated with any church. With regard to their occupational structure, they are usually unskilled workers with two to four friends.

Finally, the fifth identification type (an average level of knowledge and an average level of emotional bonding) is represented in equal proportions by both Polish (37 per cent) and Bulgarian respondents (37 per cent). Most are middle-aged, with equal proportions of the spatially mobile and immobile, of affiliations with the Orthodox, the Catholic Church or not affiliated at all. They are characterized by an average level of political alienation and have vocational or secondary school education. Almost equal proportions from different occupations can be found while they vary a great deal in their number of friends.

Table 7.3 Characteristics of types of identification with local communities in Bulgaria, Poland and Russia

Variables	1st type	2nd type	3rd type	4th type	5th type
Final Cluster Centres	High (4,96) knowledge Low feeling of bonding (2,17)	High (5,12) knowledge High feeling of bonding (5,75)	Low (2,52) knowledge High feeling of bonding (5,27)	Low (2,42) knowledge Low feeling of bonding (2,32)	Average (4,22) knowledge Average feeling of bonding (4,10)
Marital Status	Married	Married	Widowed	Unmarried	Married
Education	Secondary	University	Primary	Vocational	Vocational Secondary
Age	41-50	51-60	61-70	21-30	41-50
Occupation	Managers	Managers Farmers	Unskilled workers Pensioners	Unskilled workers	All categories
Frequency of trips outside local district	Twice a week	Several times a month	Almost never	Everyday	All frequencies
Number of friends	1-2	7 and more	No friends at all	2-4	From 0 to many friends
Level of local political alienation	Highest level	Lowest level	Low and high level	Highest level	Medium
Church affiliation	Orthodox and not affiliated	Catholic and Orthodox	Catholic	Not affiliated	Orthodox Catholic and not affiliated
Community population size	1,000-2,000	2,000-5,000	2,000-5,000, over 7,000	1,000-2,000	Over 7,000
Country	Bulgaria	Poland and Russia	Poland	Bulgaria	All countries

Source: Authors' research survey.

If we want to analyze in detail the five distinct types of identification with the local community we should first state that they are to some extent conventional. We should not look for completely logical connections and explanations between the distinguished types and all of the characteristics shown in Table 7.3. Still, a general analysis reveals the following dependencies:

Age, a demographic characteristic, influencing local bonds and identification with a local community. The youngest have the weakest identification while the oldest are very emotional. The middle-aged (40-60) show a fluctuation between the first two and the average values of identification with the local communities (5th type).

Population size - the level of urbanization seems not to influence the respondents' bonding and feeling in any of the countries. Larger size does not lead to weaker emotional bonds as the theories of urbanization claim (see 2nd and 3rd types), but in the two Bulgarian villages with less than 2000 inhabitants, low levels of bonding and feeling were observed.

Mobility (frequency of trips outside the local community) is stronger. The more they travel outside their dwelling place and have the opportunity to compare with other people and communities, the higher their 'knowledge-interest' dimension of identification becomes. The exception is the 4th type, where the young unmarried (21-30 years of age) travel everyday and the dependency is completely reversed; people with primary education show high levels of bonding (see 3rd type). An exception is observed only with the 4th type.

Social contacts and connections show a straight correlation between the identification type and number of friends of those interviewed (see 2nd and 4th type). The opposite correlation is found with local political alienation as a determinant - the higher it is the lower the general identification with the place of dwelling (the emotional or cognitive sides).

Let us summarize the above findings:

- Two types of identification dominate in Bulgaria, Poland and Russia. The first characterized by a high level of interest shown in the local community and also by strong emotional bonds with the place of dwelling and the second by an average level of knowledge and interest, and an average level of emotional bonding.
- In Russia the types of identification with local communities are more cohesive than in Bulgaria and Poland.
- The main difference between the attitudes of inhabitants in Bulgaria and Poland boils down to the fact that in Bulgaria an attitude characterized by a relatively high interest in the local community's affairs and a low level of emotional bonding predominate, whereas in Poland it is a type

characterized by a low level of knowledge and interest and a high level of emotional bonding.

The domination of particular types of attitudes can be explained as follows. In Poland a high level of emotional bonding with the local community is accompanied by a low level of interest in community affairs, resulting from a relatively high level of satisfaction in the functioning of different institutional structures within the local system. In this situation they are, on one hand, strongly linked with local communities and, on the other owing to the more effective operation of local institutions feel released - in a way - from an obligation to be interested in local problems because it is appropriate to institutional structures. In Bulgaria, it is the opposite as most are dissatisfied with the activity of various institutional structures and have a greater interest in local affairs. This results from their greater local patriotism and is also necessitated, to some extent, because they have to supplement the activity of these institutions with their social activity. On the other hand, in Russia a high degree of satisfaction with the operation of institutional structures is primarily a result of a low level of demand addressed to them.

Conclusion

The findings of the surveys carried out among the local communities of Eastern Europe do not confirm the accuracy of community-lost hypothesis in relation to the inhabitants' social bonds with their place of dwelling. The community as a place is not a social vacuum either. The inhabitants link their lives with their place of dwelling and treat it, to a large extent, as their social reference group. However, the local community is not the only one and the exceptional world of life for them. Our studies have also shown that the local identification is primarily of emotional and not of a 'cognitive-interest' nature. It means that feeling as a source of knowledge about the social world typical of traditional culture predominates over interest and knowledge as a source of social cognition typical for civil society. In this context we can't accept the view that contemporary rural local community in Easter Europe is the place of civil activity. The vitality of rural and small town communities manifested in the symbolic layer, is a result of still strong collective traditions and not an act of the citizens' choosing. These emotional bonds can prove to be a valuable cultural asset, however, emotions and traditions are not sufficient to meet contemporary challenges. 'Localities need knowledge from elsewhere about matters affecting their particular circumstances, and need to be free to build alliances and relations with other localities as well as higher levels' (Bryden, 1994). The impact of global processes on local systems is unquestionable but paradoxically the way was paved by emphasizing the importance of local factors in contemporary social and political life. This could be seen in our studies in partly similar and partly divergent sets of factors explaining the level of local identification in each country. The common core element here is the present relevance of the social mobilization theory. The specific nature of Bulgarian communities is re in the great importance played there by the theory of local roots and network theory. On the other hand, a specific Polish trait is an almost exclusive domination of political mobilization as a determinant of local identification. In turn, in the Russian communities political mobilization as a local identification determinant is as important as local roots. Empirical models of identification with local communities tend to vary within particular countries as well. The dominant model in Bulgaria is characterized by a relatively low feeling of emotional bonding and a relatively high level of interest in local affairs. Unlike in Bulgaria, an empirical model characterized by a high level of emotional bonding and a low level of knowledge and interest in local affairs predominates in Poland. In turn, a cohesive type appears to predominate in Russia with a high level of emotional bonding accompanied by a high level of interest. Thus, the contemporary essential characteristics of local communities are shaped both by common factors and specific variations, which can be observed both at the level of theory and of practical activity.

Notes

1   The empirical data presented in this chapter were gathered through an international research project, entitled: 'Patterns of Social Participation and the Social Structure of Local Communities in Bulgaria, Canada, Poland and Russia', funded by the Scientific Research Committee of the Polish Academy of Sciences (grant 1 H01F 016 09), the University of Lodz (grant 505/527) and the Universite du Quebec a Rimouski. Altogether surveys based on random samples were conducted in 3 Polish communities in the administrative province of Sieradz, central Poland; 2 Russian communities in the administrative province of Ivanovo (central part of Russia); and 3 Bulgarian communities in the former Sliven district in Bulgaria.

   The respondents were randomly chosen for questionnaire interviews from the registers of voters in particular localities. The collected data fulfil the requirements of representativeness for the communities surveyed. Data collection was completed between July 1996 and February 1997.

This chapter is based on the data from three Polish communities (617 interviews), and three Bulgarian communities (599 interviews). The total number of collected questionnaires reached 1,616. The population in these localities in 1996 was as follows: Siemkowice (PL) - 1,029 inhabitants, Byala (BG) - 1,316, Gavrailovo (BG) – 1,450, Dobron (PL) – 1,929. Luch (RUS) - 3,500, Illinskoye (RUS) - 4,238, Kotel (BG) - 7,429, and Poddebice (PL) - 8,081. All were situated 20-90 km from the nearest large city with over 100 000 inhabitants. These cities, i.e. Sliven in Bulgaria, Lodz in Poland and Ivanovo in Russia, were centres of collapsing textile industries.

2   Both were designed in a similar way: 1) eight questions concerning the respondent's familiarity with local issues and expressions of interest in the community's affairs, chosen from a comprehensive questionnaire; 2) the answers coded in a 0-1 system; 3) the sum of the points then provided a scale for each respondent from 0 to 9; 4) next, by means of the 'item analysis' procedure those items which were not significant, or weakly correlated with the entire general scale, were excluded, as well as those which correlated with another of very high significance. This solution allowed the elimination both those items which were repeating other information items (strong correlation) and those which were not relevant with regard to the general scale (lack of correlation between a particular aspect and the entire scale). Finally, we designed two 0-6 points scales reflecting both cognitive and sentiment aspects of local identification and one 0-12 points scale of general local identification.

References

Barber, B. (1973), 'Family Status. Local Community Status and Social Stratification: Three Types of Social Ranking', in Warren, R.L. (ed), *Perspectives on the American Community*, Rand McNally: Chicago.

Barbic, A. (1996), 'Cultural Identity of the Slovenian Countryside', paper presented at the Conference 'European agriculture and rural areas - on course for common future in the 21st century', Poland, Torún, September 17-20.

Beggs, J.J., Hurlbert, S. and Haines, V.A. (1996), 'Community Attachment in Rural Setting: A Refinement and Empirical Test of the Systemic Model', *Rural Sociology*, Vol. 61, No 3, pp. 407-426.

Bertrand, A.L. and Wierzbicki, Z.T. (1970), *Sociologia wsi w Stanach Zjednoczonych. Stan i tendencje rozwojowe*, Ossolineum: Wroclaw.

Boczkowski, A. (1990), 'Wybrane aspekty swiadomosci spoleczno-przestrzennej w spolecznosciach lokalnych rożnego typu', in Hryniewicz, J. (ed), *Spolecznosci loklane u progu kryzysu*, Uniwersytet Warszawski: Warszawa.

Bryden, J.M. (1994), 'Towards Sustainable Rural Communities: From Theory to Action', in Bryden, J.M. (ed), *Towards Sustainable Rural Communities*, University School of Rural Planning and Development: Guelph.

Castells, M. (1997), *The Power of Identity*, Basil Blackwell: Oxford.

Etzioni, A. (1993), *The Spirit of Community*, Simon and Schuster: New York.
Giddens, A. (1993), *Sociology*, Polity Press.
Goudy, W.J. (1990), 'Community Attachment in a Rural Region', *Rural Sociology*, Vol. 55, No 2, pp. 178-198.
Goudy, W.J. (1997), 'Community Attachment in Small Towns: Evidence from Iowa (USA)', paper presented at the 17th Congress of the European Society for Rural Sociology, Chania, Greece.
Hunter, A. (1975), 'The Loss of Community', *American Sociological Review*, Vol. 40, No 5, pp. 537-552.
Hunter, A. and Staggenborg, S. (1988), 'Local Communities and Organized Action', in Milofsky, C. (ed), *Community Organizations: Studies in Resource Mobilization and Exchange*, Oxford University Press: New York.
Jalowiecki, B. (1989), *Rozwój lokalny*, Uniwersytet Warszawski: Warszawa.
Kasarda, J.D., and Janovitz, M. (1974), 'Community Attachment in Mass Society', *American Sociological Review*, Vol. 39, No 3, pp. 328-339.
Kloskowska, A. (1983), *Kultura Masowa*, PWN: Warszawa.
Kornhauser, W. (1960), *The Politics of Mass Society*, Routledge and Keagan Paul: London.
Leach, B. and Wilson, A. (1995), 'Bringing Globalization Down to Earth: Restructuring and Labour in Rural Communities', *The Canadian Review of Sociology and Anthropology*, Vol. 32, No3, pp. 341-363.
McMichael, P. (1996), 'Globalization: Myths and Realities', *Rural Sociology*, Vol. 61, No 1, pp. 25-55.
Milofsky, C. (1988), 'Scarcity and Community. A Resource Allocation Theory of Community and Mass Society Organizations', in Milofsky, C. (ed), *Community Organizations: Studies in Resource Mobilization and Exchange*, Oxford University Press: New York.
Musil, J. (1984), *Urbanizacja w krajach socialistycznych*, KiW: Warszawa.
Poplin, D.E. (1972), *Communities. A Survey of Theories and Methods of Research*, Macmillan: New York.
Robertson, R. (1992), *Globalization: Social Theory and Global Culture*, Sage: London.
Roninger, L. (1995), 'Public Life and Globalization as Cultural Vision', *The Canadian Review of Sociology and Antropology*, Vol. 32, No 3, pp. 259-285.
Simmel, G. (1975), *Sociologia*, PWN: Warszawa.
Stinner, W.F., Van Loon, M., Chung, S. and Byun, Y. (1990), 'Community Size, Individual Social Position and Community Attachment', *Rural Sociology*, Vol. 55, No 4, pp. 494-521.
Stohr, W.B. (1990), 'On the Theory and Practice of Local Development in Europe', in Stohr, W.B. (ed), *Global Challenge and Local Response*, Mansel: London.
Turowski, J. (1974), 'Uwarunkowanie identyfikacji mieszkańców z osiedlem- na podstawie badań osiedli lubelskich', in Nowakowski, S. and Mirowski, W. (eds), *Przemiany miejskich spoleczności lokalnych w Polsce*, PWN: Warszawa.

Warren, R.L. (1973), *The Community in America*, Rand McNally: Chicago.
Wellman, B. (1979), 'The Community Question: The Intimate Networks of East Yorkers', *American Journal of Sociology*, Vol. 84, No 5, pp. 1201-1231.
Wellman, B., Carrington, P.J and Hall, A. (1988), 'Networks as Personal Community', in Wellman, B. and Berkowitz, S.D. (eds), *Social Structures. A Network Approach*, Cambridge University Press: Cambridge.
Wilkinson, K.P. (1963), *Identification with Community: A Review of Literature*, Preliminary Report no 1, State College Mississippi.
Wilson, T. (1985), 'Settlement Type and Interpersonal Estrangement: A Test of the Theories of Wirth and Gans', *Social Forces*, Vol. 64, No 1, pp. 139-150.
Wirth, L. (1964), *On Cities and Social Life Selected Papers*, The University of Chicago Press: Chicago.

8 Global Changes and Individual Responses in Rural Areas: The Dynamics of Low Income and Household Economic Status

ESPERANZA VERA-TOSCANO AND POLLYANNA CHAPMAN

Introduction

In the last few decades, the economic growth in developed countries has been associated with a process of structural change conceptualized by some authors (Amin, 1996) as *globalization*. The distinctive aspects of this contemporary phenomenon include an increasing interconnectedness, multiplicity and hybridization of social and economic life at every level, spatial and organizational, the challenge being to mobilize this diversity as a source of both social cohesion and economic competitiveness (Amin and Thrift, 1997, p. 7).

One of the immediate consequences of the globalization process has been that of *restructuring*, and more specifically, that of *regional restructuring* (Cooke, 1986), involving a lessening of the social homogeneity of regions and localities as individuals adapt to the globalization process (i.e. greater migration and mobility in general, incomers, commuting, etc.). There have also been changes in the way in which home life is arranged, and changes in political activity and affiliation, as local social structures become more heterogeneous.

Despite the identified blurring of traditional territorial and social boundaries, locality/territory becomes more important (due to the heterogeneity mentioned above). Communities have personalities and they determine their nexus of co-operation and work, this being identified as the *paradox of globalization* (Ehrensaft, 1997). As Von Meyer (1997) says, in order to understand territorial diversity and dynamics and to draw policy-elevant lessons, it is necessary to be able to create meaningful classifications and typologies of areas that allow analyses of similarities and differences among the various territorial units.

One important analytical and policy-relevant dimension for structuring territory is obviously the *rural-urban dimension.* There are some reasons that justify the decision of searching for differences between these two geographical groups. Firstly, in the last few decades rural areas of developed countries have undergone major changes in their economic system, political balance and social relations. Some of these changes include the decline in agricultural employment (Errington, 1988) and an apparent reversal of the rural-urban drift (Champion, 1981; Robert and Randolph, 1983).

Secondly, it is argued that people in rural areas face additional constraints on their ability to adapt to these structural changes. Evidence suggests that people in rural areas behave rather differently in response to situations such as that of lack of employment, training, education, etc. than their urban counterparts do. Further, particularly in rural areas, it is suggested that low income represents a vital link in the 'cycle of deprivation', as those experiencing low income are excluded from access to a range of facilities and services, for example housing and transport (Shaw, 1979; Cloke et al., 1994).

Thirdly, due to the differences between rural and urban areas, standard indicators and official statistics are not as effective when applied to the rural space. For example, the unemployment rate in rural areas might be masked by the lower participation rate in the labour market of rural women. Similarly, severely disadvantaged rural households may not be adequately represented within larger administrative units or surveys.

Lastly, and as a result of the reasons mentioned above, there has been increasing policy sensitivity towards a better understanding of the processes going on in rural areas. In particular, rural income and employment problems need to be handled in new ways. Commitment has been manifested by the UK government to 'tackle social exclusion' as one of its 'highest priorities' (Social Exclusion Unit, 1998). Furthermore, the EU 'agricultural policy' agenda is moving from purely agricultural issues to a broader concern about 'rural development' (European Commission, 1997).

There is a need to identify in some detail (involving statistical analysis to test certain hypotheses), the nature and incidence of the problems faced by rural residents, as well as to propose the kind of interventions that will direct improvements at particular groups. The main focus of this chapter then is on rural residents and, particularly, on their response to changing opportunities in rural areas of developed countries. The chapter examines changes which have taken place in rural areas, using the first five waves (1991-1995)[1] of the British Household Panel Survey (BHPS),[2] comparing them with what has happened in urban areas. In a search for differences between rural and non-rural areas on their degree of disadvantage, this chapter also examines the dynamics of low income and how it relates to household economic status. Finally, it explores the findings that result from modelling the transition probabilities into and out of low income.

Globalization, restructuring, and changes in rural household socioeconomic conditions

We have lately been witnesses to the rise of supranational political bodies, international mass migration and the spread of transnational corporations with an increasing worldwide movement of products, people, services and cultures. These 'international' phenomena have been identified by some authors with the term 'globalization' symbolizing, according to Amin (1996, p. 2), the blurring of traditional territorial and social boundaries through the inter-penetration of local and distant influences, therefore requiring hybrid and multi-polar solutions.

Certainly, this is not a new phenomenon since international exchange is several centuries old, and at the height of the imperial age between 1878 and 1914, international flows of investment, export and people exceeded current levels. However, it has to be recognized that there have been qualitative shifts in the nature of global exchanges and interconnections in the course of this century (Held, 1995, p. 20).

Those that try to debunk the 'globalization' process (Hirst and Thompson, 1996) argue that economic activity is still nationally based since most companies continue to have the bulk of their productive assets in one national location and have gained at some time from national public policies. Nevertheless, this affirmation is half finished since companies, nowadays, have no choice but to 'go/look global' very early on in their careers, for at least three reasons (Strange, 1991): firstly, because of new methods of production brought about by accelerated technological change; secondly, because of the greater transnational mobility of capital which has made investing abroad easier, quicker, and cheaper; and thirdly because there have been major changes in the ease of transportation and communication. Also, detractors of the globalization phenomena agree that there is no irreversible imperative to replace interventionist national or supranational policies by global market forces. Nevertheless, policy is becoming more and more driven by external forces, quoting Ramsay:

> The initiatives which have flowed from the revival of the project to complete the Single Market have far more to do with the reshaping and support of the Euro-multinationals, as gladiators representing the Community in the global market amphitheatre, than, with the promotion of more 'perfect' competition after models of orthodox neo-classical economics (1992, p. 27).

The discussion can not be largely restricted to questions of economic development as Hirst and Thompson (1996) have tried to do, as there is also a growing number of chains of social, cultural and political activity that are world-wide in scope; and the intensification of levels of interaction and interconnectedness between states and societies is continually increasing. Further, by accepting the 'globalization' process, we are not denying the existence of nations and regions, nor undermining the policies and measures they put in place. With or without globalization, local diversity, both within and between places, remains. This is not, however, to suggest that nothing has changed in terms of the way in which places are constituted or related to the rest of the world.

Due to the increasing worldwide movement of products, people, services and cultures, change has been the most permanent feature of the social landscape. The general term that tends to be applied to capture this change process is 'restructuring'. There are different meanings, which the word implies in the context of research into changes in the urban and regional systems.

Restructuring can be used to refer to the reorganization processes which firms undergo in order to respond to the kinds of changes they experience in the competitive world in which they exist. Massey and Meegan (1982) define these processes as: rationalization (reducing the labour force); intensification (reducing gaps in working time, 'down-time', etc.); and investment and technological change.

With respect to 'investment and technical change' as a strategy, it is possible that plant relocation or a new opening in a different geographical area may occur, the space into which new investment moves and from which disinvestment occurs itself being restructured. This process is called 'regional restructuring' (Cooke, 1986, p. 5). As a result of this regional/local restructuring, there may be a lessening of the social homogeneity of such regions and localities, changes in the ways in which home life is arranged, and changes in political activity and affiliation as local social structures become more heterogeneous. It is these changes we are interested in.

To look at this in the specific case of rural areas of developed countries, such areas have undoubtedly experienced the impact of the globalization process and of restructuring as a result of both internal and external pressures and this is reflected in a number of recent policy reforms (e.g. the EU's 'Cork Declaration' and the Rural White Papers for England, Scotland and Wales). An issue, which arises from this, is the way responses are structured to the processes of globalization, and how the responses themselves become part of the process of globalization through integration or marginalization (i.e. re-localization and new forms of employment).

It is evident that counter-urbanization has played a significant role in the rural restructuring of many parts of Britain (Harper, 1991, p. 22). Some researchers have considered whether the process is employment led, either because of the population following jobs out from the city or through new spatial divisions of labour, or whether it is housing led, or indeed, a combination of the two. At the same time, it is also accepted that rural labour markets are at the core of the problem of rural depopulation in developed countries (Hodge and Whitby, 1981, p. 3). These are two contradictory assumptions that require further research. In this chapter, we examine the patterns of movement between urban and rural areas, and explore some of the reasons for these moves being made by residents.

The implications of regional restructuring and in/out-migration vary for different rural areas and they will have uneven impacts on different social groups. However, little appears to be known about these spatial and social impacts. Neither is there much knowledge about the dynamics of rural life and rural people's living conditions. The use of longitudinal panel data, i.e. the British Household Panel Survey (BHPS), which facilitates the inquiry into the experiences of individuals in rural areas through time, may help us to provide some preliminary analysis to begin filling this gap.

The data

The British Household Panel Survey

The British Household Panel Survey (BHPS) consists of a national representative sample of approximately 5,500 households recruited in 1991, containing a total of around 10,000 individuals (see Taylor, 1996 for further information). Since we are interested in the dynamic aspect of the panel and on all five years sequence, only those individuals who were interviewed in all five waves, i.e. 1991 to 1996 were included in our sample. This left a 'balanced panel' of 7,164 individuals (adults and children).[3]

The rural/non-rural sub-sample

Defining the 'rural' and 'non-rural' sub-samples to be compared carries some difficulties both practical and theoretical. Firstly, it has to be argued that there is no clear and agreed definition of rurality (Cloke and Edwards, 1986; Errington, 1990) and that many authors have complained that studies of rural issues have been hampered by the 'undifferentiated use of "rural" in a research context' (Hoggart, 1990, pp. 245-257). Secondly, it is not clear whether the definition should be a 'uni- or multi-dimensional' one and whether rurality should be regarded as a dichotomous or continuous variable. Finally, there is the natural 'problem' in a longitudinal data set of dealing with those who move between rural and non-rural areas over the five-year period.

For the purposes of analysis, the approach here has been to use a simple uni-dimensional dichotomous variable based on the 'deep rural' definition used widely by the Rural Development Commission (Wilson, 1997).[4] This defines rural individuals as those residing in non-urban post-code sectors which fall in areas with a population of less than 3,000 individuals. While the availability of each individual's post-code within the BHPS would, in principle, have allowed the use of a definition which allowed for various degrees of 'rurality', in practice, the need for reasonable sample sizes and for a classification which made the dynamic analysis manageable, required the use of a simple definition.

Finally, dealing with rural/non-rural migrations in a consistent manner is potentially important as such movement may have a significant role in the income dynamics. For example, we can test how far migration is a 'strategy' for escape from low-income. Hence, the two main sub-samples considered, namely *rural* and *non-rural* do not contain all the same individuals for the 5 years. However, treating the data in this way does complicate the analysis and interpretation of some tables. Three further more easily interpretable sub-samples, *always rural* (individuals classified as 'rural' for the five years), *always non-rural* (individuals classified as 'non-rural' for the five years), and *movers* (individuals that have moved from 'rural' to 'non-rural' or vice versa at some stage of the five-year period) are also considered.

Household changes in rural areas

It has been argued for a number of years that rural areas of developed countries have experienced the impact of the globalization process and of restructuring as a result of both internal and external pressures (see, for instance, Boyle, 1995, p. 65). Alongside the changing spatial location of industry, retirement migrants and long-distance commuters have also been identified as an important group who have contributed to the population increases in more peripheral areas.

We have begun to address this issue here by looking at the characteristics of those that have remained in rural areas and those that have moved out of rural areas at some point during the five waves of the British Household Panel Study. We compare breakdowns by age and sex, family type, and household economic status for each sub-sample.

Looking at Table 8.1 we find that, although the proportion of types of people is more or less the same between the different sub-samples, there are some marked differences. The Wave 1 *movers* sub-sample comprises a slightly higher percentage of people of working age (both male and female) as well as couples without dependent children (compared to the always non-rural sub-sample), which gives us a preliminary indication that migration may be employment led. Also significant is the higher percentage of two or more earner households in the *movers* sub-sample as well as a smaller percentage of 'economically inactive' households when compared to the urban and rural sub-samples. Lone parents tend to move less than the rest of the categories although there has been an increase from 5.0 per cent (Wave 1) to 9.1 per cent (Wave 5) in lone parents with dependent children in the movers sub-sample.

Looking at household economic status, also worthy of note is how the percentage of households with 2 or more people in employment is higher in rural areas than in urban areas. We know nothing about what type of employment people are in but this opens a possibility for research on the level of wages and type of employment, to measure if households in rural areas need a greater number of people in employment to reach the same level of income.

Table 8.1 also breaks down the sub-sample characteristics in Wave 5, and the distribution across subgroup categories is broadly similar to Wave 1. However, not everyone remains in the same sub-group. Over time, people's household characteristics change (i.e. marriage, death, divorce, job loss, etc.). W1-W5 columns highlight the extent of the changes between Year 1 and Year 5 and shows the proportion of those within each sub-sample that did not change subgroup between Wave 1 and Wave 5.

Table 8.1 Person type, household type and household economic status breakdowns: always rural, always non-rural and movers[a] sub-samples (column percentages)

	Always Rural			Always non-rural			Movers*		
	W1	W5	W1-W5	W1	W5	W1-W5	W1	W5	W1-W5
Male working age	30.3	30.5	28.1	30.7	30.9	28.7	34.9	36.0	33.4
Female working age	27.4	26.9	24.9	29.3	29.3	27.2	32.1	33.7	31.3
Male retired	8.0	10.2	8.0	6.1	8.3	6.2	4.1	5.6	4.1
Female retired	13.9	16.3	13.9	13.1	15.3	13.1	8.4	9.2	8.4
Dependent child	20.2	15.8	15.8	20.4	16.1	16.1	20.2	15.2	15.2
% changed type[b]			8.9			8.5			7.3
Household type									
Single Non-Elderly	3.9	3.0	1.86	5.1	5.8	2.9	3.9	9.9	0.7
Single Elderly	8.0	10.5	7.69	9.4	11.6	9.2	4.3	7.5	4.3
Couple No Children	29.6	30.3	24.4	24.8	25.6	19.0	25.1	26.8	12.4
Couple: dep children	41.4	38.4	33.8	40.3	36.2	30.1	42.5	35.1	18.9
Couple: non-dep children	7.8	8.7	3.8	8.06	9.2	3.3	12.5	7.7	1.6
Lone parent: dep children	4.2	4.1	2.8	6.83	6.6	4.1	5.0	9.1	1.9
Lone par: non-dep children	1.8	2.5	1.3	2.55	2.9	1.5	2.0	1.5	1.0
2 + Unrelated adults	0.5	0.2	0.2	1.54	0.9	0.1	0.9	1.5	0.0
Other households	2.5	1.8	1.7	1.15	0.7	0.4	3.4	0.3	0.0
% changed type[b]			22.3			29.0			58.9
Household Economic Status									
Unemployed	0.2	0.0	0.0	0.3	0.2	0.0	0.2	0.0	0.0
Economic Inactive	25.1	28.3	21.0	28.4	31.9	22.2	15.6	25.9	10.2
1 earner in single household	3.3	3.2	1.6	4.0	4.4	2.0	4.1	5.4	0.7
1 earner household	24.3	24.5	7.0	23.2	20.0	6.5	20.0	20.3	5.6
2+ earners household	46.7	43.7	29.4	43.8	43.2	26.9	60.0	47.9	29.1
% changed type[b]			40.8			42.1			54.2

[a] /The movers sub-sample contains those individuals that have changed their geographical location (from rural to non-rural or vice versa) at some stage during the five year period.
[b] / % of the sub-sample whose type is the same in Wave 1 and Wave 5. For each type, (100 - sum of %s) = % changed type.

Also, the residual percentages represent the proportion that changed sub-group over the five years. From this, one can calculate, for example, that 22.3 per cent experienced a change in their household type in the *always rural* sub-sample.

A not surprising finding was the extent to which there were household type and household economic status changes within the *movers* sub-sample (58.9 per cent and 54.2 per cent compared for example, to 22.3 percent and 40.8 per cent in the *always rural* sub-sample). This instability in the *movers* sub-sample might be seen as normal due to the characteristics of the group 'per se'. They change places and therefore they are more likely to change both their household type and household economic status.

Table 8.2 breaks down 'movers' into three categories: movers towards rural areas, movers towards non-rural areas and those who show no clear pattern along the five years (they move back and forth from one area to another in the 5 year-period). Couples with dependent children are the most highly represented group among those who have moved to an non-rural area in both Waves 1 and 5 with a considerable increase between years, 37.8 per cent in 1991 and 45.9 per cent in 1995 (an 8.1 per cent increase). Among those who have moved to a rural area, however, and those where no clear pattern is defined, though it is also the best represented category, it decreases from Wave 1 to Wave 5. It is also important to note the extraordinary high percentage (17.4 per cent) of 'Single Non-Elderly' households within the group where no clear pattern is defined in Wave 5, which has increased considerably from Wave 1 (from 3.1 per cent to 17.4 per cent). This result shows that single non-elderly households have higher rates of mobility.

It is also worth mentioning the increase from Wave 1 to 5 among those who have moved to a non-rural area of the 'Lone parents with dependent children' category, from 0 per cent to 9.6 per cent.

In relation to household economic status, two or more earner households are again the most highly represented category within all three mover sub-samples. Here, it is important to mention how the percentage change is much higher for the group where no clear pattern is defined (58.7 per cent).

If we also look at the reasons for moving among those who have moved out of or within rural areas at any point during the 5 Waves of the BHPS (Table 8.3), we find that when they were asked whether they had moved for employment reasons or not, the majority answered 'No'. However, within the *movers* sub-sample, the percentage of those who moved for employment reasons is higher than in any of the other sub-samples (17.2 per cent compare to 8.8 per cent for *always rural* and 9.1 per cent for *always non-rural*). Bearing in mind that *movers* are moving in/out of rural

Table 8.2 Person type, household type and household economic status breakdowns according to migration patterns (column percentages)

	To non-rural			To rural			No patterns defined		
	W1	W5	W1-W5	W1	W5	W1-W5	W1	W5	W1-W5
Person type									
Male working age	32.2	34.3	32.2	34.2	33.5	33.0	37.4	39.3	34.7
Female working age	26.9	26.5	24.9	34.6	35.9	34.6	33.5	36.7	32.7
Male retired	10.2	10.2	10.2	2.9	4.2	2.9	0.9	3.6	0.9
Female retired	11.0	12.9	11.0	5.2	5.2	5.2	9.5	10.3	9.5
Dependent child	19.5	15.7	15.7	22.8	20.9	20.9	18.5	9.8	9.8
% changed type*			5.7			3.1			12.1
Household type									
Single Non-Elderly	4.0	4.2	0.0	4.9	6.0	1.5	3.1	17.4	0.5
Single Elderly	6.2	13.1	6.2	1.5	1.5	1.5	5.5	9.1	5.4
Couple No Children	27.2	24.2	10.9	26.0	25.7	12.1	22.7	29.4	13.5
Couple: dep children	37.8	45.9	21.2	44.0	40.0	26.8	44.4	23.4	10.1
Couple: non-dep children	8.9	2.6	0.0	8.4	10.1	2.0	18.7	9.1	2.4
Lone parent: dep children	0.0	9.6	0.0	9.1	11.9	2.8	4.8	6.2	2.5
Lone par: non-dep children	0.9	0.0	0.0	5.2	4.4	2.8	0.0	0.0	0.0
2 + Unrelated adults	1.9	0.0	0.0	0.5	0.0	0.0	0.6	4.0	0.0
Other households	12.8	0.0	0.0	0.0	0.0	0.0	0.0	1.0	0.0
Household Economic Status									
% changed type*			61.47			50.1			65.2
Unemployed	0.0	0.0	0.0	0.7	0.0	0.0	0.0	0.0	0.0
Economic Inactivity	10.5	25.9	9.3	17.6	14.6	3.8	17.2	36.2	16.5
1 earner in single household	5.3	3.2	0.0	4.9	4.5	1.5	2.4	7.9	0.5
1 earner household	26.6	23.0	10.0	25.0	25.2	8.5	11.0	14.0	0.0
2+ earners household	57.4	47.8	30.1	51.6	55.5	34.0	69.3	41.19	24.1
% changed type*			50.4			52.0			58.7

*/ % of the sub-sample whose type is the same in Wave 1 and Wave 5. For each type, (100 - sum of %₆₅) = % changed type.

Table 8.3   Reasons for moving

	Always rural	Always non-rural	Movers	To non-rural	To rural	No patterns
Moved for employment reasons						
YES	8.8	9.1	17.2	12.6	17.04	20.1
NO	91.2	90.9	82.8	87.4	82.9	79.8
Moved: Non employment reason						
Family	14.8	22.2	22.7	26.4	20.4	22.1
Housing	46.7	45.4	31.1	39.0	35.7	22.3
Other employment reasons	3.3	3.3	9.2	7.6	11.6	8.4
Retirement	0.0	0.3	1.1	0.0	2.2	0.9
Way of life	23.5	14.2	18.0	13.8	17.2	21.3
Others	11.5	14.3	17.7	12.9	12.6	24.8

areas, this result shows a close relationship between employment and geographical movements.

Migration in and out of rural areas has generated a considerable literature focused on aspects such as *push* and *pull* factors and urbanization and counter urbanization processes. The former have been identified as the movement of people to major cities seeking employment opportunities and a wider range of services, and the latter have been used to describe the redistribution of a population away from major cities and metropolitan areas towards more rural areas (Halliday et al., 1995, p. 433) in search of certain ways of life and the 'scenery'.

It can be seen that the 'classic' counter urbanization motives of scenery and way of life are not found to be as important as suggested in the literature, though the *rural* sub sample has a considerable percentage of people who moved for the perceived 'way of life' in rural areas (23.5 per cent). Instead, the main reasons given for having moved are employment, family and housing reasons. When asked for additional or non-employment reasons for moving, 'other employment reasons' was given by more people in the movers sub sample (9.2 per cent) than in either the non-rural or rural. Looking then at the 'movers' sub-sample, we discover that among those who had moved to a rural area there was a higher percentage giving employment based answers than among those who had moved to an urban area and those where there was no clear pattern defined, which could fit with the idea of globalization and counter-urbanization.

Changes in household economic status occur over time and people do not remain in the same category or in the same geographical area. These changes in household economic status and therefore in the number of earners within the household, affects annual household income and increases or decreases the probability of being disadvantaged and increases the risk of exclusion. In the next section we look at the extent to which these changes have taken place within our sample.

Patterns of household economic status in rural areas

The average movements between household economic status and location over the five Waves are given in Table 8.4. This table represents the matrix of transitions from any possible combinations of location (rural/non-rural) and household economic status from one period to the next and is formally an (inefficient) estimate of the appropriate Markov transition matrix (StataCorp, 1997, p. 652). Each row represents a household economic status/location combination for an initial time period, each column a household economic status/location for the subsequent time period, with each cell being the proportion on average who 'move' from one household economic status/location to another between periods.

The principal advantage of this type of analysis is that it accounts for both household economic status and locational mobility simultaneously. Hence, it is possible to undertake analysis of both intra and inter rural and non-rural household economic status mobility in a consistent manner.

We shall first consider intra household economic status mobility in the rural and non-rural areas, i.e. the sub-matrices containing rows 1-6 and 7-12 respectively. The highlighted figures give the average proportion of individuals who remain in the same household economic status between two periods. For both areas, the greatest degree of immobility occurs in the economically inactive category (mainly retired households). Immobility is also higher in the Single (1 earner) category for non-rural areas (80.20 per cent) than for rural ones (75.51 per cent). There is considerable movement among these single households towards economically inactive ones in rural areas (10.17 per cent) whereas, in non-rural areas, they tend to become households with 2 earners or more (9.32 per cent).

One interesting feature is that no unemployed households remain unemployed either in the rural sub-sample or in the movers one, while 4.22 per cent in the urban sub-sample do remain so. This shows either greater labour mobility in rural areas and/or a higher level of long term unemployment in urban areas.

Table 8.4 Household economic status and rural/non-rural location: transition matrix

		Rural						Non-Rural					
		1	2	3	4	5	6	7	8	9	10	11	12
Rural	1. Unemployed	0.00	24.41	0.00	34.9	40.68	0.00	0.00	0.00	0.00	0.00	0.00	0.00
	2. Economic Inactive	0.18	88.81	1.15	5.44	1.53	0.22	0.00	2.28	0.00	0.09	0.25	0.00
	3. Single (1 earner)	0.00	10.17	75.51	3.56	8.23	0.00	0.00	1.61	0.00	0.89	0.00	0.00
	4. Hhold (1 earner)	0.08	9.30	0.48	65.46	20.48	0.00	0.00	0.99	0.09	2.70	0.30	0.07
	5. Hhold (2+ earners)	0.04	1.01	0.39	11.46	83.03	0.00	0.04	0.83	0.18	0.30	2.61	0.00
	6. Others	0.00	63.87	0.00	20.24	0.00	15.88	0.00	0.00	0.00	0.00	0.00	0.00
Non-rural	1. Unemployed	0.00	0.00	0.00	1.16	0.00	0.00	4.22	26.19	13.58	35.71	19.11	0.00
	2. Economic Inactive	0.00	0.52	0.00	0.00	0.07	0.00	0.27	89.67	0.49	7.17	1.60	0.17
	3. Single (1 earner)	0.00	0.00	0.22	0.00	0.34	0.00	0.94	6.48	80.20	2.26	9.32	0.19
	4. Hhold (1 earner)	0.00	0.10	0.04	0.51	0.47	0.00	0.31	11.57	0.78	64.63	21.52	0.02
	5. Hhold (2+ earners)	0.00	0.03	0.07	0.07	0.61	0.00	0.10	2.02	1.19	10.11	85.72	0.04
	6. Others	0.00	5.83	0.00	0.00	0.00	0.00	2.47	27.81	13.98	10.79	27.76	11.33

Overall, we find that despite some tendency to remain in the same situation, mobility is still an outstanding feature within the overall sample. People do not stay within the same household economic status and the number of people in employment within the household does not remain the same. This leads us to the next section of the paper where we investigate whether changes in household economic status and in the number of people employed within the household do really put families in a more precarious situation, and if so, observe if this tendency is worse in rural areas.

Changing household economic status and the implications for poverty/social exclusion

We now turn to examine the relationship between household economic status and the risk of deprivation and exclusion. As a trigger either into or out of 'social exclusion/disadvantage', we use income as an indicator of risk. We take what we have called the *low-income threshold*: this is the figure below which somebody is more likely to suffer from poverty/social exclusion. The low-income threshold used is half the Wave 1 (Year 1991) mean income of the whole sample (which is fixed in real income terms).

The real income value of the threshold is £4,478.374 per annum for all 5 Waves. The particular level of the chosen threshold is of course somewhat arbitrary, as there is no clear-cut evidence of a sharp increase in poverty or deprivation at a particular threshold. However, using half the mean income has the virtue of being commonly used in British empirical research on incomes (see, for example, Jenkins and Jarvis, 1996, p. 14), and provides a sufficiently large number of cases in the low income sub-sample to allow meaningful breakdowns by sub-sample characteristics.

Cross-sectional analysis of household income distribution gives us a biased idea of turnover of individuals within the distribution (snapshots do not tell us about lifetime inequality). When viewed in a dynamic context, aspects such as the extent of the persistence of low income can be analyzed. In order to do this Table 8.5 provides information on the composition of the low income group by reporting the proportion of time spent in low income. Break down by household economic status is also provided.

For ease of interpretation, we consider firstly those sub-samples made up of individuals who are either always rural or non-rural. We find that 7.4 per cent of the always rural group spent 100 per cent or all five periods in low income while 33.6 per cent of this rural population experienced at least one low income spell in the period.

We find that 10.1 per cent of the always non-rural sub-sample had an income below half the Wave 1 mean income for all five interview periods. Whether this figure indicates that the incidence of persistent low income is relatively high or not is difficult to judge, and depends very much on whether one believes the cut-off is meaningful or not in terms of household deprivation. However, and in order to compare the rural and non-rural sub-samples, the cut off is very useful since it helps us to observe that the persistent low income problem is higher in the always non-rural sub-sample.

Table 8.5   Proportion of time in low income

	Proportion Time spent in low income (0.5)					
	0	>0 - <= 0.2	>0.2- <=0.4	>0.4- <=0.6	>0.6- <=0.8	>0.8 - <=1.0
Always Rural						
All	0.664	0.112	0.043	0.051	0.056	0.074
Economic Inactive	0.387	0.128	0.064	0.079	0.135	0.203
Single (1 earner)	0.938	0.061	0.000	0.000	0.000	0.000
Hhold (1 earner)	0.686	0.180	0.029	0.000	0.000	0.103
Hhold (2+ earners)	0.905	0.053	0.028	0.000	0.012	0.000
Hhold Econ Status chang	0.618	0.135	0.045	0.083	0.058	0.058
Always Non-rural						
All	0.591	0.100	0.084	0.056	0.068	0.101
Economic Inactive	0.262	0.098	0.085	0.100	0.155	0.297
Single (1 earner)	0.863	0.046	0.027	0.000	0.046	0.015
Hhold (1 earner)	0.683	0.110	0.090	0.071	0.019	0.024
Hhold (2+ earners)	0.910	0.050	0.027	0.003	0.004	0.004
Hhold Econ Status chang	0.533	0.132	0.122	0.066	0.071	0.074
Movers						
All	0.692	0.000	0.058	0.041	0.040	0.167
Economic Inactive	0.387	0.000	0.111	0.072	0.070	0.358
Single (1 earner)	0.859	0.000	0.000	0.000	0.000	0.140
Hhold (1 earner)	0.537	0.000	0.130	0.000	0.166	0.166
Hhold (2+ earners)	0.916	0.000	0.028	0.015	0.000	0.038
Hhold Econ Status chang	0.649	0.000	0.058	0.051	0.043	0.196

Note: Longitudinal sample n=7164 (always rural=968; always non-rural=5892).

The persistent low-income problem is not as acute in the *always rural* sub-sample as it is in the *always non-rural* one.

For those people that have remained *economically inactive* in the 5 Waves, again the low income problem is higher in non-rural areas, with economically inactive people being in a worse financial situation than those in rural areas.

Single person (1 earner) households seem to be the richest group in the sample. There is a very high percentage in the rural sub-sample of non-single person households, which have only one earner, compared to the other sub-samples (this group represents 7.27 per cent of the rural sub-sample). Of such households, 10.3 per cent have a persistent low income along the 5 Waves (compared to only 2.4 per cent in the non-rural sample). The more people in employment within the household the less likely the household is to have a persistently low income.

Finally, rows 6 and 12 (for always rural and always non-rural) show those people that have moved from one household economic status to another along the five Waves. Once again, the percentages are spread out along the different categories of low-income duration. According to our definition of a low-income cut-off, a minority of the population had a low income at every Wave (persistently low-income), however many more had a low income at one period or another. If we focus on the always rural sub-sample as a whole, we find that 11.6 per cent had a low income for at least 4 interviews, 19.9 had a low income for at least three interviews, 24.4 had a low income for at least two interviews, and 37.9 per cent had a low income for at least one interview in five (14.5 per cent, 21.1 per cent, 33.3 per cent and 46.5 per cent for the urban sub-sample). The relatively high proportions of the samples experiencing low income over a given period shows how income mobility is common at all points along the income range. The extent of low-income turnover has important policy implications. Since many of those on a low income would be eligible for welfare benefits, the figures indicate that the welfare benefit system has an important role in providing short-term support. Put another way, many more people are helped by the benefit system than is revealed by simply focusing on the welfare benefit caseload at a given point in time (Jarvis and Jenkins, 1996, p.18).

Modelling transition probabilities into and out of low income

This section focuses on transitions into and out of low income and the factors that influence them (focusing especially on household economic status). The results are provided by simple probit models for the probability of being on a low income in one year given a high income the previous year (entering poverty) and of being on a high income in one year given a low income the previous year (escaping poverty).

Table 8.6a-b presents the Probit model estimated effects for the conditional probability of escaping/re-entering poverty for the pooled sample as a whole and for the rural/urban and movers sub-samples. The results are generated in relation to a 'base' group. In the first instance, this consists of households with no one in employment (Household Economic Status), in the second it is males of working age (Person Type) and in the third it is couples with dependent children (Household Type). The first four columns report the probability of being on a high income in year 't' given a low income in year t-1 (leaving poverty). The first thing to note is the higher observed proportion of people moving out of poverty in the movers sub-sample (31.7 per cent compare to 28.2 per cent and 26.2 per cent in the rural and non-rural sub-samples). This is not surprising since we have found earlier on how this sub-sample is more likely to have shorter spells of low income.

In order to look at how the number of people in employment within the household influences the possibility of leaving/entering low income, we will concentrate only on household economic status variables. These variables are found to have a significant effect at the 5 per cent level of significance in both the whole sample and the rural, non-rural and movers sub-samples. In the whole sample as well as in the non-rural and rural sub-sample, the probability of leaving poverty increases with the increase in the number of people in employment. This way we can say that, for the whole sample, the probability of leaving poverty in households with 3 or more people in employment is 0.371 higher than in those households with no one in employment. The marginal increases in these probabilities are bigger in the rural sub-sample which shows how an increase in the number of earners in a household in rural areas is significantly more important than in urban areas. This supports our theory that low wages are more common in rural areas, and therefore multiple earning households more significant and necessary. Notice that the movers sub-sample behaves a little oddly due to the small sample size.

The last 4 columns provide us with the probability of being on a low income in year t given a high income in year t-1 (entering poverty). The proportion of people entering poverty in the non-rural group is higher than in the rural one (8.2 per cent as suppose to 6.2 per cent). Once again, household economic status seems to be significant at the 5 per cent level in both the whole sample and the rural and non-rural sub-samples. The probability of entering poverty for rural households with 1 worker is 0.025 lower than for rural households with no-one employed and equally, 0.087

Table 8.6a Probit model estimated marginal effects for conditional probability of low and high income in t given low and high income in t-1*

	P (high income in t| low income in t-1) (leaving poverty)				P(low income in t| high income in t-1) (entering poverty)			
Level	All	Always Rural	Always Non-rural	Movers	All	Always Rural	Always Non-rural	Movers
Household Economic Status								
1 employee	0.217 (0.000)	0.103 (0.055)	0.252 (0.000)	-0.181 (0.109)	-0.067 (0.000)	-0.025 (0.015)	-0.077 (0.000)	-0.038 (0.304)
2 employees	0.258 (0.000)	0.311 (0.000)	0.269 (0.000)	-0.213 (0.096)	-0.124 (0.000)	-0.087 (0.000)	-0.135 (0.000)	-0.073 (0.051)
3+ employees	0.371 (0.000)	0.647 (0.001)	0.339 (0.000)	0.026 (0.897)	-0.076 (0.000)	-0.054 (0.000)	-0.080 (0.000)	-0.035 (0.467)
Person Type								
Female working	-0.008 (0.623)	-0.074 (0.155)	-0.006 (0.762)	-0.008 (0.932)	0.008 (0.077)	0.005 (0.634)	0.008 (0.140)	0.027 (0.319)
Male retired	0.005 (0.869)	-0.031 (0.721)	0.026 (0.443)	-0.174 (0.232)	-0.017 (0.053)	-0.012 (0.499)	-0.028 (0.003)	0.266 (0.005)
Female retired	-0.042 (0.142)	-0.125 (0.126)	-0.021 (0.510)	-0.081 (0.674)	-0.007 (0.425)	0.005 (0.743)	-0.018 (0.046)	0.209 (0.014)
Dependent child	-0.046 (0.014)	-0.143 (0.007)	-0.037 (0.067)	-0.019 (0.845)	0.018 (0.002)	0.008 (0.510)	0.018 (0.004)	0.054 (0.109)

Table 8.6b Probit model estimated marginal effects for conditional probability of low and high income in t given low and high income in t-1*

Household type								
Single non-elderly	0.116	0.052	0.130	-0.049	-0.041	-0.030	-0.039	-0.095
	(0.001)	(0.611)	(0.000)	(0.853)	(0.000)	(0.028)	(0.000)	(0.008)
Single elderly	0.086	0.083	0.082	-0.290	0.0059	0.035	0.006	-0.048
	(0.010)	(0.401)	(0.023)	(0.141)	(0.562)	(0.127)	(0.596)	(0.446)
Couple no children	0.121	0.154	0.108	0.016	-0.034	-0.037	-0.029	-0.061
	(0.000)	(0.059)	(0.000)	(0.911)	(0.000)	(0.001)	(0.000)	(0.022)
Couple: No dep children	-0.024	-0.073	-0.006	-0.191	-0.018	0.011	-0.016	-0.079
	(0.529)	(0.481)	(0.878)	(0.234)	(0.039)	(0.654)	(0.074)	(0.014)
Lone parents: dep children	-0.054	-0.103	-0.045	-0.262	0.038	-0.005	0.043	0.029
	(0.003)	(0.112)	(0.021)	(0.009)	(0.000)	(0.831)	(0.000)	(0.612)
Lone par: No dep children	0.138	0.089	0.106	-	0.015	0.025	0.019	-0.023
	(0.005)	(0.601)	(0.042)		(0.234)	(0.492)	(0.148)	(0.711)
2 + Unrelated adults	0.291	-0.030	0.336	-	-0.032	0.072	-0.037	-
	(0.000)	(0.861)	(0.000)		(0.026)	(0.249)	(0.012)	
Pseudo R^2	0.057	0.097	0.061	0.068	0.083	0.100	0.09	0.08
Observed proportion	0.267	0.282	0.262	0.317	0.081	0.062	0.082	0.115
Sample size	6035	715	5099	219	22884	3157	18469	1258

*Table gives estimated marginal effects from a Probit model.
P>|z| in brackets Pooled BHPS data for t=1992 to 1995.

lower for households with 2 people employed and, 0.054 with 3 or more people employed. These results depend very much on the characteristics of any given household, as they are not the same for single person households with only one member who is employed and households with five members where only 1 of them is employed. For example, the probability of leaving a low income is 0.116 higher in single non-elderly households compared to the probability for couples with dependent children, while the probability of this group entering poverty is 0.041 lower than it is for couples with dependent children. The single non-elderly households seem to be the group at less risk.

Summary and conclusions

In a context of globalization and regional restructuring, this paper has provided a preliminary analysis of the changes undergone in rural areas of the UK in the last 5 years as compared to their non-rural counterparts. In particular, it has focused on the analysis of transitions into and out of low come with a focus on household economic status. The data used is from the first 5 Waves (years) of the British Household Panel Survey, 1991-1995.

We have found how people of working age (both male and female) as well as couples without dependent children tend to move geographically more than the rest of the sample, which gives us a preliminary indication that migration may be employment led.

Within the *movers* sub-sample, the percentage of those who moved for employment reasons is higher than in any of the other sub-samples. Bearing in mind that *movers* are moving in/out of rural areas, this result shows again a close relationship between employment and geographical movements.

'Single non-elderly' households seem to move back and forth from rural/non-rural areas at a higher rate than other households, which shows the not surprising finding of higher mobility among this category of households.

It can be seen that the 'classic' counter urbanization motives of scenery and way of life are not found to be as important as suggested in the literature, though the *rural* sub-sample has a considerable percentage of people who moved for the perceived 'way of life' in rural areas. Instead, the main reasons given for having moved are employment, family and housing reasons. There is much more mobility in the movers sub-sample for all types of family economic status than in any of the other sub-samples.

An initial analysis of the distribution of income among the individuals in the rural sub-sample confirms previous findings that the extent of low incomes in rural areas is significant. However, comparatively it appears less than that for non-rural areas, both in terms of the proportion of individuals experiencing low incomes and in terms of the overall inequality (persistency). It has also been observed how people in the movers category are more spread out along the income sequence patterns, with a large number of people being more likely to have short spells of low income.

The more people in employment within the household the less likely the household is to have a persistently low income. Table 8.5 showed how more than 90 per cent of the households with 2 or more earners are above the absolute low-income cut-off, for all three sub-samples.

In the rural area, the low-income households with two or more earners are more represented than in non-rural areas. The distribution of low-income households across the household economic status suggests that there is a greater incidence of low pay in rural areas than there is in urban areas, and that this contributes to low income to a greater extent for rural people.

From modelling the transition probabilities into and out of a low income, we have found that in the whole sample, as well as in the urban and rural sub-sample, the probability of leaving poverty increases with the increase in the number of people in employment. The marginal increases in this probability is greater in the rural sub-sample which shows how an increase in the number of earners in a household in a rural area is significantly more important than in urban areas.

Clearly while these results provide us with some preliminary understanding of the dynamics of change in general, and low-income and household economic status in particular, in rural areas and how different they are from their non-rural counterparts, there is still a considerable amount of research to be done. For instance, the issue of the relative costs of living in rural areas is not considered, the topic of gender has not been addressed, and nor do we know much about the quality of employment, hours worked, wages and the duration of employment spells. There is thus considerable scope to use the BHPS further to add greater depth to the findings and insights gained so far.

The results, however, are valuable, and they provide a starting point for further work.

Acknowledgements

The authors wish to express our thanks to the Joseph Rowntree Foundation and its staff for supporting the project entitled, 'Poverty and exclusion in rural Britain. The dynamics of low income and employment', undertaken by the Arkleton Centre for Rural Development Research at the University of Aberdeen. This chapter came out of this major project and it is the result of team work. We would like to express particular thanks to the rest of the team, to Mark Shucksmith, Euan Phimister, Richard Upward and Deb Roberts, who contributed to the research design and with their very valuable comments and discussions about the work.

We also received invaluable help in obtaining the necessary data from Brian Wilson (Rural Development Commission) and George Duguid (Scottish Office), as well as from Nick Buck (ESRC, Research Centre on Micro-Social Change, University of Essex).

The data used in this chapter were made available through the ESRC Data Archive. The data were originally collected by the ESRC Research Centre on Micro-Social Change at the University of Essex. Neither the original collectors of the data nor the Archive bear any responsibility for the analyses or interpretations presented here. As usual, responsibility for this work rests with the authors alone.

Notes

1   By 'Wave' the authors mean the 'interview year'.
2   The data used were made available through the ESRC Data Archive. The data were originally collected by the ESRC, Research Centre on Micro-Social Change (University of Essex). The Archive does not bear any responsibility for the analysis undertaken here.
3   All reported statistics are weighted to ensure that the results remain representative over the five years. Income related variables are deflated to 1991 prices, as well as having been equivalised using McClements equivalence scales, to ensure that incomes are adjusted for household size.
4   The available information for Scotland means that the definition for Scottish 'rural' is slightly different, being based upon the Scottish Office definition. However, the results presented are robust even with the inclusion of the Scottish based observations.

References

Abrahamson, P. (1996), 'Social Exclusion in Europe: Old Wine in New Bottles?' paper presented at the European Science Foundation Conference on 'Social Exclusion and Social Integration in Europe: Theoretical and Policy Perspectives on Poverty and Inequality', Blarney, March 1996.

Amin, A. (1997), 'Placing Globalization', paper presented at the RGS-IBG Annual Conference, Exeter 7-9 January 1997.

Berghman, J. (1995), 'Social Exclusion in Europe: Policy Context and Analytical Framework', in Room, G. (ed), *Beyond the Threshold: The Measurement and Analysis of Social Exclusion*, The Policy Press: Bristol.

Boyle, P. (1995), 'Rural in-migration in England and Wales 1980-1981', *Journal of Rural Studies*, Vol. 11, No. 1, pp. 65-78.

Cooke, P. (ed) (1986), *Global Restructuring and Local Response*, Economic and Social Research Council: London.

Dawes, L. (1993), *Long Term Unemployment and Labour Market Flexibility*, University Centre for Labour Market Studies: Leicester.

Ehrensaft, P. (1997), 'International Perspectives on Rural Employment: Introductory Propositions', in Bollman, R. and Bryden, J. (eds), *Rural Employment. An International Perspective*, CAB International: Oxon.

Errington, A. (1990), 'Rural Employment in England: Some Data Sources and their Use', *Journal of Agricultural Economics*, Vol. 41, pp. 47-61.

Harper, S. (1991), 'People Moving to the Countryside: Case Studies of Decision-Making in People in the Countryside', in Champion, T and Watkins, C. (eds), *Studies of Social Change in Rural Britain*, Paul Chapman Publishing, Ltd.: London.

Held, D. (1995), *Democracy and the Global Order*, Polity: Cambridge.

Hirst, P. and Thompson, G. (1996), 'Globalization: Ten Frequently Asked Questions and Some Surprising Answers', *Soundings*, Vol. 4, pp. 47-66.

Hodge, I. and Whitby, M. (1981), *Rural Employment: Trends, Options and Choices*, Methuen: London.

Massey, D. and Meegan, R. (1982), *The Anatomy of Job Loss*, Methuen: London.

Meyer, H. von (1997), 'Rural Employment in OECD Countries: Structure and Dynamics of Regional Labour Markets', in Bollman, R. and Bryden, J. (eds), *Rural Employment. An International Perspective*, CAB International: Oxon.

Oppenheim, C. (1993), *Poverty: The Facts*, CPAG: London.

Ramsay, H. (1992), 'Whose Champions? Multinationals, Labour and Industry Policy in the European Community after 1992', *Capital and Class*, No 48, pp.17-39.

Room, G. (1990), *'New Poverty' in the European Community*, Macmillan: Basingstoke.

Shaw, J.M. (1979), *Rural Deprivation and Planning*, Geobooks: Norwich.

Strange, S. (1991), 'An Eclectic Approach', in Murphy, C.N. and Tooze, R. (eds), *The New International Political Economy*, Reinner: Boulder.

Taylor, M.F. (ed) with Brice, J., Buck, N. and Prentice, E. (1996), *British Household Panel Survey User Manual Volume A: Introduction, Technical Report and Appendices*, University of Essex: Colchester.

Townsend, P. (1979), *Poverty in the United Kingdom,* Penguin.

Walker, R. (1995), 'The Dynamics of Poverty and Social Exclusion', in Room, G. (ed), *Beyond the Threshold: The Measurement and Analysis of Social Exclusion*, The Policy Press: Bristol.

Part IV

Local and Regional Development

Part IV

Stress and Regional Environment

9 Globalization and Rural Development: Demographic Revitalization, Entrepreneurs and Small Business Formation in the West of Ireland

PERPETUA McDONAGH AND PATRICK COMMINS

Introduction

Globalization and rural development

Although in a certain restricted sense globalization is not new, there is general agreement that a more dramatic transition from a limited international economy to a globalizing economy has been taking place since the 1970s. The term 'globalization' is now taken to refer to the economic, political and social connections that cross cut borders between countries and continents and decisively condition the fate of those living within each of them (Giddens, 1993, p. 528). More analytically, and following Wilding (1997), we may note that globalization most commonly describes trends but is also used to explain such trends, and, additionally, serves as an ideology – a set of beliefs about what trends are more desirable than others. Used as a descriptive term, globalization encompasses a number of interrelated trends including the global reach and scale of financial and capital structures, the transnationalization of technology, the intensification of global communications and information transfer, the rise of global corporations and the increasing volume and complexity of global 'cultural flows'. These flows are evident in the dissemination of common forms of consumption, sets of ideas and media outputs. At the political level, the globalization of economic forces is synchronized with a need for change in institutional and regulatory structures. For example, as the capacity of independent states to deal autonomously with vital policy issues is reduced, there is a growth of worldwide authority structures such as the World Trade Organization.

As an explanatory concept, globalization draws attention to the possible impacts of these various trends on, for example, the economic prospects of regional or peripheral economies, the viability of indigenous enterprise, local community development and demographic processes. In the particular case of demographic dynamics, population movements, in turn, may impact on local development activities. The relationships between rural population replacement and rural enterprise development are in fact one of the themes of this chapter. As an ideology, globalization is a project of powerful forces (such as financial interests) which seeks to legitimize competitiveness, deregulation, the free movement of products and services and new orders of priority in social and economic policy. Policies, for example, may be directed towards enhancing sectoral economic efficiencies nationally rather than responding to needs of disadvantaged rural regions.

Globalization does not necessarily mean the homogenization of material conditions nor the erosion of territorial distinctiveness but rather an added set of influences on local economic identities and development capabilities (Amin and Thrift, 1994, p.2). In fact, some observers (e.g. O'Hearn, 1993) have argued that a primary aim of European integration is success in global competition and this will oblige states and firms to pursue strategies that impede regional convergence thus reinforcing existing production and core-periphery hierarchies. However, Bryant (1995, p. 255) has noted that in interpreting the transformation of rural space, much attention has been given to macro-scale processes, particularly those of capitalist accumulation and uneven development. Often the role of 'local agency' is insufficiently recognized in the face of the supposedly determining influences of global integration. However, with the retreat of the central state from direct interventionism to 'provider', 'facilitator' or 'enabler' functions (Goodwin, 1998), the roles of local actors and local capacities are receiving more attention. Over the past decade, since the European Commission published *The Future of Rural Society* (CEC, 1988), policy-makers have stressed the need to maximize indigenous potential and economic diversification in response to rural decline. This increased emphasis given to 'localized action spaces' has gone hand in hand with trends that appear contradictory to the internationalization of capital and markets. One of these counter trends, or 'relocalization', is the rise in importance of medium, small and now micro-scale businesses as important job creators (Bryant, 1995, p. 256). On a similar point, Wilding (1997, p. 415) notes that the decline in the ability of states to manage the economy at the macro-level has pushed administrations into giving a clearer priority to economic policy at the more micro-level, to try to create a local economic environment attractive to international capital and conducive to the development of local economic initiatives.

In regard to rural areas, specifically, there are indications that they have the capacity to capitalize on opportunities arising from global integration. Apart from the public policy emphasis on local entrepreneurship and the revalorization of indigenous resources, rural enterprise can profit from the plant scale reductions and flexible production systems being adopted by large corporations, their tendency to externalise some functions (e.g. transport and delivery) by subcontracting, the development of niche markets and customised products, and consumer preferences for products of traceable local origin and identity. Global markets extend the potential for small rural businesses – provided they are competitive. Modern communication technologies facilitate access to information, irrespective of location. A heightened awareness of the environmental value, physical attractiveness and improved quality of life in rural areas, together with increased physical mobility, makes rural settings more attractive than formerly for entrepreneurs and employees. For certain types of rural areas, then, prospects are emerging for a 'new rural economy'.

Rural restructuring and rural population replacement

In formulating policies for rural areas, a central underlying concern has been the need to counter rural depopulation by providing employment opportunities. The restructuring of production agriculture, and indeed of agri-business, has been marked in particular by the shedding of surplus labour and this has often meant out-migration and population loss. With the exception of research in England which indicates that there is a connection between migration into rural areas and high rates of new firm formation in those areas (Keeble et al., 1992), research has paid comparatively little attention to the relationships between the 'new rural economy' and demographic processes – although studies have been concerned with the separate themes of small and medium enterprise (SME) development and changing rural demography (see, e.g., Turok and Richardson, 1991; Keeble et al., 1992; North and Smallbone, 1996; Buller and Hoggart, 1994; Boyle, 1995; Cawley 1990). Ireland's case suggests that, in the shadow of historical and continuing out-migration from rural areas, there is a stream of in-migration, even if its scale may not be sufficient to offset the outward flow. Recently Irish researchers (Tovey et al., 1996; Jackson and Haase, 1996) have drawn attention to an 'over focus' on population decline, suggesting that this comes from an assumption that the ideal is a continuous

182 *Local Responses to Global Integration*

process of replacement from within. In the context of globalization, the reality is that population trends reflect a dynamic process of interchange, creating transformations over time in the types of social groups, and consequently the types of activities, that characterize rural areas (Tovey et al., 1996, p. 32).

Focus and structure

The focus of this chapter is on rural restructuring as manifested in the development of SMEs (enterprises employing fewer than 50 persons) in three predominantly rural counties, Mayo, Galway and Clare, in the west of Ireland. More specifically, we are concerned with the relationships between the formation and development of SMEs as a state-sponsored rural development strategy and the way in which rural restructuring on this basis is related to demographic processes. The remainder of the chapter is in four parts. The first sets a context by summarizing population census data to show that out-migration (or low growth) in the indigenous population masks a secondary but dynamic process of population replacement through in-migration. Furthermore, in-comers differ from the 'usually resident' in regard to occupational and socio-economic characteristics. The second part of the chapter presents returns from a survey of SMEs in the three counties, illustrating the significance of in-comers in the formation of new rural-based businesses. The third part continues the survey analysis in assessing the impact of the new businesses on local economic and demographic structures. A final section briefly summarizes the global-local relationships emerging from the analysis.

Population replacement in the west of Ireland

In Ireland, the percentage of persons born outside their county of census enumeration increased from 19.4 per cent in 1971 to 26.4 per cent in 1996. The percentages born outside the State increased from 6.5 to 7.5 per cent in the same period. In fact, at each census during 1971-1996 all but four of the State's 26 counties recorded increases in the percentages of their enumerated populations who were born outside the country.

In the most rural and western province, Connacht, the percentage of 'non-natives' increased from 14.3 per cent to 25.9 per cent during 1971-1996. The increases in absolute numbers were particularly high during 1991-1996, with 'other county' born rising by 4,543 or 6.3 per cent and those born outside the State increasing by 6,586 or 22.4 per cent. Except for a short period in the 1970s, Connacht had net outward migration in each intercensal period from 1926 to 1991.

This population replacement process is pointedly illustrated in the case of one of the Connacht counties, County Leitrim. Leitrim has long been recognized as having all the characteristics of rural out-migration and depopulation. Between 1971 and 1996 its recorded population fell steadily from 28,360 to 25,060. Yet, in this period the numbers of 'non-Leitrim' people living in the county rose from 4,660 to 7,630, representing an increase in the percentage incidence of 'non-natives' from 16.4 per cent to 30.4 per cent. In the 1996 Census approximately one person in eleven enumerated in the county was born outside the State.

The three counties of the study area are within the less favoured areas of the country and between them have a population of 394,400 but only two large (by Irish standards) urban centres: Galway city with 57,000 inhabitants and the linked towns of Ennis-Shannon with 25,000 persons. Shannon, however, is close to Limerick City, which has 52,000 persons. Two-thirds of the three-county population live outside the centres of 1,500 or more people.

For decades the areas outside these centres have experienced out-migration and depopulation. During the 1980s in each of the counties (urban and rural areas aggregated), out-migration exceeded in-migration. Nevertheless, between 1971 and 1996, the percentage of persons residing in each of the counties but (who were) born outside the county increased steadily – from 16 to 36 per cent in Clare, 14 to 24 per cent in Galway, and from 11 to 21 per cent in Mayo.

The dynamics of population replacement are further illustrated by comparing trends in the 'native' and 'in-comer' categories over three time periods (Table 9.1). Except for the most rural county, Mayo, during the 1980s, declines or low growth in the native category were offset by in-migration.

Because of the absence of data, little is known about the 'in-comers' – their gender, ages, occupations or social class. However, some impression can be obtained by reference to census data, which gives information on persons enumerated in a county, classified by 'usual residence one year previously'. It is possible, therefore, to compare those in a county who were living at the same address one year prior to census date with those having addresses in different categories of area at that time. However, this one-year time interval reduces the number of 'non-natives' for whom information is available.

Analysis of the relevant census data (for 1991 and 1996 depending on availability) is summarized as follows. Firstly, during 1991-96, taking males and females separately for each of the three counties, the rates of increase among the in-comers exceeded those for county natives. Secondly, females formed a higher proportion of the in-comers. Thirdly, in-comers, both male and female, were younger, the majority being in the 15-35 year age group. Fourthly, most 'incoming' males were in the labour force, compared to about half of the usually resident male population. Of the males in the labour force, the largest categories of 'in-comers' were 'producers, makers and repairers' and 'professional and technical workers', whereas 'agricultural workers' were predominant among the longer established male population. Among females, the occupational differences between 'new residents' and 'usual residents' were less clear. 'Incoming' females were more likely to be in the labour force but their occupations did not vary greatly from the 'established' female population, both groups being primarily in 'clerical' and 'professional and technical' positions. Fifthly, among males, in-comers were more likely to be skilled manual workers. For females, the differentiating factor was a higher incidence of 'intermediate non-manual workers' among the new arrivals. Finally, as regards social class a higher proportion of the in-comers were classified as 'professional' and 'skilled' and a lower proportion recorded as 'unskilled', when compared to county natives.

Table 9.1   Changes in different categories of population, by birthplace

County of Enumeration	Birthplace			Net change
	County of enumeration ('natives')	Other county	Outside the State	
		('in-comers')		
1971-1981				
Clare	-179	+8937	+3801	+12559
Galway	+8125	+7806	+6864	+22795
Mayo	-3009	+3695	+4555	+5241
1981-1991				
Clare	-4808	+7915	+244	+3351
Galway	+1910	+4907	+1529	+8346
Mayo	-5355	+1584	-282	-4053
1991-1996				
Clare	+2310	-505	+1283	+3088
Galway	+2032	+3069	+3398	+8490
Mayo	-848	+346	+1313	+811

Source: Census of Population, 1971, 1981, 1991 and 1996.

Despite the time-span limitations of the data, results suggest that in-comers play a significant role in shaping the demography of the three-county area. Over 7,000 in-comers arrived between 1991 and 1996 alone. It may be premature to argue that a reversal of the 'brain drain' is underway. However, experienced and skilled workers are moving to the area. Their socioeconomic profile makes it equally unreliable to dismiss the likelihood of a break with historical trends of depopulation and human resource decline. Increasing physical mobility and new employment prospects are facilitating return and replacement migration, and are stemming from out-migration in some rural areas.

These trends are the outcome of market forces but they are also a reflection of a degree of success of State policies to promote economic diversification in disadvantaged rural regions. We now turn to a specific aspect of these policies – the promotion of SMEs and the impact of enterprises in rural areas.

SMEs as a rural development strategy

Before presenting the results from the survey of enterprises in the three counties, it is helpful to summarize the main reasons suggested by Turok and Richardson (1991) as to why policy-makers now pay particular attention to fostering SMEs in rural areas.

Emergence and potential role of SMEs

Firstly, as already indicated, SMEs create jobs. Businesses with fewer than 50 employees accounted for over one quarter of those employed in manufacturing in Ireland in 1993 (Task Force on Small Business, 1994). Secondly, new small firms are thought to provide opportunities for people who are economically vulnerable or marginalized. In rural areas, these will be on small farms, with few skills, but they may have a certain amount of assets; they will include the unemployed or underemployed, early school-leavers, those seeking their first job, women and the unskilled – sectors of the labour force often overlooked by other employers. Thirdly, small firms are frequently considered to be flexible, dynamic and innovative, being supposedly more adaptable to changing economic conditions and technological needs. Innovation may occur by introducing new products, new technologies, new processes, new markets, thereby diversifying the local economy. Fourthly, small firms are thought to be a means of achieving sustainable economic growth in a local economy. They may purchase their materials locally; local ownership and control may confer greater loyalty and economic stability than external ownership. However, it has also been pointed out that there is considerable diversity among small businesses and that there are large sectoral differences in the extent to which firms are involved in trading beyond the boundaries of their localities (Curran and Blackburn, 1994, p. 164). Fifthly, small enterprises are considered to improve the performance of other parts of the economy, for example, by limiting the ability of larger firms to monopolize the local market or charge excessive prices, by subcontracting to other local businesses, or by utilizing local services.

One impetus to the growth of new enterprise is the 'recession push factor', in which individuals are 'forced' to set up their own business because their progress in paid employment is blocked, or they even find themselves facing redundancy. On the other hand, a general buoyancy in the economy creates a climate which disposes those in secure employment to take risks in pursuing a business idea which their employment experience may have helped them to formulate. Importantly, in the context of the theme of the present chapter, a healthy economy also encourages return- and in-migration which may boost entrepreneurial talent in areas traditionally associated with a depletion of human resources and socioeconomic decline. The suggestion is that vibrant economic activity creates a stimulating business milieu in which enterprise is to a considerable extent self-generating – even if all individual firms do not survive.

Designing the survey of SMEs

The study of small-scale business enterprises in the three western counties concentrated on businesses which had received grant assistance from public sources. Although state support for enterprise development is available throughout the country it is delivered in the chosen study area by three separate public agencies (Forbairt/IDA in Mayo, Shannon Development in Clare and Údarás na Gaeltachta in west Galway).[1] These agencies represent, respectively, a national, regional and more localized approach to enterprise development and job creation, thereby allowing coverage of State-supported entrepreneurial activity at various spatial levels. To simplify our investigation and reduce variance arising from the diversity of business types, the survey was confined to small fabrication/manufacturing firms. Hereafter we use 'manufacturing' to include varieties of fabrication, such as stonework and craft activities.

To select a sample of SMEs we focused on firms employing less than 50 persons, which received grant assistance between 1990 and 1994. This time period was chosen to minimize recall problems at the time of the survey, while letting a sufficient period of time elapse to allow businesses to impact on local socio-demographic and economic conditions.

Restricted access was obtained to a central database provided by the public agencies involved with enterprise development. A relevant population of 247 enterprises within the study area was identified.[2] In early 1996 completed personal interview schedules were obtained from 'business responsibles' in 148 enterprises; these comprised 123 business owners and 25 managers.[3]

The increasing emphasis on the potential of small enterprises to generate economic diversity in rural areas and thereby offset some of the labour decline in the agricultural sector, has not been accompanied by detailed analysis of who sets up businesses in rural areas, what types of small firms are established, or what contributions they actually make to the local communities in which they locate. The interview schedule focused primarily on these issues.

Origins of business responsibles

Given that aggregate data revealed return and in-migration to the study area, an objective of the survey data was to establish whether 'in-comers' played any role in setting up or managing SMEs. In fact, the majority of respondents had recently moved to the area where their businesses were located. Of the 123 owners, 75 (61 per cent) had grown up in the three-county area (Table 9.2), but of these 'native' entrepreneurs (the terms 'owners' and 'entrepreneurs' are used interchangeably), one-third had worked outside the area for some time. They had moved to secure employment and for personal reasons, and had acquired work experience and developed their skills before returning. Most had returned before establishing their businesses.

A further 48 entrepreneurs (39 per cent) had moved to the study area, primarily from other parts of the country although, interestingly, 15 were non-nationals (Table 9.2). More than half of these resided in the study area before setting up their businesses, the majority having relocated to avail of employment opportunities within larger manufacturing enterprises.

Only 12 of the 25 managers interviewed came originally from the study area and the majority of these had lived away from home at some stage, mainly for employment purposes (Table 9.2). There were only three foreign managers in the sample; not surprisingly, they were involved with firms having multinational connections. Three out of every four managers moving to the area did so to avail of employment opportunities.

Table 9.2   Origins of business responsibles

	No. of owner entrepreneurs (%)	No. of managers (%)
From the study area	75 (61)	12 (48)
of which:		
had never lived/worked outside the area	50 (41)	5 (20)
had lived/worked outside the area and had returned	25 (20)	7 (28)
Not from the study area	48 (39)	13 (52)
of which:		
from other western counties	13 (11)	4 (16)
from the rest of the country	20 (16)	6 (24)
from Northern Ireland	02 (01)	0 (-)
from abroad	13 (11)	3 (12)

Source: Authors' survey data.

Therefore, nearly two-thirds (63 per cent) of the 148 sampled firms were owned and/or operated by 'in-comers', a fact which strongly suggests a correlation between in-migration (including return migration) and firm formation.

Socio-demographic characteristics of business responsibles

To simplify the presentation in this section, survey respondents are divided into three groups: 1) 'non-movers', i.e., owners and managers who grew up in the study area and who never resided outside it; and two categories of in-comers, i.e., 2) 'return migrants', or owners and managers who grew up in the study area but who lived outside it for some time before returning and 3) 'newcomers', i.e., non-natives who had moved to the study area from other parts of the country or from abroad.

Selected characteristics of non-movers, return migrants and newcomers are summarized in Table 9.3. Respondents, irrespective of category, were predominantly male (88 per cent); this was not surprising given that the sample concentrated on manufacturing firms and excluded the service sector where a relatively high proportion of small enterprises are known to be owned and operated by women. Nevertheless, it begs the question as to why women do not establish small manufacturing enterprises.

Discrepancies between men- and women-owned businesses have been highlighted elsewhere (Tigges and Green, 1994). One explanation may be the difficulties women face in offering security against borrowed capital, particularly if they have spent some time outside the workforce. Unfortunately, data from the survey did not facilitate exploration of this gender issue.

Table 9.3   Selected characteristics of business responsibles

Variables	Non-movers N=55	Return migrants n=32	New-comers n=61	Total n=148
Gender: % male	87	88	90	88
Age: % <35 years	20	22	8	16
% 35-50 years	53	56	54	54
% 50+ years	27	22	38	30
Have children (%)	80	78	85	82
Education: % with third level degree	18	25	56	35
% with business training	51	50	61	55
% with vocational training	34	28	26	30
Previous occupation: % employed	73	72	71	72
% self-employed	11	19	16	15
Socio-economic backgrounds:				
% family owned a non-farm business	27	25	41	32
% family owned a farm business	56	41	28	42
Operates more than one business (%)	38	44	43	41
Holds a position in the community (%)	44	47	41	43

Source: Authors' survey data.

In general, respondents were in the middle age ranges, most being between 35 and 50 years. As many businesses were relatively new - see below - the age profile suggests that younger people do not establish businesses. They seemingly need to acquire adequate skills and experience after completing their education before they can engage in enterprise development as owners or managers. They may also take time to build up a certain amount of 'own resources', for example, finance. It would appear that in the past they achieved these goals by migrating from their native place for a number of years. However, younger entrepreneurs, while accounting for only 23 respondents, were more likely to be from the area

(Table 9.3). Also, a sizeable proportion (48 per cent) of these were non-movers, suggesting that for some, new opportunities are emerging in the study area, such as education and work experience, which previously existed only in larger urban areas.

The general age profile is advantageous from both a local economic and demographic perspective. Those aged 35-50 years are likely to have most energy and drive in business development. Their stage in the life cycle suggests that they are likely to have personal commitments and responsibilities, which necessitate business success. This determination to succeed leads to a net positive impact on the local economy. Also, they are more likely to be at the stage of family formation. A majority (82 per cent) had children (Table 9.3). The age composition of *families* of return migrants and newcomers partly explains the earlier trend emerging from aggregate census data, that a high concentration of 'in-comers' are between 15 and 35 years of age.

The incidence of primary and post-graduate degrees was highest among newcomers, a factor related to the disproportionate number of managers among them. Also, they were more active in undertaking business training, principally management and marketing courses. Non-movers, on the other hand, had the highest participation rate in vocational and technical training, a factor related to the type of businesses operated. These involved more skill-intensive manual operations, for example, craft, timber product and metal fabrication enterprises, and were producing 'quality or niche' products, which is encouraging for the future.

Before becoming involved with their current businesses, 88 per cent of respondents had been otherwise employed, principally in manufacturing companies. Those remaining had been engaged with further studies, in home duties, or other activities. Only 4 per cent had been unemployed. Return migrants and newcomers had greater experience of being self-employed prior to their involvement with the surveyed firm. Given that the majority of respondents came from positions within industry, it is valid to suggest that work experience – as opposed to managerial experience – is crucial at the formation stage of SMEs. Results indicate that rural areas characterized by high rates of new firm formation are likely to be already well placed in terms of employment opportunities.

Although the majority of business responsibles came from positions of wage or salaried employment rather than self-employment, two out of every five respondents indicated that the principal owner had subsequently developed other business interests and was now the owner or part-owner of other firms. Interestingly, there was a higher incidence of multiple ownership among newcomers and return migrants than for non-movers.

Results may suggest that 'in-comers' have more 'contacts' and more capital, and consequently are presented with more opportunities than non-movers. Alternatively, they may indicate greater flexibility or risk-taking behaviour among in-comers, which instigates further enterprise expansion and development; or they may indicate that in-comers are more successful in business development – this may stem from experience gained while outside the area. Findings appear to support the hypothesis that experience gained in enterprise establishment and development can stimulate additional business opportunities, leading to further enterprise formation and new opportunities to strengthen and sustain local economies.

In general, respondents were more likely to have come from families who were self-employed, particularly within the agricultural sector; 42 per cent of respondents' parents owned a farm, 32 per cent owned a non-farm business (Table 9.3). The shift from the farm to the non-farm sector is indicative of general restructuring trends in rural areas. Significantly, a higher proportion of newcomers came from family backgrounds where parents owned a non-farm business. Other parents were employees in manual, non-manual and professional occupations. The results support the hypothesis that self-employment generates further entrepreneurship, and that those with some family collateral are more likely to develop new enterprises than those beginning from a zero base.

On the whole, findings suggest that those responsible for small enterprises in rural areas come from a sub-group of the population, which could be considered to be relatively well circumstanced, economically. Differentiating between in-comers (return migrants and newcomers) and non-movers on their personal characteristics gives the impression that in-comers are somewhat better positioned to specifically respond to the emerging opportunities and challenges of economic restructuring – at least in businesses of the kind surveyed. Consequently, they are likely to become even more significant in determining local economic vitality in rural areas in the foreseeable future, given the current policy measures favouring SME formation.

Characteristics of surveyed businesses

The age profile of surveyed firms provides an insight into the rate of small firm formation in the study area. In general, firms were relatively young, nearly two-thirds being less than 10 years established. Since the mid-1980s, the rate of new firm formation increased dramatically, with the greater policy emphasis on SMEs and with opportunities arising from economic restructuring – ongoing throughout the period. During the mid-to late-

1980s, non-movers and return migrants were more active in new firm start-ups. However, newcomers now appear to be the most important group. They accounted for more than half (55 per cent) of all new firms established between 1990 and 1994. If firms started by return migrants are also taken into account, findings indicate that 'in-comers' were responsible for establishing three out of every four enterprises during the early 1990s. Interpretation of these findings must, of course, proceed cautiously because no single factor can explain or determine entrepreneurship or business formation, but the pattern emerging is suggestive of an important link between general economic restructuring, in-migration and new firm start-ups in the study area.

By definition, firms were small, employing fewer than 50 people, and mostly private or family business. Over two-fifths (43 per cent) could be classified as micro-enterprises, typically with fewer than 10 persons employed. Nearly half (46 per cent) of these were owned and operated by non-movers (Table 9.4). By contrast, enterprises employing more than 10 people were more likely to be run by in-comers, with newcomers in particular dominating those employing 10–19 people. Thus, these various findings show that in-comers are in fact responsible for many job opportunities arising from small enterprises in the study area – a point returned to below.

Table 9.4   Size distribution of businesses

No. employed (incl. the owner(s))	Non-movers	Return migrants	New-comers	Total
1 - 2	5	4	8	17
3 - 9	25	12	11	48
10 - 19	12	6	21	39
20 - 29	6	2	10	18
30+	7	8	11	26
Total	55	32	61	148

Source: Authors' survey data.

Taken together, firms were involved in a diverse range of business activities with a high concentration in food processing, metal fabrication, timber products, electronics, light engineering, plastics, and crafts. Only a minority could be considered as fast-growing or high-tech enterprises; not surprisingly, these were more likely to belong to newcomers and return migrants. However, enterprises owned by non-movers were more skill-intensive, suggesting these to be producers of quality products. To a certain extent this has to be seen in the context of recent Irish trends in food processing whereby the growth of an international agri-food system has been paralleled by the emergence of a small-business speciality food subsector, concentrating on quality and distinctiveness, targeting niche markets and surviving dominant globalization trends (McDonagh and Commins, forthcoming).

Over half of the firms had a designated successor (usually a son of the entrepreneur) who was expected to keep the business operational after the retirement of the current incumbent. The incidence of future successorship was highest among non-movers (58 per cent), followed by return migrants (50 per cent). Only two-fifths (41 per cent) of the newcomers had a successor for their business. Findings suggest a greater commitment to business and local area among 'natives', perhaps indicative of a local strategy to maintain local community distinctiveness.

We can conclude, therefore, that rural SMEs in manufacturing are relatively new and tend to be micro-enterprises in scale. The findings of Keeble et al. (1992) regarding the link between in-migration and new firm formation are supported. The establishment and development of SMEs in the study area has been greatly assisted by in-comers, particularly since 1990, supporting the proposition that they enhance the capacity of local economies to adapt to changing conditions. Therefore, rural policy should strive to increase the attractiveness of rural areas to in-comers as a means of expanding the local pool of entrepreneurial talent.

Factors in business location and start-up

A complex set of factors influences entrepreneurial decision-making. First, considering decisions to return or move to the study area, three 'inward pull' factors emerged as particularly important: 1) the availability of employment; 2) the perceived quality of life in the study area and 3) the perceived opportunity to establish a business. Employment opportunities attracted a significant proportion (40 per cent) of the in-comers to the area, reflecting the incorporation of rural areas into wider labour markets and the changing location of jobs. Positions accepted were usually in manufacturing companies where skills and experience gained from one employer are easily marketed and transferred. Incoming respondents also assigned a high level of importance to the environmental and socio-cultural attributes of the study area. Having lived outside the area, predominantly in urban settings, they valued the peace and quiet of the rural environment and subsequently moved – a trend facilitated by increased flexibility (in terms of employment, mobility and economic conditions) afforded by industrial restructuring (see below). Similarly, identifying and acting upon an opportunity to start up a business reflects respondents' adaptability to changing economic conditions. Clearly, decisions to relocate were taken in the context of economic and social change internal and external to the study area.

Second, in relation to the main factors impacting on the decision to establish a business, respondents acknowledged the importance of a personal desire 'to be your own boss' and the attractiveness of an economic and socio-cultural environment which encouraged and facilitated this. The new emphasis on small firms from both a policy and socioeconomic point of view encouraged firm formation. Also, efforts to encourage local products and identify niche markets – a common local response to globalization – were identified as trigger factors in the decision to start some of the businesses. But, perhaps of most significance was the growing trend towards scale reduction, import substitution and sub-supply. Many enterprise ideas were formulated through experience gained, and market knowledge obtained, in the firm founder's previous workplace. Entrepreneurs were nurtured in positions of employment rather than self-employment – although they obviously benefited from the experience of having self-employed parents. Their active involvement in the workplace allowed them to gain the experience and skills to identify and capitalize on market opportunities. In nearly two-thirds of the cases, firms were established which produced similar or improved products offered by the founder's previous employer, or which manufactured component products which former employers had imported. Also, positions of employment gave the potential entrepreneur the opportunities to establish valuable personal contacts and potential customer bases. It was not unusual to find new entrepreneurs selling their products to former employers.

Third, in view of reasons cited for locating businesses in the study area as opposed to urban locations, respondents mentioned economic considerations more than qualitative concerns. However, they ranked proximity to their place of residence as the main influential factor. However, the availability of suitable premises, proximity to the local market, availability of grants and/or subsidies, and the availability of a local work force all emerged as important. All these factors can conceivably be understood in the context of contemporary economic and industrial restructuring processes and the policy context designed to respond to them. Non-movers tended to emphasize social or community values, for example, a desire to provide local employment (perhaps indicating greater commitment or loyalty to the local area), while return migrants and newcomers focused more on economic factors (local demand for product, proximity to market) and policy incentives (availability of grants/subsidies, availability of suitable premises).

To summarize: findings provide an insight into the means by which macro-forces penetrate rural economies, directly or indirectly. The wider context within which entrepreneurs must take decisions predetermines to a large extent the options available. Certain features of economic restructuring can provide a positive climate for small business development in rural areas. Findings also offer evidence not alone of a willingness, but of a desire, on the part of new entrepreneurs to locate their businesses in these areas.

Some local impacts of SMEs

In the context of increased interest in the potential of SMEs to contribute to economic development in rural areas, it was important to try to establish the role of firms in strengthening and diversifying the demographic and economic base of the local economy. Admittedly, caution is warranted in interpreting the results because any reliable estimate of the true magnitude of the direct impacts of the firms would require detailed knowledge of all the components of the local community, before and after the establishment of the firms. As such detailed information was not available, estimates are provided from survey data pertaining to: 1) demographic change, 2) jobs created, 3) diversification of the local economy and 4) local multiplier effects. Despite their limitations, findings do provide a credible picture of the positive local impacts of the firms surveyed.

Demographic change

Of the 60 per cent of the 'business responsibles' who were in-comers the majority had families, resulting in an increase of 396 persons in the study area. Return migrants and their families accounted for 137 people, while newcomers and their families totaled 259 persons. It is difficult to say what proportion of in-comers might not have remained in the area had they not their present businesses. However, it could be argued that in-comers are the most likely group to leave an area if conditions become unfavourable or better opportunities are perceived to be elsewhere. Their continued residence in the area suggests that they find economic and social conditions at least reasonably satisfactory. Non-movers together with their families numbered 255 persons. In aggregate, then, firms were directly associated with maintaining a total of 651 persons in the area. It is plausible to conclude, therefore, that firms have directly impacted on local demographic structures.

Also, in 1995, 2,484 individuals were employed by the firms, 2,037 of these on a full-time basis. While survey data cannot tell us whether they would have remained in the area in the absence of their jobs, or inform us of the number of their dependants, it is credible that firms, indirectly through their workforce, have helped to stabilise and maintain a significant proportion of the local population.

In addition, over three-quarters of the businesses contribute to local or community events, mainly through sponsorship, thereby enhancing the social fabric of the communities. A similar proportion of respondents from each sub-group held leadership or civic positions in their communities, suggesting that 'in-comers' are relatively well integrated into local structures.

Job creation

Approximately two-thirds of the 2,484 jobs were provided by in-comer firms, reinforcing earlier findings concerning the significance of return migrants and newcomers in job creation in the area. Estimates provided by respondents indicated that the majority of employees (85 per cent) came from the local area, most of the others were from elsewhere within the region.

Over half of the employees were less than 30 years of age and the majority of these were employed by newcomers. This was significant for two reasons. Firstly, it indicated that young people could secure non-farm employment and as a result could remain in the area, thereby off-setting some of the demographic decline of recent times. Secondly, stabilizing a proportion of the young adult population improves the age structure of local communities, enhances the prospects of population regeneration and maintains the local community identity.

Given the nature of the businesses selected, it is not surprising that they generated twice as many jobs for males as for females. Of the total workforce 63 per cent were men. Male employees dominated in full-time positions, accounting for 69 per cent of these jobs; females out-numbered males in part-time and seasonal positions (63 per cent and 64 per cent respectively). There was also variation in the nature of the positions occupied by men and women. Males out-numbered females by two to one in jobs classified as skilled, semi-skilled and professional while females were concentrated in the unskilled and administrative posts. While findings suggest an imbalance in the opportunities created by these firms, it must be acknowledged that they do appear to be addressing one of the more salient problems of the area, i.e., the lack of non-farm jobs, especially for males. Firms set up by returned migrants and newcomers provided most of the full-time employment but the enterprises of non-movers were the more skill-intensive.

All three types of firms had hired additional staff during 1995. In total, 301 men and 98 women had gained employment, significant in view of the fact that a large proportion of these (45 per cent) had been unemployed; a further one-fifth (21 per cent) were first time job seekers, and an additional 4 per cent had been involved with home duties. Remaining employees (29 per cent) had been employed in other jobs - mainly outside the area. Therefore, a high proportion of the jobs brought members of the local community into the workforce. Displacement from other local jobs was relatively low. Only one-tenth of the firms had laid-off staff during 1995. No significant difference emerged between non-movers' firms and those belonging to in-comers. One-fifth of the lay-offs were only temporary. In general, given that firms were established prior to 1995, it is conceivable that dominant employment trends signal growth and expansion.

In aggregate, employees earned IR£655,760 per week in gross wages and salaries or approximately IR£34 million per year – undoubtedly a significant contribution to the local economy. The mean gross weekly wage per person employed was IR£304. The average earned by those employed by return migrants was IR£169, by those in newcomer firms was IR£194, while the mean for non-mover firms was much higher at IR£312. This last figure, most likely, reflects the higher levels of skills associated with these enterprises noted above.

Diversification of local economic activities

As the businesses collectively produced a diverse range of products and in general, had been established by 'new' entrepreneurs, there was a broadening of economic activity at the local level and an increase in numbers self-employed. Many of the firm founders had come from farming backgrounds but had established non-farm businesses. Control of decision-making remained with the entrepreneur/manager at local level. Apart from contributing to the diversification of the local economy, the emergence of these SMEs enhanced local human capital and capacity. Localization in this sense is one of the important counter trends to globalization.

However, as intimated earlier, firms did produce products, which were similar to those manufactured or imported by previous employers, in which cases previous employers became the customers of the newly established firm. There are thus important vertical linkages between established and new firms, implying a certain local dynamic, which could potentially be self-propagating and lead to further new firm formation and greater local economic sustainability. But data pertaining to subcontracting among surveyed firms revealed that it related mainly to business information or support services, for example dealings with accountants and solicitors, and not to other manufacturing enterprises. None the less there is a high degree of dependence among new firms (irrespective of type of ownership) on longer established or larger businesses (limited numbers of which exist in parts of the study area). As Turok and Richardson (1991) found in their study in West Lothian, new firms appear to be imitators rather than innovators, followers rather than leaders, and are more likely to be vertically rather than horizontally integrated. These characteristics may confine their arena of activity to 'standard' products (thereby restricting the potential for diversification), or to a local base, and/or may increase their vulnerability to external shocks, and possible displacement. Either way, their ability to expand comes into question as does their capacity to substantially change the traditional character of their local economies.

Local multiplier effect

The majority of firms (again irrespective of ownership type) sourced the bulk of their raw materials outside the local area – reinforcing the lack of horizontal linkages identified above and highlighting a dependence among firms on the environment beyond their rural settings. Interestingly, the picture was reversed when sales outlets were identified; in this case, firms were primarily targeted at local and regional markets. Approximately one-fifth of the firms sell nearly all their products locally. By contrast, two-thirds export less than a quarter of their manufactured goods – primarily to European markets. A majority of newcomers (66 per cent) and of return migrants (59 per cent) were involved with export markets compared to a minority of non-movers (35 per cent) – indicating again that in-comers may be better placed to fully exploit opportunities arising from economic reorganization in modern economies.

Considering the nature of the enterprises and their product range, it seemed likely that firms might be competing against similar small scale businesses within the study area, rather than against larger rivals in other locations. Indeed, 43 per cent of respondents acknowledged that they had local competitors; 50 per cent admitted to being aware of competitors in the rest of the region, and 75 per cent knew of national competitors. The potential for duplication of effort and displacement is therefore high. By virtue of the same characteristics, the generation of additional wealth within the region would appear more limited than what policy makers would like to see.

Concluding comment

As visualized by Amin and Thrift (1994, pp. 5-10), globalization is represented by a dynamic set of economic and social processes flowing through and combining in different ways in different local settings. These processes encounter places with distinct, historically established, socioeconomic structures, experiences and practices. Territories are reconstructed as they become areas of intersecting and overlapping global flows, as well as sites of local strategies designed to assimilate globalization processes, or to resist them.

By focusing on selected demographic trends and SME development in a specific territory in the west of Ireland, this chapter illustrated aspects of global - local interactions and, specifically, elements of both integrationist and resistant strategies. Integrationist strategies centred on attracting external capital, offering attractive living conditions for external entrepreneurs, developing export markets, maximizing the use of modern information and communications technologies, and promoting the kinds of enterprises that can link successfully into modern industrial production systems. Resistant local responses evidenced included a focus on the development of indigenous resources, efforts to build local capacity, the fostering of local entrepreneurship, and a concentration by non-movers on establishing niche markets. Non-movers also show a stronger sense of identity with their localities, a greater empathy with community needs, and a high level of commitment to ensuring continuity of the business after their own retirement.

Changing socioeconomic conditions have facilitated in-migration to the study area, changing the social composition of local communities. In-comers play a significant role in establishing SMEs. Their re-location is influenced partly by the quality of life they have experienced in urban centres, by comparison, they perceive rural lifestyles to be more attractive. The opportunities for SMEs are determined to a great extent by restructuring in larger industrial enterprises. Although most SMEs are autonomous firms some are linked to multinational businesses. Inputs are sourced externally even when markets are predominantly local in scale – but some businesses have export markets. While in-comers tend to operate the larger enterprises with more modern technologies the 'non-movers' manage the more skill-intensive enterprises.

The survey also revealed strengths and weaknesses of SMEs as a response to rural problems. They have created new jobs, bringing in excluded categories of persons to the workforce. They have contributed to the generation of a culture of enterprise, to the diversification of the local economy, and to the creation of business for commercial services. However, they are limited in their innovativeness, their horizontal linkages locally are weak and their dependence on the local market limits the potential for further expansion.

A challenge for those involved with the development of rural areas in the west of Ireland is to remedy these deficiencies.

Acknowledgements

The authors are thankful to the Department of Geography, Trinity College Dublin, under Professor D. Gillmor, and also to the Department of Enterprise and Employment, Dublin, for their assistance in facilitating the enterprise survey. The financial contribution of the EU, through its AIR research programme, is also gratefully acknowledged.

Notes

1. LEADER groups and County Enterprise Boards are also involved in enterprise promotion but because of their relatively recent establishment their activities were not considered in this survey.
2. Only the western part of County Galway, the area served by Údarás na Gaeltachta, was included.
3. It was intended to include all 247 businesses selected but 31 could not be identified (closures most likely), 17 had closed, 27 could not be interviewed at a convenient time, and 24 decided not to participate.

References

Amin, A. and Thrift, N. (1994), 'Living in the Global', in Amin, A. and Thrift, N. (eds), *Globalization, Institutions and Regional Development in Europe*, Oxford University Press: Oxford.

Boyle, P. (1995), 'Rural In-migration in England and Wales 1980-1981', *Journal of Rural Studies*, Vol. 11, No. 1, pp. 65-78.

Bryant, C.R. (1995), 'The Role of Local Actors in Transforming the Urban Fringe', *Journal of Rural Studies*, Vol. 11, No. 3, pp. 255-267.

Buller, H. and Hoggart, K. (1994), *International Counter-urbanization: British Migrants in Rural France*, Avebury: Aldershot.

Cawley, M.E. (1990), 'Population Change in the Republic of Ireland 1981-1986', *Area*, Vol. 22, No. 1, pp. 67-74.

CEC - Commission of the European Communities (1988), *The Future of Rural Society*, Brussels.

Curran, J. and Blackburn, R. (1994), *Small Firms and Local Economic Networks*, Paul Chapman: London.

Giddens, A. (1993), 2nd Edition, *Sociology*, Polity Press: Oxford.

Goodwin, M. (1998), 'The Governance of Rural Areas: Some Emerging Research Issues and Agendas', *Journal of Rural Studies*, Vol. 14, No. 1, pp. 1-4.

Jackson, J.A. and Haase, T. (1996), 'Demography and the Distribution of Deprivation in Ireland', in Curtin, C., Haase, T. and Tovey, H. (eds), *Poverty in Rural Ireland*, Oaktree Press: Dublin.

Keeble, D., Tyler, P., Broom, G. and Lewis, J. (1992), *Business Success in the Countryside*, HMSO: London.

McDonagh, P. and Commins, P. (forthcoming), *Small-Scale Food Enterprises and Rural Development*, Teagasc: Dublin.

North, D. and Smallbone, D. (1996), 'Small Business Development in Remote Rural Areas: The Example of Mature Manufacturing Firms in Northern England', *Journal of Rural Studies*, Vol. 11, No. 2, pp. 151-167.

O'Hearn, D. (1993), 'Global Competition, Europe and Irish Peripherality', *The Economic and Social Review*, Vol. 24, No. 2, pp 169-197.

Özcan, G. B. (1995), *Small Firms and Local Economic Development*, Avebury: Aldershot.

Task Force on Small Business (1994), *Task Force on Small Business*, Government of Ireland: Dublin.

Tigges, L.M. and Green, G. P. (1994), 'Small Business Success among Men- and Women-owned Firms in Rural Areas', *Rural Sociology*, Vol. 59, No. 2, pp.289-310.

Tovey, H., Haase, T. and Curtin, C. (1996), 'Understanding Rural Poverty', in Curtin, C., Haase, T. and Tovey, H. (eds), *Poverty in Rural Ireland*, Oaktree Press: Dublin.

Turok, I. and Richardson P. (1991), 'New Firms and Local Economic Development. Evidence from West Lothian', *Regional Studies*, Vol. 25, No. 1, pp. 71-86.

Wilding, P. (1997), 'Globalization, Regionalism and Social Policy', *Social Policy and Administration*, Vol. 31, No. 4, pp. 410-428.

10 Seeking Local Citizenship: Towards a New Sense of the Local?

NICHOLAS MACK

Introduction

Rural development in Western Europe is characterized by a political rhetoric, and regulatory measures, which espouse a 'bottom-up approach' to shaping the development process. Local 'communities' are invited to play a key role in identifying development needs and overseeing their address, drawing on local resources and strengths. In Northern Ireland, as elsewhere, local 'communities' are extended a range of support measures by the 'Top' (the state) ranging from training and guidance, to preferential funding, and technical support to enable them to engage in the development process. Surely, is this the epitome of seeking local responses to global integration? This chapter will suggest otherwise, that this process is one reflecting 'global responses' to global integration which are then localized. In effect, that the 'Top' has been colonizing 'local life-worlds' in the invasive manner described by Habermas, rather than becoming more sensitive to them (Habermas, 1984; 1987).

A key issue addressed by this chapter is the distinction between localized responses, which essentially share a universal, 'global' culture and goals, and responses, which retain some independent identity as truly 'local'. The former is likely to place emphasis on utilizing local resources to engage in a global game. The latter tends to place some emphasis on realizing a sense of the local and its integrity in a global setting.

The focus for this chapters' exploration of the *potential* for local response to global integration begins at the interface between state agencies for (rural) development and 'localized' actors, and continues to look at how 'the local' is constructed around this interface. It will suggest that at present, whilst local and community notions are used extensively in political rhetoric and practical methods of intervention, the construction of 'the local' has been largely incidental.

The key questions to be addressed through the course of this chapter are how and why the 'Top' might facilitate a 'local space' to be created as a purpose of development intervention and in which a truly local response to global integration can be formed; a response which focuses on being 'local' but at the same time does not deny being global. The motive for doing so stems from recent policy concerns to address social exclusion and sustainable development.

In seeking to examine the condition of the 'local', this chapter aims to address issues about whether 'developing the local' can be a legitimate and realistic development goal for 'The Top' to adopt. Sociologists query the validity of the term local and community. Are social trends irrevocably toward global inclusion and individualization? Is it intervening too much to try to initiate alternative local perspectives and responses?

The rhetoric of the 'local' at 'The Top'

In EU policy, the cultural and social value of rural areas and people are regularly espoused. These values might suggest a receptivity to 'local-ness' as a resource. In large measure, however, social concerns are considered the province of individual nation states to attend to, and EU attention to be more properly focused on ensuring economic competitiveness and growth. Success here is suggested to contribute to insuring a future for rural people, and hence of their culture and diversity. However, these goals emphasize global thinking.

Capacity-building for bottom-up development has become synonymous with the term 'community development', but rather than a literal 'development of community', community development in this context has largely been about building a capacity, within the presumed (if languishing) communities of disadvantaged areas, that will enable them to engage in a process of development which has *economic* goals. In so doing, it is supposed, such communities will see themselves and their localities catch up with, indeed integrate with, the more affluent parts of Europe already heatedly engaged in the global economy.

The 'Local Development' which development agencies and cooperating communities are working towards, then, stems from EU policy and support for competitive economic 'development', equating itself to a global perspective, and global integration.

The emphasis on 'local' development has arisen to account for the substantial and complex variation in circumstances across the regions and localities of the EU, which negates the efficacy of blanket policy instruments. The appeal to community-led development is a result of the instability and limitations of a development strategy based on inward investment - a symptom itself of a competitive and globalizing economy. 'The local' has been seen as important, but perhaps largely, as a stepping stone to constructing a Europe, which is functionally effective in global competition.

In pursuing an antidote to uneven development, a rhetoric (rather than concept) of 'local', conflated with community, has been used in an idealistic fashion to galvanize local action. Yet this can be contrasted to scant attention or reflection on the condition of 'local' or community itself. Rural Sociologists and Geographers have long debated the reality of terms like community and local, and have attempted instead to provide better 'models' of localized rural society (for a full discussion, see for example Massey, 1994; Marsden et al., 1993; Mack, 1998a).

This debate appears to have gone unnoticed by policy makers and those implementing policy of bottom-up development, but perhaps this belies the unimportance placed to date on whether they exist or not for the purpose of intervention. Suffice, perhaps, to call upon the moral idea of community to rally a local response. But even whilst this may be so, the very use suggests the value of community and of local to have discursive currency, to be an inherent part of social life, and to have the capacity to influence individual action.

In agency relations for local development, social or cultural dimensions have largely been treated as incidental or as unhelpful distraction. If a need for social and cultural adjustments alongside economic re-structuring is recognized (for example, in the crisis around the role and identity of small farmers), these are expected to follow in an appropriate manner, to gather around or be nurtured, by the essential lead of globalised economic logic and welfare. The appeal to 'local' and community must be supposed to be as a transient effect - again a stepping stone to global adjustment, not particularly as ends in themselves.

The primacy of economic goals has, however, been disturbed over the past decade by the problem of structural unemployment and the associated concept of social exclusion, a term suggesting an outcast element of European society which has become not insubstantial, and if not addressed, a threat to political stability. Policy goals to increase competitiveness have become joined of late by ones to improve social inclusion or cohesion, and join the environment as components of a sustainable development. In the UK social inclusion has placed emphasis on returning political involvement and a sense of control in populations alienated from power - 'government by the people' and 'participatory democracy' are frequently used terms.

In Northern Ireland attention to social inclusion as a policy goal has been particularly strong with the provision of the European Fund for Peace and Reconciliation following the IRA cease-fires. District partnerships were formed to channel European money directly to community level - partnerships formed at a sub-regional and hence, more local spatial scale and which have generally been felt to be successful. The social goals of these partnerships have placed a greater emphasis on community structure and relationships.

Sustainable development meanwhile has created Local Agenda 21 - a part of the Rio Summit agreement, which emphasizes community involvement in the design of strategies for local sustainability.[1] The techniques of community consultation and participatory planning, of 'citizenship building' is creating the conditions in which the way 'local' is perceived is changing from the incidental to the building block.

We will return to examine the effect of these current trends on local development thinking again during the course of this chapter.

The local as rhetoric at 'The Bottom'

The perspectives to be offered here from the community level stem from the development approaches used in Northern Ireland. However, it is likely that many of the issues have a wider applicability.

The current process by which community capacity building takes place in rural development has evolved over time, moving toward the underlying rationale of economic development from a beginning, which had a more social character. This shift has left a tension among those promoting and participating in local development still to be resolved, which we will return to later. Under the auspices of what has been a largely economic development agenda, then, what has been the effect on the idea of local among local actors?

Local development is hinged upon the 'community group'. The formation of a community development group typically begins when a small group of people who want to 'do something' for the local area - who feel, in effect, a sense of local citizenship, form either voluntarily, or perhaps through the prompting of a local political or religious representative. Whilst there are various motives, this desire to do something is often (but not always) rooted in a strong identification by the individuals concerned with the community, and a desire to see it do well. The wellbeing of the community is a personal issue associated with personal identity, many having been born and bred there.

The 'proto-group' receives a mixture of support from local authority workers, the Rural Development Council or the Rural Community Network (key agencies tasked by the Department of Agriculture to promote and facilitate local development). Either of these can help the group plan a series of public meetings designed to engage local opinion about the needs and opportunities of the area, and in so doing, they seek to raise awareness of the formation of a development group, its purpose and potential. These meetings allow a committee to be assembled forming the basis of the community group. Members of the committee are nominated by the informal group or by members of the public. Those accepting their nomination then stand for election - possibly as office bearers or as general committee members. Elections are not based on canvassing - more on the standing and familiarity of those willing to sit on the committee in the local area. Typically, those first responsible for promoting the idea of a group, become elected, in effect, by default.

Through holding these public meetings, the committee can claim a form of democratic legitimacy within its local population. However, meetings rarely attract more than a hundred or so people, and many of these may leave non the wiser as to what the group is about. Typically, a vague association between the formation of a group and 'grants' is the main source of curiosity.

There is no formation, as such, of a broad vision shared across the community with which to act - the *locality* does not as such act as supposed by Cox and Mair (1991), rather, a small contingent do, claiming a remit 'on behalf of' it.

At some stage, the group will define on a map the area it seeks to represent. Typically this will involve a village or hamlet, and an area around it of perhaps 6 or 7 miles (10 km) radius. Settlement patterns in Northern Ireland are dispersed and houses are found scattered beyond the village itself. A village remains a telling reference point in the defining of local relations, but it is not always clear which households will relate to which village - proximity is not the only criterion.

It is the opinion of the group members that decides who is likely to feel part of a common social space. The members decide who would feel they belonged to the village or had a stronger association with it than any other village, by engaging in a discursive review of those known by the group members. It is largely the sense of place of the group members which is articulated, then, formed by a mental review of the networks of people they know.

The church and other community institutions (schools, sports clubs, farm union branches and the like) are also a guide. In Catholic communities these are strong indicators - because there is only one 'form' of Catholicism, meaning one local church (in or near the village) and one parish (the area served by the church) defining the space of belonging. Within the parish other institutions, sports, credit union, clubs and associations have formed with this same singular local spatial identity in common.

Amongst Protestants meanwhile, there are a number of alternative churches one can belong to - the Church of Ireland, the Methodist church, Baptist, Presbyterian or Free Presbyterian, and so on. There is more difficulty in identifying a singular sense of common place and community. The formation of community groups in Protestant communities has been slow in any case due to a wide variety of cultural reasons. The situation is made more complex where both traditions, Catholic and Protestant, live within the same geographical area.[2]

In all cases, however, community groups will without hesitation claim to have defined a common space of association - and most probably believe in it also. The extent to which those they would expect to share that space actually do so has not been evaluated, but some association is likely across a large proportion. In Northern Ireland many remain in or return to the area they were born, living near their families. Indeed, the extended family still forms the main social network for a substantial number of rural people.

A recent survey, conducted by the RDC and RCN across Northern Irelands' rural population, showed that as many as 80 per cent of respondents (N=5,552) live where they do to be near their family, whilst a further 6 per cent would like to but cannot. Only 8 per cent were living in the area away from family and were happy to do so. Sixty per cent said they had lived in their locality all their lives, whilst 30 per cent of those who had not, had nevertheless been there for 20 years or more. Further the percentage of those expressing a desire to leave the area was small even where unemployed, or more tellingly, where their own prognosis for the future of their area was for decline. Belonging to a community was important to 85 per cent of the respondents from all age groups and occupational backgrounds (Mack, 1998b).

Whether or not the boundary of belonging drawn up by the community group is correct, however, carries little significance to the larger majority entailed. They typically remain unaware they are included, or do not feel affected. The area can be agreed as much by a strong sense of place as by a sufficient level of indifference. Analysis of the role of community in the lives of respondents to the above survey, for example, suggested a passive one providing familiarity and security; important, but a role not extended into the proclivity to act collectively.

A key reason for defining the space of the group - its locality, is so that a statistical analysis and profile of the area can be prepared as a next step. RDC provides this service using GIS (Geographic Information System) linked to population census data. The data can be separated at 'Enumeration District level';[3] Enumeration Districts (ED) vary in size, but the areas defined by the group need as far as possible to follow ED boundaries. Typically, three or four EDs are involved, covering up to 2,000 households, but this is a decision of the group - there is as yet no set maximum or minimum. The statistical profile which results is designed to help the group understand the needs and population characteristics of its area - the age profile, numbers unemployed, number of married or single people, religious breakdown and so on, for the design of projects.

The area is also tested for its 'level of deprivation'. A deprivation index is used designed by Robson (1994) (hence known as the Robson Index). The index is built from a number of indicators constructed using population census data and the availability of services, which together enable an area to be ascribed a level of deprivation along a scale above or below the Northern Ireland average. Following a policy of Targeting Social Need (TSN) adopted in 1991 this index is presently used by funding agencies to target resources to areas with high deprivation scores. As such, the index score has 'value' in the group's case for project funds. The group may well alter the boundaries of its claimed area to maximize this index, cutting out more affluent places and incorporating areas of low income or unemployment. Perversely, a high deprivation score is seen as a positive result, effectively acting to devalue the local to maximize its case for support intervention from global sources.[4] The community must, in effect, think of itself as disadvantaged in relation to wider standards.

In this way, then, 'localities' for development are constructed through a combination of an assumed local sense of belonging and statistical parameters of disadvantage. These localities then assume an identity through the naming of the development group and its promotion as a 'community' body - the Kilcoo and Tollymore Community Development Association - the Fury Community Development Group, and so on.

The group then becomes the focus for a process of training and project development work. A SWOT analysis (Strengths, Weaknesses, Opportunities and Threats) is carried out with the group. Surveys and market research are done. Visits may take place to other groups in Northern Ireland or other parts of the UK or Ireland. Action plans are drawn up, followed by business plans and funding proposals.

Small projects are encouraged to help the group 'cut its teeth', but also to demonstrate to the community at large that it is doing something - to build credibility. Despite the emphasis on economic priorities, these early, smaller projects are usually social in nature. Quite often, they focus on features of 'community significance' - an old graveyard or monument might be cleaned up or a pathway improved. A programme of adult education classes or social events typically follows, alongside an obligatory effort at local fund-raising. These various activities appeal to a common sense of community and local identity.

But for real credibility most groups want to achieve a large-scale project - a community hall - a business centre, a tourism centre and so on. Expectations within the 'community' are high. In the early stages of the development programme, some groups were used by funding agencies to show an example of what might be achieved and are subsequently used as a reference. If a one million pound project is the norm, then one million pound project it should be. There is competition between localities each to get as much out of funding agencies as the other. Each wants its own community hall, its own tourism centre.

Whilst the local is undoubtedly being constructed in response to a top down (global) agenda - to compete for funding, to fund large projects, the process nevertheless belies a real sense of local which infuses the community group process. This is illustrated by reviewing some of the stages:

- The election of committee members based on local familiarity and standing (but this may also be by default).
- The willingness to adopt the game of establishing a community group by a wide number of people attending public meetings.
- The role of the village as a reference point defining a locality, and the unhesitating ascription of people as belonging to one village or another.
- The choice of initial social projects of significance to a community to win more support for a group.
- The pride and competitiveness of localities in pursuing large development projects, to be successful localities in the global game.

But is this really a local response, or rather, a localized response in which the global inhabits the space of local relations, the local 'life-world', to seek to orchestrate responses required by a global logic? The key issue is, what degree of freedom to act locally, in a local manner, is there? Are these uses of a local consciousness by community group members valued or incidental?

Regulations affecting the subsequent progress of larger projects suggests they are not; at least by the 'Top'. Construction of buildings must be put out to competitive tender, typically resulting in a non-local construction company winning the contract. Management of enterprises is normally franchised to private concerns and again, those with the required level of expertise come in most cases from outside of a disadvantaged area. The justification for this is the need to ensure a professional use of public money, that the project will not fail due to skill shortages. The risk of failure and need for professional management skills stems from the engagement of the project with competitive free market forces.

While the 'community group' seeks to satisfy criteria for a business-like approach, it is also expected to maintain a con-commitment of local accountability and to be embedded in its 'local community'. Two quite different concepts of community development have become bound together as one ideal (political) solution and the tensions, which this boundedness creates, make the result difficult to sustain. As with community co-operatives before, a combination of economic and social goals usually means economic success is limited - few sustainable quality jobs have been produced through this mechanism. However, economic goals limit the capacity of the community group to be inclusive, and often result in the group becoming detached from its community base. Coupled to this are the expectations of the local community that the group honour the various needs identified during public meetings for the variety of people who live in the area. It is typical for the group to find itself unable to escape continuing responsibility to deliver. Whilst an Annual General Meeting (AGM) is mandatory, at which committee members can change over, attendance at such meetings is generally extremely low - no-one else wants to find themselves asked to be involved. The 'trappings' of bureaucracy required for accountability do little to help. Most people do not see themselves as members of committees, but rather, look to others as the sort who should - those recognized as professionals, the councilor, the teacher, the owner of a large business.

Often, the group becomes a very localized development agency rather than a vehicle for community development, and it is treated with the same mixture of suspicion, distance and dependency as a state agency might be. The rhetoric of community development in EU and regional policy suggests that it should seek to reduce this sense of dependency, toward a situation instead of (economic) self-help and initiative. The reality is that the community group becomes seen as a provider - of grants, of new buildings, or of help and advice.

The 'Top' bemoans a lack of innovation and creativity in the proposals of community groups, yet does not (does not know how to) facilitate 'local visions' and the exploitation of diversity. A review of the purpose and goals of community groups, and the community group model, in Northern Ireland at least, may not be far away. There is a need to rationalize and separate out the two demands of present day community development - the demand to link vertically to a globally informed top-down agenda, and horizontally to a local sense of community.

Shifts in the policy climate: toward 'developing the local' and local citizenship

The tensions in the purpose of community development and the role of development groups have been increased over the past one or two years as the concept of 'Social Exclusion' has risen up the EU political agenda. Social exclusion replaces poverty, disadvantage, and deprivation as the key term representing not only economic inequality in European society but an associated social and political inequality as well. Social exclusion seeks to capture an accumulated but variable shortfall in the range of social, cultural and economic capitals that an individual can draw upon to pursue self-realization and wellbeing. It is portrayed as dynamic in contrast to the static 'fact' of being in a state of poverty, drawing in a larger part of the causal chain which brings an individual into that state, and which prevents or enables them to leave it.

The EU funded research to address 'social exclusion' from 1990 to 1994 under the Third Anti-Poverty programme or 'Poverty 3' and formulating a conceptual/theoretical framework, it began to establish the idea of inclusion in terms of citizenship. Commins (1993), for example, outlined a sense of belonging and inclusion as stemming from access to or integration with four main 'systems':

a) The democratic and legal system (civic integration).
b) The labour market (economic integration).
c) The welfare state system (social integration).
d) The family and community system (interpersonal integration).

All four systems were seen as necessary for a full sense of belonging. In keeping with the general economic trend for EU policy, EU policy toward social inclusion tends to focus on the second of the four parts of Commin's framework. Re-integration with the labour market is seen as the best solution to exclusion.

However, a wider debate within social policy circles has begun to seek a broader definition of work, and of 'rights to rights' beyond the workplace, which illustrates an acknowledgement of the need for rights and opportunities which operate *outside* of employment and foster other opportunities for active involvement in and contribution to society.[5] This debate includes (and implies an increasing emphasis on) recognition of the role of voluntary and civic (or community) bodies, set within the context of 'the challenges of massive structural change' within the EU, borne of global technical development. Civic bodies are seen as allies in 'helping to reconcile economic performance with a widespread (threat to) social solidarity'.

Subsequently, Commins has re-visited his framework in the specific context of rural development within the NESC report. 'Civic integration' expands in meaning to include; 'opportunities for local people to participate in or influence decision - making, and the availability of structures to implement *local* development'. 'Social integration', meanwhile, retains its emphasis on service provision but now places it alongside opportunities to develop personal talents and skills and to develop the capacity to participate in collective action for local development. Sense of belonging is also emphasized under this heading through the encouragement of community arts, cultural expression and the creation of a local identity, as well as through communal development for supportive networks.

The result presents roles for rural development, which include facilitating a greater capacity for local involvement in the development process, based on broad individual integration and inclusion. In this respect, rural development is not so much about the environment or the economy, but about social change. Rural areas become the focus for instigating a social change aimed at enhancing participation, and a devolved responsibility or citizenship for rural resources and local equity.

The issue of social inclusion, then, can be cast in terms of citizenship - of creating the conditions in which individuals can contribute to finding new solutions to common problems, and in so doing, achieve personal wellbeing. This re-emphasis on social developments as much as on economic ones, however, aggravates the tensions between the roles of community development groups in furnishing top-down economic development and a local sense of community (social integration). Social inclusion is an objective faced with a society and culture in transition, one increasingly influenced by new technology. The trends operate on the whole to reduce (or change) the sense of (geographic) place and increase the pressure to be 'mobile'. The resources required to be included in this way are substantial - not only money, but education, continual learning, computer literacy, and a large degree of self-confidence. Can these resources ever be equitably distributed? Can such an equitable distribution be sustained?

It has long been recognized by proponents of sustainable development that capacities for adaptability and resilience to external change are central. Identifying and measuring indicators for these characteristics is therefore a means to gauge sustainability. Where do these features arise from, however? Bryden (1994), in addressing the circumstances for sustainability, places a great deal of emphasis on 'rebuilding' the fractured connections and relations between people, people and 'nature', and people and place. Essentially, this view implies re-integrating the so called 'included community' with the presently 'excluded' one, that is providing reference points for returning the included from their drifting lifestyles to the local, face-to-face world the excluded have been largely 'abandoned to'. Bryden and Commins (1997) call for the need for appropriate institutional frameworks for the joint resolution of social and environmental problems, which link the concepts of community and sustainability. They add: 'A sense of community and the existence of real communities are key ingredients for a social ecology supportive of sustainable development'. It is through community organization, add Bryden and Commins, that people can reinforce attitudes and practices, and also institutionalize mutually agreeable strategies for sustainability. The principle of the 'bottom-up approach' employed in rural development, places an emphasis on participation which 'harnesses the creativity and solidarity of rural communities' (Cork Declaration).

Recent rural development policy discourse has begun to highlight, in this new context, the positive contributions rural areas can provide, and the associated contribution the 'social resource' of rural settlement patterns and sense of community can make to regional quality of life and competitiveness in its own right.[6] This perspective moves away from seeing rural localities in terms of disadvantage only, but also in terms of strengths and contributions.

The next round of rural development support (for years 2000-2006) stemming from the EU's Agenda 2000, also emphasizes the need for rural areas to realise the theoretical virtues ascribed to them in justifying expenditure and intervention to date - environmental and cultural goods, new services to society, and new 'settings' which essentially inspire inward investment, community regeneration and contribute to overall quality of life. Localities must become more apparent as such as elements in a global quality of life.

Capacities for adaptability and resilience are also seen to stem from the resource of community - resilience, from its contribution to inclusion and mutual support, and adaptability through a greater involvement in development as a continual process. Rural development, therefore, now has both a stronger need but also a new rationale for encouraging and building on a re-discovery of the local. Area-based strategies and partnerships pre-figure a new localism - an increased capacity for local say and local responsibility.

A key question, though, is to what extent we can expect there to be the willingness and wherewithal for people to become involved in community or voluntary groups when the trends are firmly toward individualization. Without some receptivity to collective action, the role of community groups of any sort in rising to these new challenges will be limited. Without some significant shift in the locus of power in decision-making over local life; in other words, a reality to the notion of citizenship, such a willingness would not seem likely to materialize.

The community and voluntary sectors need a new sort of legitimacy, both internally and externally in society at large, to become a real alternative for citizenship and self esteem. One source for this may be a greater role in policy and planning decision-making, but if so, it must be built on efforts to establish a genuine broader participation at grassroots level if it is not to become another form of top-down authority. How might this be achieved?

New routes for local development

> It is everybody's *responsibility* to take part in deciding and shaping the future of the areas in which they live - a kind of 'social contract' linking rights with responsibilities (Melo, 1997).

For broader involvement in community-led development to take hold in the 'consumer-led' sense of inclusion,

> What is needed by community workers is a philosophical basis and an effective practice for strengthening face-to-face communities, to meet the psychological needs of belonging, practical needs of mutual care, and the political need of participation and campaigning (Smith, 1997).

These needs have at most been only partially met in the current approach to local development. From the perspective of RDC research and strategy, the components for a wider framework for inclusive local development are being explored. This 'Development of the Local' framework obliges a shift in the relationships between 'The Top' and 'The Bottom'. It has ramifications for the way 'the local' and the consciousness of being local is employed in the development process. What does this framework consist of? Its two main strands are a concept of Collaborative Planning and Development and of local Quality of Life Strategies.

To help realize sustainability, capacity is needed for adaptability. 'Planning' becomes more important than 'the plan'. Targets and physical planning frameworks are usually based on aspirations. Regional and National authorities have less control over events and trends than before (or more awareness that this has always in fact been the case). Planning itself is shifting to be more collaborative (Healey, 1998). Planning as a process means power shifts from the centre (the holder of plans) to an intermediary point, which enables the active employment of a flow of information to and from localities and strategic bodies. Engagement with communities needs to be on a more continuous basis and to involve a broader community base in orchestrating adaptability. The local has a role in feeding back information monitoring and evaluating change. It is not merely a recipient of globally informed development goals.

Collaborative development also encompasses the greater involvement of the community in the effective day-to-day provision of services; involvement in the design of service delivery, but perhaps also active involvement in enhancing the scope and reach of service resources as the cost of providing them escalates. The rationale for this sort of involvement requires a new perspective on community and local life, which a broad base of people can understand. Building quality of life (forming quality of life strategies) provides a framework for participation in the community and in the engagement of development agency support. Quality of life strategies enable the role and contribution of 'the local', both positive and negative, to be addressed and appreciated. It is no longer marginal. Given the emphasis on rural areas contributing to *regional* quality of life, rural communities also need to be more involved in managing rural resources toward the expediting of stewardship roles, the provision of new (environmental and aesthetic) services, the creation of 'settings and places', and so on.

This broader-based framework for local development sees the local as a more integral building block in the functional stability of a globalizing society, not transiently, but permanently. It places an emphasis on individuals-as-citizens being fully engaged in appraising quality of life, and (flexibly) contributing to its management and sustainability. Appraising and managing it in a meaningful way requires the additional contextual framework of a locality and a sense of collective responsibility. Forming these requires attention to issues of identity and identification (sense of belonging or association). These issues need teasing out, making the 'development of the (a) local' a key concern.

How are these various relations to be facilitated? Firstly, tools for broader and deeper (reflective) engagement are needed in addressing locality and the structuration of local quality of life. The term structuration (Giddens, 1984) gains practical currency in helping to describe a process by which local actors can identify factors contributing to their life experiences in an area, the extent to which these are shared, the extent to which they remain global or local, and to which they can be changed or influenced locally. This approach places emphasis on the cultural resources through which social actors relate to one another, their ways of thinking, ways of organizing and ways of conducting life, the way these are maintained, reproduced, or transformed. Further, this approach places emphasis not only on rational, technical knowledge, but also on emotive, moral and intuitive ones.

Building participatory techniques, which enable these areas of experience to be tapped is a key step in the new framework. Facilitative techniques are needed for adapting the concept of 'structuration' to practical realization. The concepts of Participatory Action Research or Participatory Inquiry are key elements in building this approach (see, for example, Reason, 1994). Likewise, the use of arts-based techniques of 'Active Reflection', and Frierean methods of discussion (see Friere 1979). This must then be translated into appropriate monitoring and evaluation frameworks, which can capture qualitative dimensions, building communicative linkages between actors, both locally and at agency level.

Whilst local monitoring and evaluation frameworks are important, building from the bottom up, a further strand of the framework is the development of management indicators and participatory planning techniques, which seek to create linkages between localities and 'The Top'.

Work here builds on the surge of activity stemming from Local Agenda 21 in the development, design and use of development indicators. The ethos of participatory planning at local authority level has been introduced and developed here, providing in the meantime additional tools and techniques for broadening participation and developing collective visions. Likewise, the Healthy Communities programme has contributed to the idea of indicators, encouraging communities to identify key indicators of local quality of life which they can then play a role in monitoring and by which they can judge progress (Murray, 1998).

The indicator process goes beyond consultation, to identifying appropriate roles the community and the development authority can take up in reference to the same, common set of goals and indicators. This forms the basis of collaborative development.

Adjustments required within intermediary planning and development bodies to accommodate local participation and collaborative development are a key element associated with this work. Given that a culture of development for global goals is prevalent within these bodies which is 'upward and outward' rather than downward, such adjustment is itself a substantial issue. Change must take place on both sides of the agency/local actor interface. These various areas of work leave out the question of economic development, yet this is the primary concern of rural development to date. How does it fit into a 'development of the local' model? Along with a capacity for collaborative planning, (marginal) local areas need a degree of self-reliance in order to ensure adaptability and resilience. As Robertson (1998) puts it, 'more self-reliant local development will play a key part in the transition to people-centred, environmentally sustainable ways of economic life... a key part, but only one part, of a new, multi-level approach to economic activity worldwide', one which links local economies to a new approach to globalization.

Social economy initiatives, built from local community needs and participation, also help create links between marginal, non-competitive localities where private enterprise has failed to thrive, and global economic development (see, for example, Pearce, 1993). The links must be made, however, by building from more innovative hybrids of social and economic enterprise, blending voluntary and paid labour, utilizing LETS (Local Exchange Trading Systems) for example.[7] These constitute responses, which have a distinct and necessary local basis and consciousness which must come before any attempt to forge links into global economies can be sustained.

In turn, business network models currently held up as solutions to competitive, adaptable development, stress the shared, strong social milieu of individuals, and the element of trust it supports, as a key ingredient in their effective reproduction (see, for example, Harrison, 1992). A common vision of the locality can inform and enhance individual enterprise and co-operative projects between such enterprises. The new framework for collaborative development suggested here, then, and which is being pursued by the RDC as a development agency, consists of four main strands:

- Developing a *structurated* sense of the local as a domain of action. This approach does not assume a 'functional community' or locality but facilitates its construction out of actor life-worlds. Structuration is made practical by use of the idea of formulating *quality of life strategies.*
- Quality of life strategies, beginning as value statements, are translated as far as possible into a local framework of action, which includes indicators by which to monitor progress collectively.
- Economic development is also translated into local goals in a social economy framework, but not exclusively.
- Wider use of indicators also forges links between local actors and broader development authorities (local councils, area-based partnerships, and so on) to define mutual roles and common goals.

The objective is to enhance social inclusion in the development process, build foundations for sustainable development, but not isolate the 'local' from the global, rather, re-balance the relationships between the two.

The RDC, through its action research unit, is collaborating with a range of partner institutions and local communities in developing this approach within a participatory action research model. For example, within a LEADER II programme with the Centre for Rural Studies, Queens University Belfast, to develop models and techniques of participatory planning, and with bodies a wide apart as the Arts Council and Community Theatre to GIS and telematics departments of the universities, to develop other aspects of the framework.

Concluding remarks

> Every journey includes stops in places; continuity requires discontinuity (Thrift, 1995).

The key issue placed at the centre of this chapter has been to distinguish between 'local responses', which share a universal or globally oriented culture and goals (and which are, as such, not local, but localized), from ones which are grounded in a locally informed culture. In each case, culture is to be understood in terms of knowledge, experience, and identity. The view expressed has been that to date, it is the former, localized response with which the various development agencies, policies and planning processes have been concerned. However, to improve on the capacity for social inclusion, and to achieve the ambition of sustainable development, the building block of local citizenship was suggested which in turn requires more attention to a development of the local itself, and hence, local responses, as a context for action. It is not suggested that these become mutually exclusive goals - it is impossible to extract 'the local' from the global - rather, the aim should be to enhance the local as a component of the global - to integrate localities, not replace them for a seamless, referenceless whole.

Experience in community development suggests that for many, perhaps the majority of those in local communities who engage in local development, it is the nuts and bolts, the doing of it, which is important. Abstract concepts, whether 'local development' or 'development of the local'; of vision-building, of quality of life strategies and the like, are seen as of no relevance. But for those working in development - policy, planning or practice, working with strategic knowledge, these concepts and differences do have meaning. It is important to decide what it is we wish to encourage, enhance, and try to facilitate. Likewise, for those working in local community development, a stronger legitimacy and wider value base may be vital if their efforts are to reach wider and deeper among local people.

This last raises the question of legitimacy. If being local is insufficient or inconsequential to local actors, who wish, rather, to identify with a global society, can there be any justification for seeking to encourage a local consciousness and focus for action? The points made in answer to this question have been threefold. Firstly, there is ample evidence to suggest that being local does have value to the majority of people in rural (and urban) areas, in Northern Ireland at least. Secondly, from a strategic perspective being local enables a distinct and effective contribution to a sustainable global development - it can and should be encouraged, rather than sublimated to a representation of relative disadvantage. Thirdly, being local is not a separate alternative to being global. In other words, the issue is to refocus 'the local' into what is already there. Fourthly, however, perhaps from an actor's perspective being local is not an option - only the extent to which it is made use of. Local and locality may continue to be substantially 'contingent places' constructed by an array of social actors, local and non-local, further interlinked with non-social bio-geographic and technical entities (Callon, 1986). Intervention for a development of the local sets out to amplify the awareness of these linkages and contingencies and the role of the local as a discursive context (Mack, 1998a) and in the structuration of daily life. It is this consciousness, its inclusiveness, intensity and content, which forms the basis for a development of a new local, and of local citizenship.

Notes

1 Local Agenda 21 is a component of Agenda 21 - an 'action plan for the 21st century' stemming from the Rio 'Earth Summit' of 1992. Agenda 21 states that local authorities and local communities will have to be involved if development is to be sustainable. It urges local authorities to draw up Local Agenda 21 plans for their areas by 1996.
2 Mixed communities are common, although they two often maintain separate use of the same space by using different shops, sides of the road, or social areas.
3 These are defined for the purposes of distributing and collecting household information for the electoral register and hence for the distribution of voting cards at elections, as areas which can be serviced by a single enumeration officer.
4 EU money forms the main source of support, coupled in Northern Ireland to the International Fund for Ireland (contributed to by the USA, EU, Canada, and New Zealand).

5   See, for example, the following EU documents: European Commission, 1994 and European Commission 1995.
6   See, for example, the White Papers on Rural Development for England, Scotland and Wales respectively, and the Cross-Sectoral Policy Group Report published by the RDC in 1998.
7   LETS systems utilise a local currency generated by trade between members of the system. The currency has no value outside the locality and has the potential to help re-build local economies (see, for example, Williams, 1996).

References

Bryden, J. (1994), 'Towards Sustainable Rural Communities. From Theory to Action', in *Towards Sustainable Rural Communities: The Guelph Seminar Series*, Canada, University of Guelph Publications.
Bryden, J. and Commins, P. (1997), 'Rural Development: Some Observations on New Policy Orientations and the Cork Declaration', paper presented to the Agricultural Economics Society Conference, Edinburgh.
Callon, M. (1986), 'Some Elements of a Sociology of Translation: Domestication of Scallpops and the Fishermen of St. Brieucs Bay', in Law, J. (ed), *Power, Action, Belief. A New Sociology of Knowledge?,* Routledge: London.
Commins, P. (1994), *NESC Report. New Approaches to Rural Development*, Teagasc: Dublin.
Commins, P. (ed) (1993), *Combating Social Exclusion in Ireland 1990-1994*, A Midway Report, EU Poverty 3 Programme, Combat Poverty Agency.
Cox, K.R and Mair, A. (1991), 'From Localized Social Structures to Localities as Agents', *Environment and Planning A*, Vol. 23, pp. 197-213.
European Commission (1994), *European Social Policy: A Way Forward for the Union*, European Commission: Luxemburg.
European Commission (1995), *Medium Term Social Action Programme 1995-97*, Social Europe 1/95, European Commission: Luxemburg.
Friere, P. (1979), *Pedagogy of the Oppressed*, Sheed and Ward: London.
Giddens, A. (1984), *The Constitution of Society*, Polity Press: Cambridge.
Habermas, J. (1984), *The Theory of Communicative Action: Reason and the Rationalisation of Society*, Vol. 1, Polity Press: London.
Habermas, J. (1987), *The Philosophical Discourse of Modernity*, Polity Press: Cambridge.
Harrison, B. (1992), 'Industrial Districts: Old Wine in New Bottles?', *Regional Studies*, Vol. 26, No 5, pp. 469-483.
Healey, P. (1997), *Collaborative Planning; Shaping Places in Fragmented Society*, Macmillan Press: Hampshire.
Mack, N. (1998a), 'Cultural Empowerment: (Re)building Locality and Facilitating Collective Vision as Interventions Toward Sustainable Rural Development', in Reqeuir-Desjardins, D., Spash, C. and van der Straaten, J. (eds), *Environmental Policies and Societal Aims*, Netherlands, Kluwer Press.

Mack, N. (1998b), *Rural Belonging - Gauging the Status of the Rural Community in Northern Ireland*, RDC Action Research Publications.
Melo, A. (1996), 'From Global Thinking to Local Action', in Conference Proceedings Report 'Making Partnerships Work', NICVA: Belfast.
Murray, M. (forthcoming), *Social Capital formation and Healthy Communities: Insights from the Colorado*, Healthy Communities Initiative.
National Economic and Social Council (1994), *New Approaches to Rural Development*, NESC Report No 97, Dublin Castle: Dublin.
Pearce, J. (1993), *At the Heart of the Community Economy. Community Enterprise in a Changing World*, Calouste Gulbenkian Society Publication: London.
Reason, P. (ed) (1994), *Participation in Human Inquiry*, Sage Publications: London.
Robertson, J. (1998), *Transforming Economic Life: A Millennial Challenge*, Schumacher Briefings. Green Books: London.
Robson, B., Bradford, H and Deas, I. (1994), 'Relative Deprivation in Northern Ireland', *Occasional Paper No 28*, Policy and Planning Research Unit, DoENI.
Smith, G., (1996), 'Ties Nets and an Elastic Bund: Community in the Postmodern City', *Community Development Journal*, Vol. 31, pp. 250-259.
Thrift, N. (1995), 'Inhuman Geographies: Landscapes of Speed, Light and Power', in Cloke, P., Doel, M., Matless, D., Phillips, M., Thrift, N., *Writing the Rural: Five Cultural Geographies*, Routledge: London.
Williams, C. (1996), 'Local Purchasing Schemes and Rural Development: An Evaluation of Local Exchange Trading Systems (LETS)', *Journal of Rural Studies*, Vol. 12, No 3, pp. 231-244.

11 Rural Development Policy in Finland in the 1990s: Towards Flexible Specialization or Spatial Taylorism?

PETRI RUUSKANEN

Introduction

Finland is one of Europe's least densely populated countries, and according to the OECD Reviews of Rural Policy, it is among the three most rural countries in the OECD, along with Norway and Turkey. Under the OECD definition, 57 per cent of its population live in rural areas, which account for 98 per cent of the country's territory (OECD, 1995a). At the same time the problems experienced by rural areas in Finland are the same as anywhere else: an aging population, depopulation, a declining economy, scarce employment opportunities and so on. Hence, it is often stated that rural policy is of special importance for Finland.

Finnish rural policy has been basically a state-led agricultural policy. Since the 1960s, however, it has been based on a blend of agricultural subsidies, an industrializing regional policy and the establishment of a welfare state (see Granberg, 1989; Pyy and Lehtola, 1996). When Finland started planning closer integration with the EC in the 1980s, the old policy nevertheless became a problem. As in many other countries, rural development policy in Finland faced significant reorientation in response to demands for economic integration (see OECD, 1993). As a result, post-Fordist concepts such as differentiation, networking, flexibility and entrepreneurship now form the body of Finnish rural policy documents.

The concept of rural policy in Finland - also called 'new rural policy' to distinguish it from the earlier, 'old' rural policy - gained official status in the early 1980s, and it took its present form by the national Rural Development Project (1988-91). The project is described in the main publication: *Rural Development Programme. Objectives, Strategies and*

Measures of Finnish Rural Policy in the 1990s (RDP 1991a; 1991b). The status of the new rural policy was strengthened in 1992 with the establishment of a Rural Policy Board, and further in 1995, when the Co-operative Group for Rural Policy was formed (Malinen, 1996, p. 42). In addition, the Ministry of Agriculture and Forestry appointed a committee, which published its report *Rural Programme. Active Rural Areas* in 1996 (CRP, 1996). The strategy and the main operating methods of the new rural policy have remained virtually unchanged all along.

There has been quite a lively discussion in Finland recently about the changing meanings of rurality and the evolving rural policy (see Granberg, 1995; Oksa and Rannikko, 1996), and as a sequel to this, the present chapter sets out to discuss the rhetoric and 'implicit themes' of the new rural policy (see Billig et al., 1989). It focuses in particular on the Rural Development Programme (RDP 1991a, 1991b; also RPC, 1992) which lays down the strategy for the rural policy of the 1990s and explains the background to this strategy. Rural policy will be considered as an expression of a 'mentality of government', a concept of how the authorities should use their powers to improve the wellbeing of rural areas, and crucially, the nature of the persons upon whom the authorities must act (Rose, 1992, p. 145). It has to be remembered in any case that this perspective on rural policy is by no means the only one possible. Other standpoints would yield other characteristics as being the essential ones (Weber, 1976, pp. 47-48). Before going on to consider the rhetoric of contemporary Finnish rural policy, it would be useful to briefly sketch the development of the rural policy in Finland.

From the 'old rural policy' to the 'new rural policy' of the 1990s

Finland has always considered itself a forerunner in rural development. Indeed, governments have adopted various measures to support rural sources of livelihood in order to keep every part of the country inhabited. The aim of Finnish rural policy has usually been described as being to promote the idea of social and regional equality. Nevertheless, it can be argued that the interests of the state have always been a major factor behind rural issues. Actually, the basic long-term trend in Finnish rural policy has been embedded in a nation building project, industrialization and social policy.

Peasant landowners have had an important position in the formation of state and nation in the Grand Duchy of Finland from the late 19th century onwards. Under pressure from Imperial Russia, the dominant Swedish-speaking elite adopted the Finnish language and promoted the idea of national unity and the 'Finnish folk culture'. The peasantry constituted the core of the nation in the nation building project, the folk, while the aim of the elite was to achieve a kind of civic education for the freehold peasants, making them aware of the needs of the nation and their patriotic duties. Thus, the peasantry became a useful resource for the elite in their nation building project. At the same time, the elite used cultural means to defend the traditional agrarian ethos against the threats of industrialization (Alapuro, 1988). Thus, a double bond was created between the state and the peasantry, which legitimated the position of the elite in a strong paternalistic state administration and paved the way for a rural policy. Later, from the 1940s onwards, the governing coalition assimilated the interests of the workers' movement and enabled the construction of a universalist welfare society (see Haatainen, 1993).

In the aftermath of the war, the 'Winter War' of 1939-40 and the Continuation War of 1941-44, the rural areas underwent important changes, the outward signs of which were extensive government-led projects such as resettlement, industrialization and the construction of a welfare state (Uusitalo, 1995, p. 43). Up to the 1960s, rural policy meant primarily agricultural policy as the country was faced with a shortage of agricultural products and government intervention was geared to promoting self-sufficiency in this sphere. Furthermore, agricultural policy and resettlement activity were intended to support national independence and cohesion within society under the unstable political conditions of the post-war period. Agricultural policy gradually adopted aspects of social policy while welfare rationality spread throughout society, aiming at equality of results rather than equality of opportunities. To promote employment in the rural areas, the government also reinforced its agricultural policy with an industrializing regional policy from the late 1960s onwards (Granberg, 1995, p. 84; see also Pyy and Lehtola, 1996; Tykkyläinen, 1996).

Up to the 1980s, rural policy rested on a strong, paternalistic central government, which planned the economy and, together with organizations such as the Finnish Employers' Confederation, the Confederation of Finnish Trade Unions and the Central Union of Agricultural Producers, judged how the national income should be distributed amongst the various sectors of the population. In the public discourse of the 'old' rural policy, the persons at whom the policy was targeted, primarily the farmers, were not considered entrepreneurs whose main objective was to maximize profits. Until the late 1960s, they were rather considered as social actors whose moral duty was to serve the public interest and later as a social group which is a natural partner of the collective bargaining process

(Alasuutari, 1996, pp. 38-73). However, rural policy has undergone a considerable reorientation since the late 1980s. The globalization process and the increasing integration of the world's economy have meant that the rural policy rhetoric based on the vocabulary of the welfare state has been transformed into a market-led policy rhetoric. The new rural development policy of the 1990s now draws a sharp distinction between itself and the old rural policy, so that the new policy is described in the national rural programme as 'abandoning the preservation of the status quo in favour of a forward-looking development strategy', which makes it easy for the reader to figure out the backwardness of the old policy (RDP, 1991b, p. 9; RPC, 1992, p. 7). Post-Fordist regimes, especially the flexible specialization outlined by Piore and Sabel (1984) and industrial networking have now been brought forward as solutions to the problems of competitiveness confronting rural areas. Instead of agricultural subsidies and the welfare state, 'entrepreneurship', 'enterprises' and 'new sources of livelihood' now form the core of rural policy. Consequently, the government is transferring responsibility for rural development to local actors.

Entrepreneurship has become a keyword in rural policy in the 1990s (Ruuskanen, 1995a) to the extent that rural enterprises and entrepreneurs have become the main objects and agents of rural development (Uusitalo, 1995, pp. 63-77). As Mokry (1988, p. 115) puts it, the concept of using entrepreneurship as an economic development tool is an extremely attractive one for policy-makers. At the same time, the word can suggest innovativeness, a dynamic economy, the liberty epitomized by independent small businessmen, liberalistic self-help, increasing communal vitality, working with local people - or almost anything else. Its simultaneous attractiveness and ambiguity (or rich content) make the question of *what rural policy means when it talks about promoting entrepreneurship, flexible specialization and new sources of livelihood* so interesting.

The rhetoric of the new rural policy

As described briefly above, government interests have always been a central factor behind rural policy in Finland. The rural population was an important tool in the emergence of the state, the nation and the Finnish identity, when the country was building up its independence in the late 19th and early 20th centuries and agrarian reforms and agricultural policy were important means for stabilising the country at times of political turmoil. Later, the rural population had an important role as a source of manpower in the government-led drive for industrialization (see Rannikko, 1989).

Besides alleviating structural changes in rural areas and promoting regional equality, rural policy has always included the aspect of governing as such. Actually, in the words of Foucault (1991), we have been living in an 'era of *governmentality*' with respect to the administrative state ever since the eighteenth century. Foucault uses the word 'governmentality' to mean,

> The ensemble formed by institutions, procedures, analyses and reflections, the calculations and tactics that allow the exercise of this very specific albeit complex form of power, which has as its target population, as its principal form of knowledge political economy, and as its essential technical means apparatuses of security (1991, p. 102).

As Miller and Rose (1990) have pointed out, the concept of governmentality is useful for analyzing the complex ways in which authorities shape and regulate economic, social and personal activities. Miller and Rose especially emphasize language-oriented analysis of the political rationales on which government policies are based, for example. It is quite obvious that rhetoric is a natural characteristic of administrative documents and of the government of society. At the base of this approach, one finds the conviction that administrative rhetoric and discourse as such play a role in what rural policy is and what it will become (see, also, Summa, 1992). As the speech act theorist Austin (1982) has shown, speech does not merely reflect reality, but it also has a performative nature - by saying something, one is often and at the same time doing something.

In the same spirit, Foucault (1972, p. 49) defines discourses as 'practices that systematically form the objects of which they speak'. He maintains that discourses and practises should be treated as if they were the same thing. He is especially interested in what Dreyfus and Rabinow (1982, pp. 45-49) call serious speech acts, i.e. *what experts say when they are speaking as experts*. Such speech acts may constitute a relatively autonomous realm and they gain their autonomy by passing some sort of institutional test.

The texts of rural policy, such as policy planning documents, are a good example of serious speech acts. The aim of the Rural Development Programme (RDP) is to control the changes and threats confronting rural areas, and both the experts and the institutional test can be identified in the policy-making procedures:

> The National Programme is based on the findings of 23 groups of experts and of individual experts - a total of more than 100 persons representing almost 50 organizations. The Co-ordinating Group examined these findings and integrated them into a consistent whole (RDP, 1991b, p. 8).

Furthermore, the programme was later submitted to the Parliament (see Valtioneuvosto, 1993). The wording of the *Rural Development Programme* is here considered to exemplify the mentality of government. The programme simultaneously constitutes a state of affairs - a picture of the causes and effects behind the problems confronting rural areas - and recommends how these problems can be solved or controlled. At the same time, it also puts forward expectations regarding how people should learn to recognize themselves as subjects (see Foucault 1982, 1991; Miller and Rose, 1990; Rose, 1992). In doing this, the programme uses rhetorical techniques to make the audience accept its outlook on the world. The task of the analyses of administrative rhetoric in the next chapters can be described in the same way as Foucault puts it:

> Commentary questions discourse as to what it says and intends to say; --- in other words, in stating what has been said, one has to re-state what has never been said (1973, p. xvi).

In analyzing the rhetoric of the programme, I shall focus on argumentative strategies built into it. What are the statements of the reasons for rural policy? What are its objectives and how will those objectives be achieved? How does the policy describe the subjects living in rural areas, and what expectations does it have of them?

Why rural policy?

> Rural policy covers all objectives and measures designed to ameliorate rural conditions and improve the situation of rural areas in Society and in the regional structure (RDP, 1991a, p. 373; RPC, 1992, p. 7).

As quoted above, the concept of rural policy is defined very broadly in the Rural Development Programme: It covers all the objectives and measures which improve and ameliorate the situation of rural *areas*. Thus, it is the rural areas and their situation, which form the primary object of rural policy and not the rural inhabitants and their wellbeing. Why then, as stated by the programme, do we need to improve the conditions of these areas?

> The primary commonly accepted goal is to keep every part of Finland inhabited. Without that it will be impossible to utilize the existing infrastructure and natural resources, to secure the national defense or to promote regional wellbeing and equality. A dispersed, relatively self-sufficient societal structure is not so prone to environmental and other crises. A populated countryside also

permits the development of renewable domestic sources of energy to supplement or replace coal, oil and nuclear power (RDP, 1991b, p. 10).

We can see that the statement of the reasons for rural policy is mainly based on macro-scale rationales concerning national economy and society as a whole. Measures are needed to keep all parts of the country inhabited so that they can serve as economic growth reserves and secure the national defense. The defense question is especially interesting, as this statement has been left out of the English version of the document (RPC, 1992, p. 8), probably on the grounds that such an argument is convincing only for Finnish readers. It has even been stated elsewhere that the rhetoric of external threats is a particularly efficient method of controlling both the economy and the people in Finland (see Anttonen, 1996; Vartiainen, 1996). In any case, it seems to be the state and not the inhabitants that lie at the centre of the rationality behind rural policy.

The programme mentions numerous threats looming on the horizon for rural areas. The population is aging and moving to the centres, mainly in response to structural changes in the economy and there are also global trends, which threaten the future of these areas.

> Businesses and enterprises are threatened by internationalization and the more open world markets --- cost-benefit calculations and management by results in the public sector are impeding the preservation and development of rural services (RDP, 1991b, pp. 11-12; RPC, 1992, p. 9).

These external factors which threaten rural business and enterprises - economic integration and globalization - compel the state to be more effective and trim its budget, which makes it impossible to develop rural services. This appeal to an external threat makes the audience aware that as the needs of rural areas increase, the means available to the state are diminishing. All the same, rural policy emphasizes the importance of rural areas for the whole country.

> Both culturally and mentally rurality is a part of the Finnish people, our roots are in countryside. An inhabited countryside is an aim, which the Finns hold in high esteem and universally accept (Valtioneuvosto, 1993, p. 5).

While global economic trends threaten the future of rural areas, rural policy assigns almost a mythical meaning to rurality. The culture of rural areas forms 'a cultural entity', which in turn constitutes a national identity. According to official rural policy, rurality is culturally and mentally a part of every Finn. In the first place, this argument refers to a sense of community - the future of rural areas is a matter of common interest. Secondly, it assigns the rural population the honourable task of keeping that base alive in the face of an external threat.

At this stage of argumentation, rural areas seem to form an integral whole. When talking about rural policy measures, however, this rhetoric is abandoned. In fact, the programme recognizes three types of rural areas:

> *Economically integrated rural areas.* These have the widest opportunities for development. Large towns nearby create opportunities for paid employment and lively local markets for rural enterprises.
> *Intermediate rural areas.* These include areas limited almost exclusively to agriculture and areas that have achieved functional diversification. They are mostly some distance away from the large towns, but reasonably close to medium-sized towns. They contain well-appointed local centres and villages.
> *Remote rural areas.* These are problem areas where the long distances from the towns prevent commuting and deprive the areas of local markets. Their occupational structure is non-diversified (RDP, 1991a, p. 29).

In the era of the nation building project and the old rural policy, it was expedient to regard rural areas as an integral whole - as the place where the 'independent peasantry' lived. The peasantry constituted the core of nation and its moral duty was to act in the public interest, secure the national defense and ensure an adequate food supply. As noted above, this argument is still useful when stating reasons for a rural policy. The era of the new rural policy has changed all that, however. Now, in the face of economic integration and globalization, it is appropriate to classify the countryside into several types of rural area, differing in their market position, and to abandon the 'outdated' notion of government regulation and adapt instead to trends in global markets and integration.

Objectives, strategies and measures

The same market-oriented rhetoric can be found in the objective definition of rural policy. Its goals in the 1990s have been summarized as follows:

> *The goal of rural policy* is to revitalize the countryside, alleviate structural problems, improve rural sources of livelihood and services, strengthen the viability of rural communities, enhance *the competitiveness of rural areas, and increase their attraction as places to live and as locations for enterprises.* ---
> *The essence of rural policy is to create new sources of livelihood and services*

that will strengthen the countryside but as yet have no organizations to watch over their interests (RDP, 1991b, p. 8; RPC, 1992, p. 7; italics in the original).

The key words of the new rural policy are *competitiveness, enterprise* and *new sources of livelihood*. The mention of new sources of livelihood which 'have no organizations to watch over their interests' obviously refers to the important position of corporations in the 'old' rural policy, which now has to be reduced. As noted earlier, the emphasis on competitiveness as the most important objective means in the policy rhetoric 'changing over to a forward-looking strategy'. Again the distinction between 'old' and 'new' is clear. Where agriculture was once an inherent value in rural policy, this attitude is now outdated and belongs to the past. There is no room for such backwardness in the globalized world and on the open world market. The objective of a self-sustaining agriculture, which was previously the central basis of rural policy, has given way to a 'relatively self-sufficient social structure' (RDP, 1991a, 12). According to the new rural policy, centralization of agriculture will be the inevitable result of globalization. The volume of production will be reduced, the acreage of farms will grow and agriculture will become centralized (RDP, 1991a, pp. 37-40 & p. 133). This seems to be a natural law of globalization, which will of course reduce job opportunities in the agricultural sector.

The jobs lost in agriculture will be replaced by 'creating new sources of livelihood and services'. Such themes as entrepreneurship and enterprise stand out very prominently. Almost all branches of administration emphasize the new notions of entrepreneurship and the spirit of enterprise as a solution to the diminishing job opportunities in their sectors. The development of new sources of livelihood will be supported by promoting small businesses, independent enterprises and entrepreneurship (RDP, 1991a, pp. 37-41). 'Resistance to change' and 'the prevailing climate of opinion' are obstacles to this development, however. People are unfortunately 'satisfied with the present' (RPC, 1992, pp. 28), they do not apply for entrepreneurial training and entrepreneurship (RDP, 1991b, p. 32). Furthermore the cultural patterns of rural entrepreneurs seem to resist new, flexible production models such as networking (see Ruuskanen, 1995b; CRP, 1996, p. 109), which effectively prevents the creation of the 'new sources of livelihood' in small business enterprises which is the objective of the policy:

> The greatest obstacle to small-scale rural enterprise is a lack of will or know-how (RDP, 1991a, p. 40).

As a consequence, the policy emphasizes the creation of the correct attitude as a tool for solving the problems:

> Entrepreneurship and training for rural entrepreneurs have to be promoted so that changes in attitudes, spontaneous activity and independent initiative will be supported (RDP, 1991b, p. 48).

As Burke (1989, p. 271) notes, we convince our audience through reasons which we hold *in common*. Most of us indeed want to be spontaneous individuals, but this does not mean that everybody, or even most of us, would be able or want to become an entrepreneur. Rural policy nevertheless appeals to this common agreement when persuading its readers of the need for a new *entrepreneurial spirit*. At the same time it implicitly deplores a state of affairs in which the rural population *has lost its own initiative* and is stuck in attitudes of the past. This situation will be corrected by entrepreneurial training. The same emphasis on attitudes and spirit when speaking of entrepreneurship can be seen when the policy emphasizes the importance of entrepreneurship education in primary school (RDP, 1991a, p. 139). Young people will 'be educated in entrepreneurship at school and through their hobbies' (RDP, 1991a, p. 171). Thus, the idea of people acting on their own initiative turns out to be a paradox: on the one hand, the state tells people to be spontaneous, and on the other, it starts a massive civil education process to promote entrepreneurship as an economic ethos and to make people dissatisfied with the present.

Toward flexible specialization or spatial Taylorism?

What, then, are these small-scale rural enterprises which, according to rural policy, can be run by spontaneous independent entrepreneurs and which will create about 300,000 new jobs? (RDP, 1991a, p. 81) Central issues mentioned in the strategy are 'diversification', 'know-how', 'expanding entrepreneurship which covers all trades', 'interaction between rural areas and centres' and 'spontaneous activity instead of public regulation'. This means that:

> Crucial aspects are commuting, subcontracting, distance work and possession by townspeople of a stake in the rural areas (RDP, 1991a, p. 78; see also CRP, 1996, p. 9).

In rural policy discourses, the rural areas themselves are transformed from a place of active production into a residual of the centres: manpower reserves and consumption landscapes. The main new rural forms of livelihood outlined are connected with entrepreneurship, i.e. first of all subcontracting and distance work. The explicit background to the stress on 'entrepreneurship', 'subcontracting', 'diversification' and so on is the model of flexible specialization, with its emphasis on differentiation, flexibility and industrial networking (RDP, 1991b, p. 72).

In the ideal model of flexible specialization as outlined by Piore and Sabel (1984), the strategy of permanent innovation would enable small firms organized in horizontal networks and vertical chains of cooperation to compete with the mass production model dominated by large firms. On the one hand, small rural enterprises can diversify their production and seek competitive advantage in narrow, specific market segments, or niches. A niche market strategy is not an easy way to attain competitiveness, however, as market niches often appear and disappear very rapidly. This places many demands on the producer if he (or she) is to achieve a specialized knowledge of a particular market and the development of products for it (see OECD, 1995b). The other possible strategy is vertical networking, i.e. subcontracting by a core group of companies in the centres to small rural firms.

There is a big difference, however, between the flexibility of 'active versatility' and that of 'passive pliability'. With the first type of flexibility small firms utilize their capacity to react and adapt to exploit temporary market niches, whereas the second type is characterized by an ability and readiness to submit to outside pressure and to accept long-term risks and lasting cutbacks in labour standards and profits (see Semlinger, 1993, pp. 164-168; Amin, 1991, pp. 128-135).

For larger manufacturing companies it may indeed be rational to hire-out their peripheral tasks in order to seek flexibility reservoirs in the labour market. Atkinson (1987), for example, distinguishes three goals for employers in seeking greater labour market flexibility:

1. *numerical flexibility*, which is concerned with how employers adjust the numbers of people employed or the hours they work to changing workloads,
2. *functional flexibility*, which is concerned with how they adjust the deployment of these people, and
3. *distancing*, which represents the replacement of employment contracts by commercial contracts such as subcontracting agreements.

Each type of flexibility impinges differently on different groups within the labour force, which as a result becomes segmented into a 'core' group of employees surrounded by 'peripheral' and 'external' groups. A strong trade union can nevertheless restrain this flexibility within a firm, which makes outsourcing attractive, as small-scale entrepreneurs - self-employed persons and small employers - are supposedly more willing (or can be forced) to accept flexible working hours, an intensification of work or a squeeze on their profits. At the same time, outsourcing makes it possible for the larger firms to achieve more flexible financing by shifting part of the investment burden to subcontractors. It even seems that the conscious efforts of the core-periphery strategists favour the more systematic use of an external workforce rather than organizational restructuring within firms (Hakim, 1990).

Outsourcing and the segmentation of the labour market can give rise to new firms by a pull-push mechanism. On the one hand, the process opens up new business opportunities by creating a demand for small-scale suppliers, but on the other hand it creates an 'unemployment push', which may force people outside the core labour market to establish small firms of their own. The latter seems to be very common among small rural entrepreneurs in Finland, especially where the smallest industrial firms are concerned (see Niittykangas, 1992, p. 90). This double mechanism affecting the formation of new companies may also produce wider and sharper segmentation of the 'external' labour market than of the 'internal' labour market.

Let us examine more closely what kind of entrepreneurship and flexibility Finnish rural policy is actually talking about. Instead of emphasizing labour and marketing skills, technologies and industry, or region-specific assistance to firms, which are demands of 'active versatility', the policy stresses entrepreneurship as a resource for subcontracting and distance work:

> In developing the centres, research and development investments and nation-wide and international communication will be crucial. Correspondingly, the reform of rural entrepreneurship will be emphasized through entrepreneurial training (RDP, 1991a, p. 79; CRP, 1996, p. 50).

It can be seen that rural policy does not stress the innovative characteristics of rural entrepreneurship. Instead, as cited earlier, the emphasis is on a change of attitude to be achieved through entrepreneurial training. One celebrated case of a project which combines the key words of the new rural policy, i.e. 'entrepreneurship', 'networking' and 'interaction between rural areas and centres', is 'The Finnish Woodwork Project', which was financed by the Committee for Rural Policy in 1992-1994 and again from 1997 onwards (see CRP, 1995). It is quite obvious that development in the forest sector has always had a powerful effect on Finnish rural policy. Up to the 1960s, for example, the government supported a rural economy based on a combination of small-scale farming and lumbering, as this provided the manpower reserve required for the seasonal jobs of felling and transporting the timber from the forests (Rannikko, 1989). Now that subsidies to agriculture are being progressively reduced, the idea of the Finnish Woodwork Project is to increase the value added on sawed timber through networking.

> The first woodwork unit in the chain, i.e. the sawmill, can be rather small, possibly sorting, cutting and packaging the products. The next link or links in the chain, again possibly small units, work [up] the timber further, possibly into components or blanks. Several component manufacturers may combine their input to the final product. The product is then manufactured in large enough quantities to meet the demand of the market (Vanhanen, 1996, p. 68).

The Finnish Woodwork Project was organized at two levels: the modelling and building of the network were the tasks of certain 'Lead Companies', presumed to be larger, medium-sized companies which were already equipped for the export trade, while a regional organization was responsible for the rural activities and sought out potential entrepreneurs to act as links in the production chain. At the beginning of the project the role of the local-level entrepreneurs was described as follows:

> We have an immediate challenge, especially in the timber industry, to create new systems for the purchasing of raw materials and the production of goods. Firms are dividing their production into components, which they hire out to subcontractors. In this way firms can exploit the entrepreneurial potential released from traditional rural means of livelihood. This makes it possible to promote structural changes in sources of livelihood in rural areas from primary production to industrial production. --- As regards regional development, it is important to recognize that models based on hard, unpleasant industrial work can most easily be created in the rural parts of Finland, where the culture and values support hard work and the development process that is needed (Finnish Woodwork Project, 1992).

The idea of networking is that the production chain should spread its tentacles from the forested rural areas out into the world market. In this way, a Lead Company can ensure a supply of its raw materials and simultaneously out-source the inferior, tedious work, making use of smaller rural enterprises in which 'wages are lower and working skills poorer', as Vuorinen (1989, p. 28) puts it, for example, - as flexibility reservoirs. The role of the small rural entrepreneur in a networking model of this kind is to be passively flexible. The ideal model for a flexible woodworking network is presented in Figure 11.1 (CRP, 1995, pp. 52, 61-62).

The model for a flexible network is quite similar to that usually described as representing Taylorism, the basic idea of which was to improve productivity by breaking each labour process down into components. Redesigning jobs makes it possible to rationalize each fragmented task, but at the same time it enables control to be exercised over the 'laziness' of the workmen (see Taylor, 1972, p. 33). Now 'the management take over all work for which they are better fitted than the workmen, while in the past almost all of the work and the greater part of the responsibility were thrown upon the men' (Taylor, 1972, p. 37). In other words, Taylorism means distinguishing between management, conception, control and execution, which at the same time leads to polarization and de-skilling within the labour process (see Taylor, 1972; also Lash and Urry, 1987, pp. 164-165; Harvey, 1989, p. 125).

It seems that the interpretation of flexible specialization and industrial networking in Finnish rural policy is rather a new application of Taylorism than a version of the model described by Piore and Sabel (1984). In their model, firms in the network have distinctive but overlapping specialities and expertise and they also share a common culture (Piore, 1995, p. 190). Conversely, in the ideal model for a flexible manufacturing network, which is outlined in Finnish rural policy documents, 'the Lead company' breaks the labour process down and hires-out the inferior, 'tedious' tasks to self-employed entrepreneurs away from centres, on the grounds that lower wages and poorer labour standards will probably be accepted more willingly in rural areas, where employment opportunities are scarce and 'the culture and values support hard work'. Hence the model is based on the different, not the common culture between the core companies and the small rural suppliers.

At the same time, the leading company can control the whole chain since it commands the key functions – product development and marketing – and controls the flow of information in the chain. This asymmetrical distribution of power in the chain gives the leading company the ability to pressure small-scale enterprises into various forms of passive pliability. Now distinguishing between management, conception, control and execution is not carried out inside a single plant, but it is decentralized regionally. Thus, this model tries to combine the efficiency of Tayloristic work organization and the work ethos usually associated with small rural entrepreneurs.

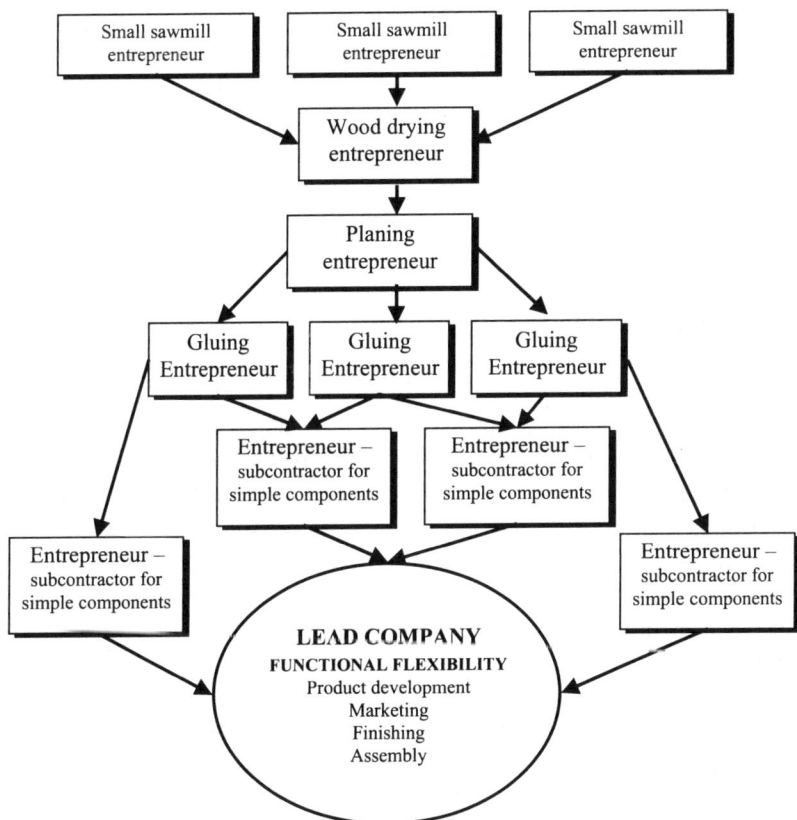

Figure 11.1 The ideal model of flexible manufacturing network

When Taylor advocated his famous model of 'scientific management', he justified it in quite a persuasive manner: 'What other reforms --- could do as much toward promoting prosperity, toward the diminution of poverty, and the alleviation of suffering?' he asked (Taylor, 1972, p. 14). In much the same way, the rural policy of today argues that promoting 'spatial Taylorism' 'revitalizes the countryside', 'alleviates structural problems', 'improves rural livelihoods and services', 'strengthens the viability of rural communities' and so on. The state - in the name of seeking benefits for rural areas - concurs with the process and itself promotes a kind of spatial

Taylorism in which semi-skilled work is transferred from the centres to peripheral areas. This process is reinforced by the education process, which attempts to alter rural patterns of thought through entrepreneurial education. In a rural policy of this kind, the structural problems of rural areas, lower wages and a poorer educational level, become a source of competitive advantage. At the same time, rural policy measures may nevertheless undermine the long-term market position of small rural enterprises by acceding to patterns dictated by the lead companies. This does not encourage their own innovations, technologies and labour and marketing skills, i.e. 'their capacity to react and adapt to exploit temporary market niches' or 'the strategy of permanent innovation'.

Discussion and conclusions

For several years now the structural change in the economy, flexibility in the labour market and the breaking down of the structures of the welfare state have been central themes of societal discussion in Finland as in the whole of Western Europe. The background to this lies in the restructuring of national economies and the demands of global integration, often described in such terms as competitiveness, efficiency and flexibility. Entrepreneurship and flexible specialization with its various dimensions are solutions that have been proposed for the problems of rural areas, among others.

Jessop (1994) describes the macro-scale change in economic policies in the globalizing world as a transition from a 'Keynesian welfare state' to a 'Schumpeterian work-fare state', where the latter refers to a new form of state which seeks structural competitiveness in the national economy by intervening on the supply side and subordinates social policy to the needs of labour market flexibility and/or the constraints of international competition. At a time when the entrepreneurship has become something of a magic spell for an economy, it is more than fitting to choose Joseph A. Schumpeter as the symbol of this new form of state, as his theory of capitalism and economic development introduced the entrepreneur as a key figure to the conception of industrial dynamics. With his specific economic *ethos*, the entrepreneur is the propelling force in the dynamics of a competitive economy (Schumpeter, 1961, p. 81).

In this transition in state intervention, the forms of 'governmentality' are also changing. In the era of the Keynesian welfare state and the old rural policy, the 'government' of 'the economy' occurred primarily through paternalistic, centralized systems of economic planning. These systems are diminishing in the face of globalization, however, and giving way to more complex forms of governmentality. In a sense, governments are minimizing their direct political intervention controlling the economy more and more 'at a distance' (Miller and Rose, 1990, pp. 14-15). In the case of Finnish rural policy rhetoric, this means that there will be a 'gradual shift from dependence on public organizations to development by local initiative. Supervision and controls to be reduced, co-ordination increased' (RPC, 1992, p. 31). Control of the economy at a distance is carried out by attempting to transform the subjectivity and mentalities of individuals. Attempts are being made to restore the economic ethos described by Schumpeter (1976, pp. 131-142) as a crumbling prime mover of capitalism by means of entrepreneurship education starting at the primary-school level.

The idea of rural policy is that the transformation of the economy requires a change in attitudes and culture - the new economic form should be complemented by a new economic 'spirit' (Weber, 1976). Where the Keynesian system presupposed collective commitment and a kind of 'mass consumerism', the ideal subject in the Schumpeterian State is an individual with a spirit of enterprise. The idea of the rhetoric of the enterprise culture is to spread the mentality required in the work of a small-scale entrepreneur until it becomes a general identity for all individuals regardless of their position in the labour market (see Gibb, 1987).

The themes of enterprise and entrepreneurship have also permeated into Finnish rural policy. The interests of the state have always occupied a central position in Finnish rural policy, the rural population having played an important role in the nation building process on the one hand, while on the other, the government later had to convince the rural population of the inevitability of EU integration and the reduction in agricultural subsidies. Now the government has to offer something to justify this integration policy. To rationalize its rural policy, therefore, it constructs a narrative in which rural areas have a central place in the national culture and identity, establishing a collective representation of rurality that is intended in a way to convince its audience of the need for a rural policy. This shared heritage shifts the moral obligation for keeping the heritage alive to the rural population.

At the same time, however, globalization and the more open world markets have reduced the possibilities for the state to offer welfare services or other support. The rural policy convinces its audience that changes in the old system of agricultural and welfare subsidies are needed, but globalization and the integration of the world's economies determine that no increase in government subsidies to rural areas will be possible in the future, notwithstanding the situation of the rural inhabitants. Conversely, there are pressures to break down the existing system of agricultural subsidies and the structures of the welfare state. The focus of the new rural policy is on so called 'new sources of livelihood'. The implicit theme in rural policy is that rural inhabitants should be more responsible for their own wellbeing and not ask the state to provide agricultural subsidies and other social and welfare services. In these days of globalization, the state is unable to take care of the welfare of rural population, nor does it feel any obligation to do so. The most important factor as regards the prosperity of rural areas is people's own initiative and entrepreneurship. The rhetoric that is emphasizing entrepreneurship does not emphasize the innovative characteristic of this undertaking. Instead, entrepreneurship is seen as a general principle of work and a system of attitudes to which people can be educated. Rural inhabitants have to become self-employed entrepreneurs, subcontractors and distance workers. Entrepreneurship, as a new mentality for the individual, will replace the 'dependence on public organizations' created by the welfare services. In this process, the state renounces its paternalistic authority and replaces it with a drive to educate people to be 'spontaneous', 'autonomous' and 'self-governing' entrepreneurs. At the same time, however, this promise of autonomy may turn out to be 'an authority without love', as Sennett (1981, pp. 84-121) puts it, because the risks and cutbacks linked with a flexible globalized economy now appear to be a natural part of the entrepreneurial risk to be borne by the individual.

The rural policy rhetoric described above could have undesirable social consequences. The rhetoric emphasizes local initiative, but at the same time it advances network practices that will centralize know-how and information concerning market processes in the core companies in the centres, and promotes semi-skilled manufacturing in rural areas. The structural problems of rural areas - such as lower wages and poorer levels of education - become competitive advantages, a lever by which the rural policy can ensure that every part of Finland is inhabited, which is the objective of the state. Instead of promoting the competitiveness of rural areas and regional equality and improving social conditions for the rural inhabitants, the policy may lead to a spatial division of labour in which the task of the latter is merely to acquiesce passively to the flexibility demands of core sector companies. The consequence may be a form of spatial Taylorism in which self-employed people and owner-managers of small-scale enterprises accept cutbacks in their terms and conditions of employment in order to be able to continue to live in their home district. This shift of rural policy towards 'autonomy without love' may not balance the economic opportunities of rural and urban areas in the face of globalization, but it may undermine the long-term possibilities of local initiative in rural areas and will certainly exacerbate the social inequality between them.

References

Alapuro, R. (1988), *State and Revolution in Finland*, University of California Press: Berkeley and Los Angeles.
Alasuutari, P. (1996), *Toinen tasavalta. Suomi 1946-1994*, Vastapaino: Tampere.
Amin, A. (1991), 'Flexible Specialization and Small Firms in Italy: Myths and Realities', in Pollert, A. (ed), *Farewell to Flexibility*, Blackwell: Oxford.
Anttonen, P. (1996), 'Myyttiset uhkakuvat ja puolustuseetos Suomen ja suomalaisuuden konstituoinnissa', *Elektroloristi*, 2/1996 <http://www.joensuu.fi/~loristi/ 2_96>.
Atkinson, J. (1987), 'Flexibility or Fragmentatation? The United Kingdom Labour Market in the Eighties', *Labour and Society*, Vol. 12, No 1, pp. 87-105.
Austin, J.L. (1982), *How to do Things with Words*, Oxford University Press: Oxford and New York.
Billig, M., Condor, S., Edwards, D., Gane, M., Middleton, D. and Radley, A. (1989), *The Ideological Dilemmas. A Social Psychology of Everyday Thinking*, Sage: London.
Burke, K. (1989), 'Revolutionary Symbolism in America', in Simons, H.W.S. and Melia, T. (eds), *The Legacy of Kenneth Burke*, The University of Wisconsin Press: Madison.
Cooperative Group of Rural Policy (CRP) (1995), 'Puu-Suomi - kannolta maailmalle', *MMM:n julkaisuja*, No 5, Helsinki.
Cooperative Group of Rural Policy (CRP) (1996), 'Maaseutuohjelma. Toimiva maaseutu. Maa- ja metsätalousministeriön asettaman työryhmän ehdotukset ja perustelut', *Maaseutupolitiikan yhteistyöryhmän julkaisu*, No 1, Helsinki.
Dreyfus, H.L. and Rabinow, P. (eds) (1982), *Michel Foucault: Beyond Structuralism and Hermeneutics*, The Harvester Press: Sussex.
Finnish Woodwork Project (1992), *Puu-Suomi -projektin tiedote*.
Foucault, M. (1972), *The Archaeology of Knowledge*, Pantheon Books: New York.
Foucault, M. (1973), *The Order of Things. An Archaeology of Medical Perception*, Tavistock Publications: Bristol.
Foucault, M. (1982), 'Subject and Power', in Dreyfus, H.L. and Rabinow, P. (eds), *Michel Foucault: Beyond Structuralism and Hermeneutics*, The Harvester Press: Sussex..
Foucault, M. (1991), 'Governmentality', in Burchell, G., Colin, G. and Miller, P. (eds), *The Foucault Effect. Studies in Governmentality*, Harvester Wheatsheaf: Hertfordshire.

Gibb, A. (1987), 'Enterprise Culture - Its Meaning and Implications for Education and Training', *Journal of European Industrial Training*, Vol. 11, No 2, pp. 1-38.
Granberg, L. (1989), *Valtio maataloustulojen tasaajana ja takaajana*, Suomen tiedeseura: Helsinki.
Granberg, L. (1995), 'A Break in Agricultural Policy. From Peasant Values to Welfare Rationality', in Granberg, L. (ed), *The Peasant State. The State and Rural Questions in 20th century Finland*, University of Lapland: Rovaniemi.
Granberg, L. (ed.) (1995), *The Peasant State. The State and Rural Questions in 20th century Finland*, University of Lapland: Rovaniemi.
Haatanen, P. (1993), 'Suomalaisen hyvinvointivaltion kehitys', in Riihinen, O. (ed), *Sosiaalipolitiikka 2017. Näkökulmia suomalaisen yhteiskunnan kehitykseen ja tulevaisuuteen*, WSOY: Porvoo-Helsinki-Juva.
Hakim, C. (1990), 'Core and Periphery in Employers' Workforce Strategies', *Work, Employment and Society*, Vol. 4, No. 2, pp. 157-188.
Harvey, D. (1989), *The Condition of Post-Modernity*, Basil Blackwell: Cambridge.
Jessop, B. (1994), 'The Transition to Post-Fordism and the Schumpeterian Workfare State', in Burrows, R. and Loader, B. (eds), *Towards Post-Fordist Welfare State?*, Routledge: London and New York.
Lash, S. and Urry, J. (1987), *The End of Organized Capitalism*, Polity Press: Cambridge.
Malinen, P. (1996), 'Changing Rural Policy of Finland', in Oksa, J. and Rannikko, P. (eds), *New Rural Policy. Finnish Journal of Rural Research and Policy*, English Supplement.
Miller, P. and Rose, N. (1990), 'Governing Economic Life', *Economy and Society*, Vol. 19, No 1, pp. 1-31.
Mokry, B.W. (1988), *Entrepreneurship and Public Policy. Can Government Stimulate Business Startups?*, Quorum Books: Connecticut.
Niittykangas, H. (1992), 'Maaseudun yritystoiminnan kehittymismahdollisuudet', *Jyväskylä Studies in Computer Science, Economics and Statistics 21*, Jyväskylän yliopisto: Jyväskylä.
OECD (1993), *What Future for Our Countryside? A Rural Development Policy*, OECD: Paris.
OECD (1995a), *OECD Reviews of Rural Policy. Finland*, OECD: Paris.
OECD (1995b), *Niche Markets as a Rural Strategy*, OECD: Paris.
Oksa, J. and Rannikko, P. (eds) (1996), *New Rural Policy. Finnish Journal of Rural Research and Policy*, English Supplement.
Piore, M.J. and Sabel, C.F. (1984), *The Second Industrial Divide. Possibilities for Prosperity*, Basic Books: New York.
Piore, M.J. (1995), *Beyond Individualism*, Harvard University Press: Cambridge.
Pyy, I. and Lehtola, I. (1996), 'Nordic Welfare State as Rural Policy', in Oksa, J. and Rannikko, P. (eds), *New Rural Policy. Finnish Journal of Rural Research and Policy*, English Supplement.

Rannikko, P. (1989), 'Metsätyö-pienviljelykylä. Tutkimus erään yhdyskuntatyypin noususta ja tuhosta', *Joensuun yliopiston yhteiskuntatieteellisiä julkaisuja*, No 12, Joensuun yliopisto: Joensuu.

Rural Development Project (RDP) (1991a), 'Maaseudun kehittämisohjelma. Suomen maaseutupolitiikan tavoitteet, strategiat ja keinot 1990-luvulla', *Sisäasiainministeriö, kunta- ja aluekehitysosasto, moniste 10*, Helsinki.

Rural Development Project (RDP) (1991b), *Maaseutupolitiikan linjat 1990-luvulla -tavoitteet, strategiat ja keinot*, Sisäasiainministeriö ja maa-ja metsätalousministeriö: Helsinki.

Rural Policy Committee (RPC) (1992), *Rural Policy in Finland*, Ministry of the Interior and Ministry of Agriculture and Forestry: Helsinki.

Rose, N. (1992), 'Governing the Enterprising Self', in Heelas, P. and Morris, P. (eds), *Values of the Enterprise Culture. The Moral Debate*, Sage: London.

Ruuskanen, P. (1995a), 'Laajennettu yrittäjyys - reaalinen toimintamalli vai ideologinen tautologia?', *Hallinnon tutkimus*, No 3, pp. 170-180.

Ruuskanen, P. (1995b), 'Maaseutuyrittäjyys puheina ja käytäntöinä', *Chydenius-Instituutin tutkimuksia*, No 5, Chydenius-Instituutti: Kokkola.

Schumpeter, J.A. (1961), *Theory of Economic Development*, Oxford University: New York.

Schumpeter, J.A. (1976), *Capitalism, Socialism and Democracy*, George Allen and Unwin Ltd: London.

Semlinger, K. (1993), 'Small Firms and Outsourcing as Flexibility Reservoirs of Large Firms', in Grabher, G. (ed), *The Embedded Firm. On the Socioeconomics of Industrial Networks*, Routledge: London and New York.

Sennett, R. (1981), *Authority*, Vintage Books: New York.

Summa, H. (1992), 'The Rhetoric of Efficiency: Applied Social Science as Depoliticization', in Brown, R.H. (ed), *Writing the Social Text. Poetics and Politics in Social Science Discourse*, Aldine de Gruyter: New York.

Taylor, F.W. (1972), 'The Principles of Scientific Management', in Taylor, F.W. (1972), *Scientific Management*, Greenwood Press Publishers: Westport.

Tykkyläinen, M. (1996), 'The Legacy of Postwar Settlement Policy', in Oksa, J. and Rannikko, P. (eds), *New Rural Policy, Finnish Journal of Rural Research and Policy*, English Supplement.

Uusitalo, E. (1995), 'Rural Policymaking Procedures. Promotion of Economies in the Partnership for Rural Development', *Maaseutupolitiikan yhteistyöryhmän julkaisu*, No 1, Helsinki.

Valtioneuvosto (1993), *Suomi eurooppalainen maaseutumaa, Valtioneuvoston maaseutupoliittinen selonteko eduskunnalle*, Helsinki.

Vanhanen, H. (1996), 'Finnish Woodwork: From Project to Process', in Oksa, J. and Rannikko, P. (eds), *New Rural Policy. Finnish Journal of Rural Research and Policy*, English Supplement.

Vartiainen, J. (1996), 'Kansantalous - valtiota vai kansalaisia varten?', *Helsingin sanomat, Kuukausliite, huhtikuu*, pp. 83-86.

Vuorinen, P. (1989), 'Verkostotalous ja modernien yritysten toimintaympäristöt', in Eskelinen, H. and Virkkala, S. (eds), *Talouden verkostot ja alueellinen muutos. Joensuun yliopisto, Karjalan tutkimuslaitoksen monisteita No 4*, Joensuu.

Weber, M. (1976), *The Protestant Ethic and the Spirit of Capitalism*, George Allen and Unwin: London.

12 Revisiting the Rural: A Southern Response to European Integration and Globalization

APOSTOLOS G. PAPADOPOULOS

Introduction: reaffirming the 'rural'

The reaffirmation of the rural can be found in Howard Newby's seminal work, where he expressed a widely accepted reservation on what rural is, by saying that,

> There is, now, surely, a general awareness that what constitutes 'rural' is wholly a matter of convenience and that arid and abstract definitional exercises are of little utility (Newby, 1986, p. 209).

With such a justified skepticism, Newby 'bypassed' the definitional issue by referring to an 'implied meaning, for the time being' (1986, p. 210). However, this implicit meaning of the rural is conceived differently in Western or Northern Europe than it is in Southern Europe to say nothing of Eastern Europe. Our characterization of Southern Europe does not, of course, entail any meaning of a European 'South' posed against some notion of a 'North'.[1] However, it cannot go unmentioned that the heritage of the 'sociology of development' debates and, more particularly, that of dependency, modes of production and agrarian political economy approaches has played an important role in the fundamental reformulation of what constituted rural in the developed capitalist countries in the 1970s and 1980s (Newby, 1980).

In our view, any regional or territorial aggregation of the rural should reconsider the basic constructions, which, in fact, define the common issues of the rural 'problematic'. The term 'rural' is being built upon two more or less obvious facts: First, the term obtained a meaning due to a geographical cleavage between the city and the countryside providing for a social etiquette. Second, the division of the social field into two worlds whose relationships were unclear, gave rise to a more or less coherent rural world which represented certain types of relationships between structural and spatial characteristics (Mormont, 1990, p. 28).

In that respect, the term 'rural' has been evidently associated with some sort of distinctiveness, which is attributed to rural life and to agriculture. Rural research seems to have been polarized across two extreme ends: the first being the investigation of internal mechanisms and characteristics of past rural society and the second concerning the changes triggered by rural society's increasing integration into wider contemporary society (Marsden et al., 1990). The 'rural' has been somehow characterized by stability and introversion whereas it is intensely subjected to change and extroversion.

The much discussed 'end of the peasantry', which was the hallmark of rural society, is an evident reality for the more developed countries of the EU. The older definition of agriculture, as an 'art of the locality', underlining the 'infinite diversity that characterizes the French countryside' has worn-out and it has been replaced by a different rationality, which combines new techniques of cultivation with economic calculation and speculation (Mendras, 1970, p. 48, 124, 131-132). For France, according to Mendras and Cole, the 'traditional peasant civilization is passing away with the dying-out of the last generation of genuine peasants' (1991, p. 21). In fact, for Mendras, the French peasant has not exactly disappeared but 'will in his turn settle into the perpetual change of technological innovation and economic contingency' (1970, p. 14).

For French as well as for British rural sociology, agriculture has comprised a large part of what constitutes the rural. For French rural sociologists, the focus has been the rural community as a socioeconomic and cultural entity, while they 'continued to emphasize the importance of *localization* in all social processes' (Bodiguel and Hervieu, 1990, p. 238). Thus, for French speaking sociologists, the sociology of the rural may be considered as 'a sociology of the localized effects of social change more than a sociology of space' (Mormont, 1990, p. 29), or else we may be 'moving towards a sociology of regional differences' (Bodiguel and Hervieu, 1990, p. 238).

Mendras, succumbing to a 'neo-ruralist discourse', sees the modern French countryside as 'becoming a living entity once again, although it has radically changed its character' (Mendras and Cole, 1991, p. 22). The transformation of rural sites to consumption sites or else 'post-productivist' places appears to convey new meaning(s) for the 'rural'. However, Hervieu - in our interpretation - appears to be ambivalent against the salient discontinuities in French rural society pointing towards a redefinition of the constituents of the 'rural' and of their interconnections (farmers, food, rurality, nature etc.) (Hervieu, 1988; 1991).

The 'rural' was constructed at a time when peasant societies were being integrated into the wider society. What constitutes the rural is embedded in the social, economic and cultural history of national societies. The historicity of the term is highly dependent upon its conception by different national societies. For example, a comparison between French and British conceptions of the 'rural' and of rural space shows that they are conditioned by separate national traditions. As it is presented, the French approach has been 'explicit, deductive and universalistic', whereas in reverse the British approach has been 'implicit, inductive and contextual'.[2] Those approaches reflect diversified rural contexts. That is, in France rural communities have been historically a key element of national identity, still retaining a symbolic role as the heartland of an essentially rural nation, whereas in Britain rural areas have been variably considered as pragmatic constructs in order to implement policies within a long urbanized nation. From the latter arise two seemingly contrasting rationales in rural research. In France, rural research has been largely preoccupied with the 'peasant question', whereas in Britain rural research has been more closely linked to policy-making, especially focusing on land use and the environment (Bodiguel et al., 1990, p. 43).

It may now be said that what constitutes rural cannot be simply attributed any more to particular social or spatial characteristics.[3] Rather the rural 'derives from the social production of a set of meanings' (Mormont, 1990, p. 36). More specifically, it should be seen as a multiplicity of social spaces, which can overlap with a given geographical space. Consequently, the rural arises as a category that each society adopts and reconstructs thus making a 'social construction' (Mormont, 1990, p. 41). This line of thinking has produced two interrelated arguments in recent British rural research.

The first argument simply says that the rural increasingly emerges as a set of social representations which should, in fact, be distinguished from its socio-spatial referent. For Halfacree, it is of prime importance to distinguish between rural locality and its social representation, since the latter takes on increased significance in the current era (Halfacree, 1993). Along this line of thinking, Murdoch and Pratt propose a re-conceptualization of the relationship between 'rural' and 'urban' by giving precedence to a plurality of 'post-rural' (reflexive) meanings constructed upon 'rural experiences' (Murdoch and Pratt, 1993, pp. 424-425).

The second argument builds upon the increasingly evident fact that the rural represents simultaneously a world of social, moral and cultural values, thus giving credit to multiple 'rural geographies'. This cultural geography of the rural signifies the introduction of deconstructionist re-thinking of the rural in already 'post-rural' spaces (see, e.g. Cloke et al., 1994). In fact, the aim of this line of thinking has been to produce a more detailed and systematic interpretation of rural spatial formations in order to 'refashion the rural' in qualitative terms (Cloke, 1994, pp. 164-165).

As a consequence, an all-encompassing concept of the rural is neither viable or at stake any more. In general, three positions appear to exist in the British context. One position which supports a 'classic' treatment of the rural and stresses the use of class analysis and of political economy thinking (Miller, 1996). A second position which aims at reconfiguring the subject matter and the approach to the rural and favours a 'penetrating' or a post-structuralist treatment of rural space (Phillips, 1998). Finally, a third position located somewhere in the 'middle', which succumbs to a more relativist consideration of the rural and in effect accepts the multiplicity and multi-dimensionality of rural space (Ilbery, 1998).

Returning to our basic discussion on the definition of the rural in Europe, the references made to the French and the British rural research traditions provide a significant context for reconfiguring the rural in Southern Europe. Drawing some very crude analogies, we argue that as regards the identification of the rural with the 'peasant question' and 'rural community' there are some similarities between Southern Europe and the French rural tradition. However, it should be underlined that the policy-making and land-use element of the rural becomes increasingly important in Southern Europe, especially within the EU economic environment. Consequently, both rural research traditions reflect differentially upon the constructions of the 'rural' in Southern Europe.

In this respect, it would be useful to consider diverse types of rural tradition in Europe as discussed by Hoggart et al. Three of them are particularly useful for our discussion here (1995, pp. 91-109). Hoggart et al. juxtapose an *agrarian tradition* with a *naturalist tradition*. They distinguish between a conception of rural areas as primarily productive surfaces on which the exploitation of natural resources is related to the construction of a distinct rural culture and a conception of rural space as an arena for consumption, which points to a predominantly urban-centred notion of rurality. In this continuum, a *Mediterranean tradition* is described on the basis of either a close integration between city and countryside or is attributed to an inability to find grave distinctions between the two.

Having said that, we will now consider the prospects of reconfiguring Southern Europe's rurality by referring more explicitly to trends and characteristics of the rural in Italy (especially Mezzogiorno), Greece, Spain and Portugal. Our discussion will be developed across three themes, which, in our opinion, intersect with the basic preconceptions of rurality and may well provide the axes along which rural Southern Europe unfolds. These are: a) *the differentiation of farming,* which refers to the diverse effects of the socioeconomic modernization processes upon the agricultural sector of Southern European countries; b) *the peripheral construction of the rural,* which considers the regionalization and spatial perception of rural regions in Southern Europe; and c) *the crosscutting conceptions of the rural,* which expand rurality to consider traditionally non-specifically-rural components and examine the diffused spatial characteristics in southern regions.

The discussion which follows is based upon three assumptions: first, that all Southern European countries are treated together as a heterogeneous whole; second, that our intention is not to construct a single 'Mediterranean' model of rural change;[4] and, third, that there is not a unified model of rurality counter-posed to Southern European rurality. Thus, we present some basic characteristics of Southern European rural economy and society without neglecting its divergence from and/or convergence with the rest of Europe.

Reconfiguring 'rural' Southern Europe

The late entry or the slow pace of agricultural modernization in the countries of Southern Europe lies in the core of what basically differentiates the 'northern' from 'southern' rural trajectories (Hoggart et al., 1995, pp. 81, 85). The intensified trends of agricultural modernization, resulting from the growing pace of European integration processes as well as from national economies' integration into the world economy, have caused significant strains in the rural restructuring in Southern European countries.

Although it is evident that what constitutes rural in Southern Europe largely involves agriculture and family farming, equal attention will be given here to the employment characteristics and rural restructuring in the countries of our concern.[5]

The differentiation of farming in Southern Europe

Today, all four Southern European countries represent 32 per cent of the total population (1993) and 28 per cent of the economically active population (1992), accounting for 32 per cent of the surface (1993) and 40 per cent of the total utilized agricultural area of the EU15.

In the post-1980 period, although the proportion of the agriculturally employed population has been nearly halved (apart from Greece where it was reduced from 30 to 21 per cent) in all four countries, it still ranges from 21 per cent in Greece to 8 per cent in Italy. This significantly exceeds the EU average (5.5 per cent), not to mention UK and Germany where the agriculturally active population is limited to 2-3 per cent of the total active population (EC, 1996a, p. A112). Moreover, in the same period, although the share of agriculture in GDP was virtually halved in all four countries, it still exceeds the EU average (1.8 per cent) varying from 7.5 per cent in Greece to 2 per cent in Portugal (both Italy and Spain just exceed 2.5 per cent) (Eurostat, 1995a, p. 250; EC, 1996a, p. A22-23).[6]

Although Greece seems to keep a slower pace in the decline of agriculture as a productive sector in the national economy, all four countries maintain trends which had prevailed in the main core of the European economy long ago. However, in respect to agriculture's significance for the total national economy, one may note a differentiation between Greece and Spain, where agricultural and food products account, respectively, for 33 per cent (three times the EU average) and 17 per cent (twice the EU average) of their total exports, and between Italy and Portugal which follow the EU average (EC, 1996a, pp. A22-23).

The countries of Southern Europe account for 57 per cent of the total agriculturally employed population and 71 per cent of the farm enterprises, whereas they produce only 34 per cent of the total final agricultural output of the EU12 (1993/4) (EC, 1996a, pp. A22-23, A26-27). Although one may notice a significant trend towards a decline of agriculture in the economy of Southern Europe, this trend is, neither uniform or attains the same importance in each of the four countries.

Overall, the continued significance of southern agriculture in the EU may be attributed to the structural characteristics of family farming in those countries. The average agricultural area used ranges (1990) from 4 to 7 hectares in Greece, Portugal and Italy and exceeds 15 hectares in Spain (the EU average, i.e. 14.4 ha). In the period 1980-1990, more than 1.3 million agricultural holdings ceased to operate in the EU12. Forty eight per cent of those holdings were situated in the countries of Southern Europe, a decrease which amounted to 10 per cent (the largest decline being in

Portugal by 22.2 per cent and Spain by 12.4 per cent) of the agricultural holdings existing in 1980 (Eurostat, 1995b, pp. 123-127). The average size of agricultural holdings has increased significantly in all countries apart from Italy (from 3.6 to 4.0 ha in Greece, from 4.3 to 6.7 in Portugal, from 12.9 to 15.3 ha in Spain).

The reduction of the agricultural holdings may be largely attributed (88 per cent of the total) to the decrease in the number of holdings smaller than 5 hectares. In fact, the agricultural holdings of less than 5 ha account for 61 per cent in Spain, in Greece and Italy they amount to 78-79 per cent of the total and for 82 per cent of the total in Portugal (Eurostat, 1995b, pp. 123-127).

Contrary to other EU countries, the agricultural holdings of less than 5 ha contain a varying amount of agricultural land. In fact, they range from 7.2 per cent in Spain to 29 per cent of total agricultural land used in Greece (18-19 per cent for Portugal and Spain, respectively) (EC, 1996a, pp. T144-149). Nevertheless, Southern European agriculture in general follows the trends which are also evident in the other EU member-states. Clearly, the small agricultural holdings lose significance as their number is reduced and the size of agricultural land declines, whereas the holdings with over 50 ha increase in number and size of agricultural land used.

The large majority of agricultural holdings in Southern Europe are family farms, which mostly employ family labour. In Greece, the proportion of wage labourers is very small (4.5 per cent). In Portugal it is lower than the European average (18.2 per cent) and in Spain and Italy, the proportion exceeds the European average (31.1 and 37.3 per cent respectively). The significant size of agricultural wage labour in all three countries apart from Greece may be largely attributed to the significant share of large land-holdings (EC, 1996a, pp. T114-115).

However, the number of people employed in family farms is far larger than the one denoted by the size of the agriculturally employed population. In 1989, the total number of people employed in family farming was 16.4 million in the EU. All four countries contain 68 per cent of this population (amounting to 11.2 million people from whom 5.3 million were Italians and 2.8 million Spaniards), the large majority of which are family members (apart of permanent or seasonal wage labour). In all four countries, the number of permanent labour employed in family farms has decreased significantly during the last fifteen years (1980-1993). The average annual work unit (AWU) per person in the family farms of Southern Europe amounted to less than half (ranging from 0.39 in Italy to 0.48 in Portugal) (EC, 1996a, pp. T116-117). This implies that the largest proportion of those occupied in agriculture is, in fact, under-employed within agriculture.

Notably, a large number of family members are 'farm helpers', who work part-time in farming. The majority of those farm helpers are women, who as farmer's wives or daughters perform a large number of unskilled or semi-skilled tasks within the farm enterprise and account for a significant part of the agricultural labour. More than half of family farm operators in Southern Europe (from 52 per cent in Portugal to 77 per cent in Italy) spend less than 50 per cent of their time within their family farms. The operators employed full-time within their family farm in Southern Europe range from 11 per cent in Italy to 22 per cent in Portugal. This proportion is significantly smaller than the EU average (26 per cent). The size of pluriactivity among family farm operators ranges from 26 per cent in Greece (30 per cent in Italy and 35 per cent in Spain) to 36 per cent in Portugal (EC, 1996a, pp. T120-121). Nevertheless, family farm operators appear to be significantly aged. In fact, the operators aged over 55 years in Southern Europe range from 55 per cent in Spain to 61 per cent in Italy. Whereas the proportion of operators over 55 years of age average to 59 per cent in the four Southern European countries, they account for 42 per cent in the rest of EU countries (Eurostat, 1996b, p. 142-143).

Labour intensive family farms seem to predominate in Southern European countries, while in the north farms concentrate on large-scale capital intensive field crops and livestock which need a smaller labour force. The average annual work units required for 100 ha are much higher in Southern Europe than those required in Northern Europe (with the exception of the Netherlands). For example, whereas 20-21 AWU are required in Greece or Portugal to cultivate 100 ha, in the UK the number does not exceed three (Eurostat, 1995a, p. 262; Eurostat, 1995b, p. 139).

It seems that Southern European agriculture has not quite followed the north-western model of agricultural modernization, where there was an elimination of marginal family farms, concentration of land and professionalization of farmers. Instead, a large part of family farms in the south remain small, labour intensive and mainly employing family labour. The oversized farming population is, in fact, under-employed, while a good part of family farm operators are aged. The land concentration process is slow, but most of farm closures have to do with small farms. This eventually benefits the larger farms which consolidate the available land and construct an enlarging agricultural sector based on economies of scale. On the other hand, it may be argued that three characteristics, small family farming, intensive agricultural labour and pluriactivity, construct an emerging image of a Mediterranean agricultural structure going slowly into modernization, but which increasingly shows signs of differentiation and family farm readjustment. Rural regions undergo significant restructuring from the displacement of marginal family farms, while new forms of family farming based upon technology, capital resources and human ingenuity gain recognition and power.

The peripheral construction of the rural

Changing the focus of our analysis, we will first refer to how these rural regions are conceived within the EU. The whole of Greece and Portugal, the Mezzogiorno in Italy and a large part of Spain are considered as areas which are 'lagging behind in development', belonging to Objective 1 Regions (areas whose economic performance is limited to less than 75 per cent of the average GDP of EU).

The basic idea of the European integration process is that there is a 'transitional' period (1989-99), when, in fact, opportunities are given to lagging regions in order to converge with the levels of income and wealth of the more advanced regions. In such a case, a 'catching-up' process is institutionalized for the 'late-comers'.[7] This naturally means that,

> Lagging countries and regions are forced to follow an intensive development pattern based upon modern production and process rationalization, instead of a theoretically more appropriate pattern based on a widening of the production base and on low productivity sectors (Camagni, 1992, p. 362).

The results of such a convergence process are diverse since the improvement of national economic performance is linked to the resurgence of certain regions. In the case of Italy, intra-national disparities have grown considerably since the 1970s. The 'Third Italy' phenomenon, which constituted a successful diffused-manufacturing case, provided a 'local development' model for the rest of Southern Europe (Hadjimichalis and Papamichos, 1990). A mixture of small business predominance, the existence of traditional manufacturing, intensive agricultural employment patterns and tourism succeeded in mobilizing local resources gaining a lot from labour flexibility. What is considered imperative for the emergence of *rural industrial districts* is the existence of traditions of local entrepreneurship, the mobilization of local resources, and new technological practices aiming at niche markets. In relevant analyses, petty bourgeois and family farming patterns are considered as providing the basis for nurturing modern small-medium enterprise cores (Paloscia, 1991, Hoggart et al., 1995, pp. 159-168). Such an approach has taken the form of a 'development model' supported by EU policies in parallel with its regional and agricultural policies of integration. However, the latter seem to have diversified effects upon rural regions. For example, it is increasingly argued that EU integration policies create new inequalities established not only between but also within regions (Camagni, 1992; Hadjimichalis, 1996). As shown in a recent EC report, the case of Italian Mezzogiorno is relevant here. The north-south divide in the country increased in the period 1991-1994, as evidenced by a downturn of GDP per head and unemployment rate indicators of the rural regions of Mezzogiorno (EC, 1997a, p. 85).

Diffused manufacturing sites in the rest of Southern Europe, due to the establishment of 'intermediate development regions' which are mainly located in proximity to advanced areas along the main transportation axes, may include the Spanish Mediterranean Axis from Barcelona to Malaga, the Ebro Valley Belt (Barquero, 1991), the development sites on the Atlantic belt north of Lisbon in Portugal, and the Athens-Thessaloniki central axis in Greece. However, the geographically remote and economically marginal regions cannot, of course, benefit from such processes, unless they construct endogenous development paths on the basis of some sort of local particularity (Camagni, 1992, p. 363).

'Endogenous development' constitutes a pattern of local development, which pays particular emphasis upon the internal organization of resources (human, entrepreneurial and material) and characterizes concrete regions or localities that enable a complex inter-relationship with wider economic and social structures. To justify their etiquette, endogenous development regions should be able to 'auto-reproduce' themselves (van der Ploeg and Saccomandi, 1995, p. 18). However, endogenous development cannot be conceived far and outside from exogenous conditioning or enabling factors. As Lowe et al. argue,

> The attractiveness of rural areas in this changing economic context will not necessarily lead to endogenous development, for even where rural regions are successful this success may well be attributable to a whole range of local and non-local factors. Where regions remain peripheral it might be the case that they simply cannot generate development from within and will therefore be particularly reliant on development from without (1995, p. 103).

In this respect, the classification of Southern European regions according to the performance of their structural characteristics shows that although there is a general tendency for convergence, the predominantly rural regions do not manage to reduce the gap. Convergence is more likely to be achieved by those regions which seem to follow a development path towards a future either of urbanization and industrialization or of environmental attraction to tourism and associated activities (Pompili, 1994, p. 688).

Inter-regional diversity in Southern Europe, which is also reinforced by EU policies, has created large income disparities and differentiated economic performances. For example, lists showing the economic performance of all Community regions on the basis of per capita income, unemployment rate, employment figures etc., allow for classifying southern regions of the EU as the poorest and in immediate need to take action for promoting their 'social and economic cohesion' (EC, 1994).

The social and economic cohesion of the rural areas in Southern European countries is increasingly connected to the 'success story' of a region or productive sector within one region. It seems that rural localities, following the image of urban ones, may variably or inter-changeably acquire the status of 'hot spots' or 'cold spots' of globalization processes (Whatmore, 1994), thus being responsive to 'external' calls. As a result, regional economies and societies become increasingly extrovert (by opening up to external challenges and opportunities) and consequently more vulnerable to global slumps and market fluctuations. In this respect, rural localities are faced by a strenuous dual option. The choice between integration or convergence and marginalization or divergence from set targets is hardly a choice for rural regions in Europe. The globalization processes as well as the European integration process have been set long ago and any thought of countervailing those processes may be considered an 'ideological issue'. Moreover, issues of reaction such as the nationalist and secessionist movements acting in Europe (the same in the north – e.g. UK, Belgium- and in the south – e.g. Italy, Spain) provide some evidence on the regional-local resistance against global identities and European integration.

In fact, the European unification and integration process should not be seen outside the wider globalization process. The text of Agenda 2000 aiming at a 'stronger and wider union' explicitly states that a major challenge for the EU is to 'adjust with the continuous globalization process' since it is 'in a position to bear benefits from this process' and that the EU should also adapt to 'a world of multiple poles' (EC, 1997b, p. 15). This is argued aside from a declared regional policy which favours regional development by introducing or supporting differentiation of economic development strategies, institutional cooperation and growing interest in networking both within regions and with external actors (Bachtler, 1997, pp. 86-87). So that regionalization appears as a tendency that accompanies globalization and European integration processes.

In this connection, Southern European countries show significant inter-regional as well as intra-regional diversity. This is evident if one examines the structural dualism affecting all four countries of Southern Europe and which pertains similarly to agriculture (large scale against small-scale family farming), regional development (main development axes against remote-peripheral areas) and cross-sectoral mixtures (locally-successful entrepreneurship against marginal-survivalist practices) (Mottura and Pugliese, 1991; Belo Moreira, 1991; Etxezarreta, 1992; Kasimis and Papadopoulos, 1994).

For Southern European societies, rural has been intersecting with urban space and it is identified with sets of small-scale family farming and survival activities located in remote and peripheral areas from main development and transport axes. This inter-sectoral mixture of activities provides in our view the basis upon which Southern European rural regions may 'resist' wider processes of integration and dependency. In fact, according to Bazin and Roux, there is an enormous diversity in the types of resistance of rural southern regions against their marginalization:

> It is necessary to find the best possible means of linking the four levels of decisions and actions - local, regional, national and European - to promote and multiply local development actions, to reinforce old activities like agriculture and what is left of traditional rural industry, to seize any new opportunities brought by rural tourism, scattered cottage industry and the new technologies. Organizations dealing only with these disadvantaged areas could be created or strengthened as they would be linked directly to the local district associations. Their role would be to identify the local agents of economic innovation and development, to define with them ways of achieving regional resistance to marginalization, to gather outside resources to implement them (Bazin and Roux, 1995, p. 346).

In this context, resistance to the marginalization of rural Southern Europe would be to reconstruct its own meaning of the rural by mobilizing reflexive mechanisms (Amin and Thrift, 1995), relating not only to negotiation but also to the institutionalization of alternative agricultural strategies and networks (Amin and Thrift, 1994; Whatmore, 1994, p. 61).However, such an eventuality can be materialized to the extent that local actors meet exogenous or external demand for alternative agricultural and/or rural niche markets and exploit any existing 'structural holes' on the institutionalized and sovereign socioeconomic networks.

Crosscutting conceptions of the rural

Next, we will refer to three issues in order to show the various ways through which the city is connected with the countryside in Southern Europe. The first issue is the shift of the in/out-migration pattern in Southern Europe. The second issue refers to the different models of urban development in Southern Europe compared to the rest of Europe. Finally, and more importantly, there is the increasing informalization and labour flexibility in the Southern European economies.

First, the migration movement was evident in all Southern European countries from the mid-1960s to mid-1970s. All of the countries were, at that time, net contributors of labour force, thus, working for the development 'miracle' of Western and Northern European market economies. The migrants originating from rural economies facing economic problems and high demographic growth resulting into rising unemployment rates poured into the labour-hungry countries of the North. By 1973-74, at the time of the so-called 'recruitment stop', the main recipient countries for migrants were: (former) West Germany (with 2.6 million, i.e. 12 per cent of the labour force), France (with 2.3 million, i.e. 10 per cent of the labour force), Belgium (200,000, i.e. 7 per cent of the labour force), the UK (750,000), Switzerland (600,000), Sweden (220,000) and the Netherlands (80,000, i.e. 1 per cent of the labour force). Correspondingly, the main national groups of immigrant workers in the EEC countries were: Italy (858,000),[8] Spain (527,000), Portugal (469,000), Yugoslavia (535,000), Greece (332,000), Turkey (582,000) and North Africa (701,000) mainly to France (King, 1994, p. 226).

Southern European countries had contributed 2.2 million of migrant labour to the more developed economies of Europe by the mid-1970s. The economic recession of the 1970s caused a discontinuous flow of migrant labourers' return to the countries of their origin. However, the impact of return migration on regional development in southern regions of the Community is difficult to assess because of the different factors (scale of return, age and employment profile of the returnees, economic geography of the area of settlement etc.) intervening in the process.

However, for twenty years the economic restructuring of Southern European countries has led to in-migration waves. This time they were directed at the southern areas of the Community. In recent years, all four countries have received around 3 million immigrants, including 1.5 million in Italy alone, 778,000 in Spain, over 500,000 in Greece and 155,000 in Portugal (King et al., 1997a, p. 4). These immigrants, who constitute a significant proportion (2.3-2.5 per cent) of these countries' population, are employed in niches of the Southern European labour markets which are largely identified as low paid, low status, precarious, illegal and marginal (see, also, King and Black, 1997). Moreover, different nationalities perform particular jobs in specific geographical localities (Hoggart et al., 1995, pp. 123-125).

It should be noted here that still the Southern European labour force is today used (e.g. Portuguese in construction works in France, Italians as contract labourers for European firms etc.), as unskilled or lowly-skilled labourers for performing low paid jobs, thus contributing to labour flexibility and intensity within the common European labour market (Montagne-Villette, 1994).

Second, the Mediterranean cities have been more compact and more densely populated than the ones in the north, where large parks and remote suburbs have been developed.[9] Moreover, in the Mediterranean cities wealthier groups tend to gravitate to the centre while the periphery is mostly abandoned to poorer strata. There is a great diversity of land ownership patterns in Mediterranean cities, where, however, large properties are rare and fragmentation of urban land ownership and partial re-development may be considered as more systematic. Mixed land uses predominate, whereas the informal sector is widely diffused. Moreover, throughout the whole of Southern Europe there is a speculative real-estate market (established quite recently) as well as an informal land and housing sub-market (Leontidou, 1990; 1994).

Informality in the urban sector is also evident in illegal housing taking the form of *bairros clandestinos* in Portugal, *viviendas marginales* in Spain, *borghetti* and *borgate* in Italy and *afthereta* in Greece. The informal sector in Southern European cities includes a number of characteristics such as the self-built settlements, due to unplanned urban development and mixed land-uses, and the increased significance of social polyvalence due to the size of pluriactivity, small-scale production and labour flexibility.

Finally, the employment patterns in Southern European countries follow different trajectories than they do in the rest of Europe. Notably, the household, which is the cell of economic activity in the Southern European societies, is significantly larger than in the rest of Europe. In Greece, Spain and Portugal the average number of persons in each household was still above three in 1991, while Italy also exceeded the European average (2.6). Furthermore, the proportion of single person households in all Southern European countries varies from 11-20 per cent of the total number of households, i.e. significantly lower than the European average (26 per cent) (Eurostat, 1995a, p. 161). Finally, the late departure of young adults from home (which often comes only with marriage), the care of the elderly which falls almost exclusively on the family and the significant intergenerational reciprocity within the same family are some characteristics of a different ('strong') family system prevailing in Southern European countries when compared to the ('weak') family system prevalent in Northern Europe (Reher, 1998).

The activity rate in all Southern European countries apart from Portugal is lower than 50 per cent, i.e. significantly less than the European average. This is due to the low participation of women in the labour force. That is, only one out of three women belongs to the labour force (Eurostat, 1995a, pp. 182-83).

In terms of labour flexibility, in all four countries there is a significant amount of self-employment. The proportion of those self-employed reaches 35 per cent in Greece, 25 per cent in Italy and Portugal and 22 per cent in Spain (1994). The proportion of self-employment is far larger than the EU average (15 per cent), while in most countries this proportion does not exceed 12 per cent (EC, 1996b, pp. 48-49).

Although part-time employment has an admirably low share in all four countries of Southern Europe (5-8 per cent against 15.4 per cent of the EU average), the share of fixed-term employment has been significant. Overall, Spain has shown the largest proportion of employees on fixed-term contracts, which in fact rose from 15.6 per cent in 1987 to 33.5 per cent in 1992, while the rest were around the EU average (10.4 per cent). The agricultural sector has had the highest proportion of fixed-term contracts with an EU average of 28.4 per cent, but Spain has shown a remarkable 57.6 per cent, Greece 38.7 per cent and Italy 37.6 per cent. In industry, there have been relatively fewer fixed-term contracts, with a EU average of 9.1 per cent, but again Spain made 36.7 per cent of the total, Greece 13.2 per cent and Portugal 12.1 per cent (Eurostat, 1995a, pp. 192-193).

Consequently, the economic activity of relatively large households in Southern European regions is a first indication of the increased need for household survival and of significant availability of family labour. The large proportion of women who remain 'economically inactive', i.e. outside the formal labour force, indicates that their activity goes unrecorded as 'family help' or else as 'informal employment' (see Bagnasco 1990; Hadjimichalis and Vaiou, 1990). Furthermore, the large share of those self-employed indicates the diffusion of petty entrepreneur, small property owner and family farm activities in southern regions. Also, the increased significance of fixed-term contracts in both agriculture and industry provides a strong indication of labour flexibility in the countries of Southern Europe.

Modelling rurality in Southern Europe

Returning to our discussion on the reconstruction of the rural in Southern Europe, we are content that it cannot be conceived in terms of 'post-productivist' or 'beyond agriculture' themes as for western European countries (Marsden, 1995). What is more, the differentiation of family farming in rural Southern Europe is related to the diffusion of employment patterns to all productive sectors which is not of the sort described by 'post-rural' characterizations. The survivalist target of both informality and pluriactivity constitutes a permanent characteristic of Southern European rural social structures. In fact, the extent and expansion of pluriactivity have been important indications of the polyvalent social structures in Southern European countries. Thus, the sustainable development of family farming in Southern Europe is closely linked to a number of 'informal activities' (Pugliese, 1993, pp. 154-156).

The adaptation of the rural population of Southern Europe to external conditions of production is strongly related to off-farm employment, to the use of immigrant labour for unskilled and temporary work, to the flexible use of the labour force as well as to the utilization of some forms of non-wage, contract labour, self-employment, non-taxed and non-declared activities which all aim at income diversification (Hadjimichalis and Vaiou, 1990). All of these informal activities may be considered as part and parcel of survival strategies of rural households, which of course blur the particularity of the agricultural sector (Reis et al., 1990). The inter-sectoral character of the survival models in Southern Europe entails a strong regional aspect, which, in fact, refers to the expansion of the globalization processes and to forms of local resistance against them. The strain between the survivalist and the productivist models remains, up to now, unresolved since pockets of resistance can be found through the use of informal activities and of labour flexibility (Baxter and Mann, 1992).

One may distinguish two levels in the analysis of the significance of the globalization process in the restructuring of rural areas in Southern Europe. The first level is that of the petty-commodity unit of production, which in rural areas is related to family farming, and its differential persistence under diverse social and economic conditions. In Southern Europe, the family farm is a production unit capable of responding to market calls by increasing its differentiation and variable integration to the external economy (Reis et al., 1990; Pugliese, 1993; Papadopoulos, 1998). The second level is that of the local society structured on the basis of the characteristics and the trajectories of different family farms, or on the basis of recognizing the existence of local differentiation in the operation of wider labour processes which refer to the restructuring of agricultural activities (Marsden et al., 1992; Lem, 1997). Both levels provide significant ground for 'revisiting' the rural in Southern Europe not only conceptually but also in terms of policy-making and implementation. The recognition of the 'growing centrality of rural space', affirms the strategic significance of providing alternative regional constructions of rurality outside the dominant mainstream discourses on rural space and its official interpretations (Marsden, 1998).

Conclusion: what prospects for rural Southern Europe?

The goal here has been to discuss a set of rural meanings which do not necessarily comply with or lead to a 'northern' path of development. The rural in the south of Europe mainly relates to the difficulties of separating the city from the countryside. Posed differently, it has to do with the bonds between the city and the countryside, bonds which are strong enough to negate distinctions on the basis of employment patterns, land use, economic activities, politics, and culture. Despite the differentiation caused by urbanization and migration in Southern Europe, the latter processes were not accompanied with a wide disengagement from the rural.

Notably, labour flexibility, informalization and pluriactivity provide some sort of social fiber (or social glue) which knits together those threads which are normally (in terms of western rationality) considered as purely local or conjectural threads in social structuration. Local or national social and economic networks have been, by large, institutionalized in Southern European countries long before they became theorized as providing some sort of 'institutional thickness' for endogenous development models (Amin and Thrift, 1994). Local networks of socioeconomic activity should be interpreted, in many common cases, as modes of survival for farmers, petty-entrepreneurs, professionals, traders and economic actors in general.

On the other hand, what remains distinctive for the rural in Southern Europe is the way this social fiber, which consists of various mixtures of family farming, private property, survival strategies and pluriactivity, maintains its scope in terms of agricultural sustainability within the countryside. On this basis, the pervasive nature of agricultural activity and of the rural space is quite evident not only in Greek society, but also in the Portuguese, the Italian and the Spanish societies (Reis et al., 1990; Etxezarreta, 1992; Pugliese, 1993; Papadopoulos, 1998). Furthermore, as Reis et al. argue,

If one takes into account the links between farm families and 'urban' families with a rural origin, then the cultural relevance of the rural milieu becomes yet more notable (Reis et al., 1990, p. 398).

The responses of the rural South to integration and globalization processes are often reflexive and spontaneous rather than calculated, rational and planned. What is missing (or delayed) is, to a large extent, the formulation of an entrepreneurial tradition of the magnitude and the character of the 'Danish' or of the 'Western' model. On the other hand, one may refer to a 'Spanish' (and correspondingly Greek, Italian and Portuguese) type of entrepreneurship and competitiveness. In one way or another, for example in Greece, rural social differentiation has not yet (if ever) reached its closure due to the continuous survival of small production units (Kasimis and Papadopoulos, 1997). Consequently, there are many modes of thinking or acting that more or less diverge from the much-praised 'Western model'.

Even the notion of agricultural sustainability in Southern Europe, does not point towards a kind of 'return' or 'revitalization' of agricultural production practices which have become extinct, but rather it can be identified with farming practices implemented in different rural areas of the south and are increasingly marginalized by the initial implementation and later by the reform of Community agricultural and regional policy.[10] Thus, the rural in Southern Europe may be confronted as an aspect of social reality that needs to be supported instead of just be regulated or de-regulated. A similar view is shared by *Agenda 2000* which appears to be in favour of integrating rural structural policy into the wider economic and social context of the countryside, and treating rural diversification as a necessary supplement to agricultural activity, considered in a flexible manner (EC, 1997b, p. 29).

The trajectory of the rural in Southern Europe has taken the form of autonomous sustainable development within rural localities. Again, in other instances, this has included a number of small entrepreneurial initiatives which are based upon labour flexibility, informal activities or economic diversification. For Southern Europe, the social identity part of the rural is daily experienced and negotiated either in the form of clashes against state (EU imposed) measures or in the form of obtaining benefits and/or subsidies from state bureaucracy. Anyhow, agricultural policy (both national and EU) and/or policies for the rural areas have taken the form of social policy transforming the rural population into clients of the state (Pugliese, 1985; Djurfeldt, 1993; Kasimis and Papadopoulos, 1994, p. 209).

The state and EU policies implemented for rural areas, aside from the target of enhancing agricultural competitiveness, have an explicit welfarist aims i.e. to accommodate the demands of the rural population in order to avoid extreme marginalization and social deprivation. On the other hand, the impact of policies aiming to increase agricultural competitiveness and differentiation of family farming in Southern European countries has led to social differentiation in rural areas by intensifying regional diversity and disparities (within and across rural areas), increasing inequalities among the local social strata and accentuating differences between small and large farms, farmers and non-farmers, family farms and capitalist farms. Such duality and fragmentation of the social structure in the rural areas of Southern European countries has led to different interpretations of the rural and to various not always compatible notions of resistance against homogeneity and integration. European integration itself – as seen in the pursued EU policies – is an ambivalent process as regards the integrity of rural social structures. An inherent contradiction of European integration takes the form of a 'policy shift':

> In the more recent past, the CAP and other EC policies, notably regional policy, have contributed to reducing the distinctiveness of national initiatives for the countryside by establishing a European framework for rural policy. Today, the member states have a new rural lexicon. Nonetheless, as the recent history of the CAP and international agreements such as GATT so amply demonstrate, adherence to national frameworks for rural policy-making and appeals to the particularities of national circumstances remain a strong force in EC decision-making (Hoggart et al., 1995, p. 90).

Any reservations regarding the treatment of rural Southern Europe cannot of course be associated with a retreat towards the re-nationalization of agricultural and/or regional policy within the EU, but rather lead to a reconsideration of policy measures and frameworks allowing for rural heterogeneity in Europe. Rural restructuring in Southern Europe cannot be just reflective of exogenous modernization patterns, but rather should leave room for choice among endogenous patterns of social reproduction. This aims at a 'relocalization' of family farm practices and at a 'conscious resistance' to globalizing and homogenizing trends of the European and global economy. Putting forward the flag of agricultural heterogeneity in rural Southern Europe may only lead to an increasing victimization of southern rural areas. Also, the end of the domination of 'endogenous development' arguments heralds the need for a new synthesis between endogenous and exogenous development factors. Thus, resistance of rural south to globalization and European integration may imply a confrontation with the modernizing forces which invariably take the form of subsidies, structural adjustments and incentives (Whatmore, 1993).

Instead, a 'modernization project' (even within a more integrated EU) may well support a reconstituted image of rural restructuring, one which encompasses social networks, local empowerment, socio-spatial heterogeneity and cultural diversity (see McAleavy and de Rynck, 1997). In this sense, 'revisiting the rural', as it has often been conceived in the past, i.e. in 'Northern European' terms, may give rise to refashioning the rural in order to convey meaning for Southern European countries.

Rural Southern Europe has to overcome the idyllic, folkloric or pastoral preconceptions of rurality and synchronize itself with the new conceptions of and challenges facing rural space, yet based upon its very historical particularities, social fabric, economic complexity, political structure and cultural diversity.

Acknowledgements

I would like to thank Maria Fonte, Henk de Haan, Charalambos Kasimis and Constantina Safilios-Rothchild for their comments and the discussions I have had with them on earlier drafts of this chapter.

Notes

1   In some treatments of the Southern European development patterns, what predominates is a 'Southern perspective' against a perspective arising from the North of Europe (Hadjimichalis and Papamichos, 1990; Hadjimichalis, 1996). This may be an interesting aspect at the level of policy-making as well as for interpreting the uneven development of capital accumulation at a European scale. It is our contention that the 'conjuncture' plays a far more important role than it is normally attributed to; such that, we consider the rural as a 'social formation' resulting from spatial localization of social relations which take differential meaning depending upon both the political and cultural contexts.
2   This paragraph is based upon the discussion developed in Bodiguel et al., 1990 and upon the views expressed in Hervieu 1988; 1991.
3   The significance of the rural for the construction of national (and/or regional - local) identity can be attributed to its symbolic and cultural connotations as for the character of peasant powerlessness, of idyllic rural community life and of authoritarian regimes. As for the national construction, one may refer to the

4. 'rural' as an 'imagined community' (in the sense of Anderson's (1997) use of the term) based upon the representations of space (not of language) and, consequently, of the meanings attributed to spatial formations of the rural.

4. The Mediterranean, as a historical arena, has been considered in terms of a territorial aggregation of economies and cultures that need specific focus and cannot be merely seen as appendices of the western economy or culture (see Braudel, 1992). On the other hand, the Mediterranean is a geographical entity (crosscutting different continents) which is significantly compartmentalized and its socioeconomic situation is considerably fragmented (King et al., 1997b). Surely, although the name serves as an etiquette where a number of not-easily-classified-'miscellaneous' development cases are included, it still maintains the connotation of a 'backward' region which is non-modernized and actually resists restructuring due to socioeconomic and cultural reasons (see e.g. EC, 1995).

5. There is an increasing emphasis placed upon the local labour markets and on labour processes in rural space (Marsden et al., 1992), which aims at a better understanding of labour flexibility in the face of globalization and European integration processes affecting rural areas in Southern Europe.

6. However, in terms of real agricultural income per annual work unit, Greece and Spain have shown a clear increase during the period 1973-1992, whereas Italy has shown a decline during the same period and Portugal in the period 1980-1982 (Eurostat, 1995a, p. 255).

7. In the period 1989-1999, the catching-up effort which needed to be made by each separate country of Southern Europe for converging with EU average has been considered as significantly diverse. According to a recent Community report referring to the impact of structural policies upon the EU member countries, Portugal and Spain show signs of real convergence, Greece appears to have achieved stabilization after a period of divergence, while Mezzogiorno seems to have diverged (EC, 1997a).

8. Italy has played a double role as both a receiver and contributor of migrant labour. Still today 6 million Italians are emigrants (King, 1994).

9. This paragraph draws heavily from Leontidou, 1994.

10. The legitimization of the productivist model of agricultural production by the CAP worsened both inter-regional and intra-regional income and land differences in all EU member states and especially affected Southern European agriculture, which was initially non-competitive and protected by national policies. Furthermore, the liberalization turn initiated by means of the reform of CAP in recent years seems to further exacerbate the development problems of Southern European agriculture by increasing the uneven modernization and subsidization (Corbera, 1994; Sarris, 1994).

References

Amin, A. and Thrift, N. (1994), 'Living in the Global', in Amin, A. and Thrift, N. (eds), *Globalization, Institutions and Regional Development in Europe*, Oxford University Press: Oxford.
Amin, A. and Thrift, N. (1995), 'Institutional Issues for the European Regions: From Markets and Plans to Socio-Economics and Powers of Association', *Economy and Society*, Vol. 24, pp. 41-66.
Anderson, B. (1997), 2nd Edition, *Imagined Communities*, Nepheli: Athens (in Greek).
Bachtler, J. (1997), 'New Dimensions of Regional Policy in Western Europe', in Keating, M and Loughlin, J. (eds), *The Political Economy of Regionalism*, Frank Cass and Co Ltd: London.
Bagnasco, A (1990), 'The Informal Economy', *Current Sociology*, Vol. 38, No 2/3, pp. 157-174.
Baxter, V. and Mann, S. (1992), 'The Survival and Revival of Non-wage Labour in a Global Economy', *Sociologia Ruralis*, Vol. 32, pp. 231-247.
Bazin, G. and Roux, B. (1995), 'Resistance to Marginalization in Mediterranean Rural Regions', *Sociologia Ruralis*, Vol. 35, pp. 335-347.
Belo Moreira, M. (1991), 'Portuguese Agriculture and the State: An Outline of the Past 25 Years', in Friedland, F.H., Busch, L., Buttel, F.H. and Rudy, A.P. (eds), *'Towards a New Political Economy of Agriculture*, Westview Press: Boulder.
Bodiguel, M. and Hervieu, B. (1990), 'The Metamorphosis of French Rural Sociology', in Lowe, P. and Bodiguel, M. (eds), *Rural Studies in Britain and in France*, Bellhaven Press: London.
Braudel, F. (1992), *The Dynamics of Capitalism*, Alexandreia: Athens (in Greek).
Camagni, R.P. (1992), 'Development Scenarios and Policy Guidelines for Lagging Regions in the 1990s', *Regional Studies*, Vol. 26, pp. 361-374.
Cloke, P. (1994), '(En)culturing Political Economy: A Life in the Day of a Rural Geographer', in Cloke, P., Doel, M., Matless, D., Phillips, M., Thrift, N., *Writing the Rural: Five Cultural Geographies*, Paul Chapman Publishing Ltd.: London.
Cloke, P., Doel, M., Matless, D., Phillips, M., Thrift, N. (1994), *Writing the Rural: Five Cultural Geographies*, Paul Chapman Publishing Ltd.: London.
Corbera, M. (1994), 'The Common Agricultural Policy and the Development of Agriculture: Problems and Perspectives', in Blacksell, M. and Williams, A.M. (eds), *The European Challenge: Geography and Development in the European Community*, Oxford University Press: Oxford.
Djurfeldt, G. (1993), 'Classes as Clients of the State: Landlords and Labourers in Andalusia', *Comparative Studies in Society and History*, Vol. 35, pp. 159-182.
EC (1994), *Competitiveness and Cohesion: The Trends in the Regions. Fifth Report for the Social and Economic Situation and Development of Regions in*

Europe, Office for Official Publications of the European Communities: Luxembourg.

EC (1995), *Development Prospects of the Central Mediterranean Regions (Mezzogiorno-Greece)*, Office for Official Publications of the European Communities: Luxembourg.

EC (1996a), *The Situation of Agriculture in EU. Report 1995*, Office for Official Publications of the European Communities: Luxembourg.

EC (1996b), *Tableau de Bord 1995*, Office for Official Publications of the European Communities: Luxembourg.

EC (1997a), *The Impact of Structural Policies on Economic and Social Cohesion in the Union 1989-1999: A First Assessment Presented by Country*, Office for Official Publications of the European Communities: Luxembourg.

EC (1997b), *Agenda 2000: For a Stronger and Wider Union*, Office for Official Publications of the European Communities: Luxembourg.

Etxezarreta, M. (1992), 'Transformation of the Labour System and Work Processes in a Rapidly Modernizing Agriculture: The Evolving Case of Spain', in Marsden, T., Lowe, P. and Whatmore, S. (eds), *Labour and Locality: Uneven Development and the Rural Labour Process*, David Fulton Publishers: London.

Eurostat (1995a), 4th Edition, *Europe in Figures*, Office for Official Publications of the European Communities: Luxembourg.

Eurostat (1995b), *Agriculture: Statistical Yearbook*, Office for Official Publications of the European Communities: Luxembourg.

Hadjimichalis, C. (1996), 'The Southern Fringes of Europe and European Integration', *TOPOS Review of Urban and Regional Studies*, No 11, pp. 3-22 (in Greek).

Hadjimichalis, C. and Papamichos, N. (1990), 'Local Development in Southern Europe: Towards a New Mythology', *Antipode*, Vol. 22, pp. 181-210.

Hadjimichalis, C. and Vaiou, D. (1990), 'Whose Flexibility?' The Politics of Informalization in Southern Europe, *Capital and Class*, No 42, pp. 79-106.

Halfacree, K.H. (1993), 'Locality and Social Representation: Space, Discourse and Alternative Definitions of the Rural', *Journal of Rural Studies*, Vol. 9, pp. 23-37.

Hervieu, B. (1988), 'From the End of Peasants to the Renewal of French Rural Societies: French Rural Sociology in Question', *Greek Review of Agrarian Studies*, Special Edition in English, No 4, pp. 78-87.

Hervieu, B. (1991), 'Discontinuities in the French Farming World', *Sociologia Ruralis*, Vol. 31, pp. 290-299.

Hoggart, K., Buller, H. and Black, R. (1995), *Rural Europe: Identity and Change*, Arnold: London.

Ilbery, B. (1998), 'Dimensions of Rural Change', in Ilbery, B. (ed), *The Geography of Rural Change*, Longman: Harlow.

Kasimis, C. and Papadopoulos, A.G. (1994), 'The Heterogeneity of Greek Family Farming: Emerging Policy Principles', *Sociologia Ruralis*, Vol. 34, No 2/3, pp.206-228.

Kasimis, C. and Papadopoulos, A.G. (1997), 'Family Farm and Capitalist Development in Greek Agriculture: A Critical Review of the Literature', *Sociologia Ruralis*, Vol. 37, No 2, pp. 209-227.

King, R. (1994), 'Migration and the Single Market for Labour: An Issue in Regional Development', in Blacksell, M. and Williams, A.M. (eds), *The European Challenge: Geography and Development in the European Community*, Oxford University Press: Oxford.

King, R. and Black, R. (eds) (1997), *Southern Europe and the New Immigrations*, Sussex Academic Press: Brighton.

King, R., Fielding, A. and Black, R. (1997a), 'The International Migration Turnaround in Southern Europe', in King, R. and Black, R (eds), *Southern Europe and the New Immigrations*, Sussex Academic Press: Brighton.

King, R., Proudfoot, L. and Smith, B. (eds.) (1997b), *The Mediterranean Environment and Society*, Arnold: London.

Lem, W. (1997), 'Restructuring, Work and Identity: Perspectives on Region Class and Gender in Southern Europe', in Keating, M and Loughlin, J. (eds), *The Political Economy of Regionalism*, Frank Cass and Co Ltd: London.

Leontidou, L. (1990), *The Mediterranean City in Transition: Social Change and Urban Development*, Cambridge University Press: Cambridge.

Leontidou, L. (1994), 'Mediterranean Cities: Divergent Trends in a United Europe', in Blacksell, M. and Williams, A.M. (eds), *The European Challenge: Geography and Development in the European Community*, Oxford University Press: Oxford.

Lowe, P., Murdoch, J. and Ward, N. (1995), 'Networks in Rural Development: Beyond Exogenous and Endogenous Models', in van der Ploeg, J.D. and van Dijk, G. (eds), *Beyond Modernization: The Impact of Endogenous Rural Development*, Van Gorcum: Assen.

McAleavy, P. and De Rynck, S. (1997), 'Regional or Local? The EU's Future Partners in Cohesion Policy', *Working Paper RSC No 55*, European University Institute, October.

Marsden, T. (1995), 'Beyond Agriculture? Regulating the New Rural Spaces', *Journal of Rural Studies*, Vol. 11, pp. 285-296.

Marsden, T. (1998), 'Economic Perspectives', in Ilbery, B. (ed), *The Geography of Rural Change*, Longman: Harlow.

Marsden, T, Lowe, P. and Whatmore, S. (1990), 'Introduction: Questions of Rurality', in Marsden, T, Lowe, P. and Whatmore, S. (eds), *Rural Restructuring: Global Processes and their Responses*, David Fulton Publishers: London.

Marsden, T, Lowe, P. and Whatmore, S. (1992), 'Labour and Locality: Emerging Research Issues', in Marsden, T, Lowe, P. and Whatmore, S. (eds), *Labour and*

Locality: Uneven Development and the Rural Labour Process, David Fulton Publishers: London.
Mendras, H. and Cole, A. (1991), *Social Change in Modern France: Towards a Cultural Anthropology of the Fifth Republic*, Cambridge University Press: Cambridge.
Mendras, H. (1971), *The Vanishing Peasant: Innovation and Change in French Agriculture*, The MIT Press: Cambridge, Mass.
Miller, S. (1996), 'Class, Power and Social Construction: Issues of Theory and Application in Thirty Years of Rural Studies', *Sociologia Ruralis*, Vol. 36, pp. 93-116.
Montagne-Villette, S. (1994), 'Mobility and Illegal Labour in the EC', in Blacksell, M. and Williams, A.M. (eds), *The European Challenge: Geography and Development in the European Community*, Oxford University Press: Oxford.
Mormont, M. (1990), 'Who is Rural? or How to be Rural: Towards a Sociology of the Rural', in Marsden, T, Lowe, P. and Whatmore, S. (eds), *Rural Restructuring: Global Processes and Their Responses*, David Fulton Publishers: London.
Mottura, G. and Mingione, E. (1991), 'Agriculture and Agribusiness: Transformations and Trends in Italy', in Friedland, F.H., Busch, L., Buttel, F.H. and Rudy, A.P. (eds), *Towards a New Political Economy of Agriculture*, Westview Press: Boulder.
Murdoch, J. and Pratt, A.C. (1993), 'Rural Studies: Modernism, Postmodernism and the Post-Rural', *Journal of Rural Studies*, Vol. 9, pp. 411-427.
Newby, H. (1980), 'Trend Report: Rural Sociology', *Current Sociology*, Vol. 28, No 1, pp. 1-141.
Newby, H. (1986), 'Locality and Rurality: The Restructuring of Rural Social Relations', *Regional Studies*, Vol. 20, No3, pp. 209-215.
Paloscia, R. (1991), 'Agriculture and Diffused Manufacturing in the Terza Italia: A Tuscan Case-Study', in Whatmore, S., Lowe, P. and Marsden, T. (eds), *Rural Enterprise: Shifting Perspectives on Small-Scale Production*, David Fulton Publishers: London.
Papadopoulos, A.G. (1998), 'Flexible Agriculture: Survival Strategy and Resistance to Marginalization or Form of Integration into the Agro-Food System?', in Zioganas, C. (ed), *Competitiveness and Integrated Development of the Rural Sector: New Challenges for Greece*, ETAGRO: Thessaloniki (in Greek).
Phillips, M. (1998), 'Social Perspectives', in Ilbery, B. (ed), *The Geography of Rural Change*, Longman: Harlow.
Pompili, T. (1994), 'Structure and Performance of Less Developed Regions in the EC', *Regional Studies*, Vol. 28, pp. 679-693.
Pugliese, E. (1985), 'Farm Workers in Italy: Agricultural Working Class, Landless Peasants, or Clients of the Welfare State?', in Hudson, R. and Lewis, J. (eds), *Uneven Development in Southern Europe*, Methuen: London and New York.

Pugliese, E. (1993), 'Labour Market and Employment Structure in the Mezzogiorno', *Journal of Regional Policy*, Vol. 13, pp. 147-157.

Reher, D.S. (1998), 'Family Ties in Western Europe: Persistent Contrasts', *Population and Development Review*, Vol. 24, No 2, pp. 203-234.

Sarris, A.H. (1994), 'Consequences of the Proposed Common Agricultural Policy Reform for the Southern Part of the European Community', *European Economy: Reports and Studies*, Vol. 5, pp. 113-132.

Van der Ploeg, J.D. and Saccomandi, V. (1995), 'On the Impact of Endogenous Development in Agriculture', in van der Ploeg, J.D. and van Dijk, G. (eds), *Beyond Modernization: The Impact of Endogenous Rural Development*, Van Gorcum: Assen.

Whatmore, S. (1993), 'Sustainable Rural Geographies?', *Progress in Human Geography*, Vol. 17, pp. 538-547.

Whatmore, S. (1994), 'Global Agro-Food Complexes and the Refashioning of Rural Europe', in Amin, A. and Thrift, N. (eds), *Globalization, Institutions and Regional Development in Europe*, Oxford University Press: Oxford.